FRAMING THE NATION

FRAMING THE NATION

Languages of 'Modernity' in India

AJANTA SIRCAR

NEW YORK LONDON CALCUTTA

Seagull Books 2011
Copyright © Ajanta Sircar 2010

ISBN-13 978 1 9064 9 730 9

British Library Cataloguing-in-Publication Data
A catalogue record for this book is available from the British Library

Typeset by Seagull Books, Calcutta, India
Printed and bound by Hyam Enterprises, Calcutta, India

That is the story of the Enlightenment in the colonies. It comes in the hands of the policeman and the marriage is consummated in the station-house.

—Partha Chatterjee, *Nationalist Thought and the Colonial World: A Derivative Discourse?* (1986)

CONTENTS

ACKNOWLEDGEMENTS

For the many ways they helped to give it substance and shape, this book is indebted to the following people:

Prof. Laura Mulvey, for a very privileged glimpse of academics at its best. I cannot adequately express the intellectual horizons she has opened for me. It is my pleasure to concede that the Enlightenment *was*, really, worth the trouble.

Prof. Pam Cook, who despite her busy schedules always had time to help and encourage me during my years at the University of East Anglia (UEA), Norwich, UK. To her, too, my less than adequate gratitude.

Mr Suresh Chabria, former Director, National Film Archive of India, Pune, and the library staff of the film section, Mrs Shinde and Ms Lakshmi, for going out of their way to make me feel welcome during my stay and accommodating my many requests at short notice.

Warren Buckland, Jon Cook, Andrew Higson, Ashish Rajadhyaksha, Roger Sales, Paul Willemen and Anil Zankar, all of whom, at different stages of its formulation, gave of their time and scholarship to help me put my ideas into better shape.

Ms Alita Thorpe and Ms Aileen Davies at the UEA, for their kindness and patience.

Maria and Howard Creswell for food (!), affection, *family* at Norwich.

Lakshmi and Mark Holmstrom and Uma Kambhampati and Vijay—the 'Indian' half of my family in England, on whom, consequently, I made the same demands.

Nayef Al-Yaseen (the impasse over Japan and feminism notwithstanding), Minako Araki, Miles Booy, Conor Houghton and Yoriko Kitagwga, for making UEA a place I will always fondly remember.

Raghavan Uncle and Aunty and Padmaja who, over the years, have played a huge part in making Hyderabad 'the nicest city in the world'!

And finally, to my father, without whom none of this would be possible. And because he left before I had ever adequately said 'thank you', to his memory, this book is dedicated, with love.

INTRODUCTION

I was typical of a generation of European intellectuals who, in their
youth during the 60s, fell in love with Hollywood in its sunset years
. . . [That] obsession was [then gradually] forced to mutate and take
political issues on board as cinephilia grew into film theory
(Mulvey 1996: 19).

Theory with a capital 'T' arrived in the Indian academy in the early 1980s.
In the first flush of intellectual excitement this generated, it seemed the
promise of light that would wipe away all signs of the exhaustion that had
stained the national psyche with the fading of the Nehruvian dream. The
fascination with popular cinema, especially that of Bombay, also found a
new lease of life at this point.

To look back, then, at the beginning, this book grows out of the intellectual energy generated by that moment and the new kind of engagement
with popular cinema this enabled in India, a transition both similar and
different from the one that Laura Mulvey, describing the European context

of the 1960s, charts from cinephilia to 'film theory'. It also grows from both a passion for the movies as well as a commitment to that still-very-partially realized promise of the Enlightenment—the growth of capabilities, both individual and collective, without the intensification of social relations of power and dominance. Yet, necessarily, to mark time is to also mark distance. And part of the project of this book is to map the distance that 'film theory' itself has travelled, in the Anglo-American academy as well as in India; to examine how the one has played off the other as also the questions that come to the fore as the new kind of study of cinema in India assumes 'disciplinary' forms.

In 1994, the first department of Film Studies was established in India at Jadavpur University, Calcutta. In 1995, the Indian Institute of Advanced Study, Shimla, hosted the first film-theory-oriented study week on 'Making Meaning in Indian Cinema'. These have now been followed by several national-level seminars, workshops and conferences as well as a whole spurt of research projects on the different popular cinemas in all parts of the country. In addition, the publication of the *Encyclopaedia of Indian Cinema* by the British Film Institute, London, in 1994, has been a significant marker of the growing visibility of Bombay/popular Indian cinemas in Anglo-America. How, then, do we make sense of this new *academic* interest in popular Indian cinemas? What should be our agendas as a new body of knowledge takes shape around the twin signifiers, film theory and Indian popular culture? While necessarily still inchoate, these are some of the questions this book tries to explore.

LOCATING THE 'POPULAR'

Analysing the emergence of the new 'disciplines' of knowledge that emerged in nineteenth-century Bengal, political theorist Partha Chatterjee notes that, as it travelled from its originary setting in Enlightenment Europe to the colonies of the non-West, 'modernity' changed dramatically in complexion. Taking issue with Michel Foucault, Chatterjee argues that the Foucauldian thesis about the new nature of power that emerged in the post-despotic/'modern' state of the West, one that radiated from innumerable nodes in the social body rather than being located in any one source, only holds in those cases where this state power could fulfil one fundamental criterion—that of representativeness. Necessarily in the non-West, then, Chatterjee contends, the socio-political project of 'modernity' would be irreparably compromised, even subverted, given the fundamental nature of colonial rule (1995b: 2–29).

Following Chatterjee among others, modernity functions in this book as a sliding signifier, carrying different connotations at different times and places. The British colonial intervention was instrumental in introducing a specifically post-Enlightenment notion of modernity into India. By fixing the colonized people onto a civilizationally lower scale not only did the colonial rhetoric provide the ethical justification for colonial rule but such a transplantation of conceptual worlds was also necessary if India were to be transformed into both an efficient supplier of raw materials for British industry and a market for British goods. In the process, however, the colonial rhetoric intersected with preexisting feudal ideologies and was reinflected by traditional elites to strengthen already existing social hierarchies. Through a process of emulation as well as contestation, the nationalist movement then marked the culmination of the process by which the indigenous elite in India worked out its own hegemonic possibilities within the overarching framework set in place by colonial rule. The fashioning of a distinctly *Indian* modernity was crucial to this enterprise.

Modernity, therefore, has been an enormously contested idea, one redefined and contextualized across a whole range of socio-historical locations. As Chatterjee has pointed out, in travelling from the West to the colonies, the Enlightenment notion of the 'modern' sharply changed track. Spilling over the embankments of exclusive colonial enclaves, it found new life in the 'native quarters'. Energized by very different desires and strategies, 'modernity' took on completely new forms (ibid.: 8). In the process, discourses on modernity would be irrevocably intertwined with questions of nationalism.[1]

As part of a larger ongoing philosophico-cultural debate, this book attempts to track the interweaving narratives of modernity and 'nationhood' in India. Its specific point of entry is an analysis of the ways in which these intertwined narratives found articulation through a particular *kind* of language in the 1980s—the language of popular[2] culture. My attempt, in the following sections, has been to argue that the changing terms of this popular articulation of modernity/nationhood, from the 1950s to the 1980s, was symptomatic of the ideological reconfiguring of Indianness in the post-Nehruvian era.

To map these inflections in the language of the popular, I have examined the changing cultural hegemony of 'Hindi' as it has operated as a signifying system.[3] My assumption is that Hindi, as a signifying system, has historically generated overlapping, but also distinct, ideological and political resonances from 'English'. Moreover while English has comprehensively occupied the domain of the 'formal', signifying the conceptual world of education/law/administration, it is Hindi which has exerted maximum influence from the terrain of the popular, especially through the institutional site of Hindi/Bombay cinema. Further, the transition from the Nehruvian 'socialist' era to the moment of 'globalization' has decisively rewritten the terms of traffic between the two. While English in India has lost its traditional mystique, Hindi has gained a new sense of cultural capital.[4] It was in the 1980s—the decade when the liberalization project was launched—that these foundational changes first become discernible.

Hindi gained decisive new visibility in the public sphere through the Official Language Act (1965, amended 1967). Subsequently, the nationalization of Hindi also received a major boost from the mushrooming television network which, with the Special Extension Plan (1984), now covers more than 70 per cent of the nation's population.[5] Culturally, the consumerism spawned through television has been simultaneous with—or the obverse of—the emergent project of Hindutva.[6] As we shall see, these diverse phenomena in the realms of language, technology, culture and politics can be comprehended through the changed notion of cultural distinction that Hindi currently conveys. Having mapped the social dynamics of Hindi as language, I have traced the ways in which the national imagination configured through Hindi has historically been mobilized by the Hindi/Bombay film industry. This framing argument of the book will be discussed at length. Such a move is based on what Eric Hobsbawm and Terence Ranger (1983) have described as 'the invention of tradition'. Hobsbawm and Ranger have argued that, for nations to be imagined, 'traditions' have to be invented. Moreover, as we shall see, in an *anticolonial* nationalism such as India's, discourses on 'traditionalism' would be doubly important. This is especially relevant to Hindi which, as a signifying system, has exerted its major impact on the cultural self-definition of the nation not as language[7] but through the 'neo-traditionalism' (Rajadhyaksha 1980: 20–67) that Bombay cinema has visually represented. From this perspective I contend that the gradual dominance of Hindi as language and Bombay as film industry points to a very specific configuration of the national imagination in terms of what it means to be Indian.

FASHIONING AN *INDIAN* MODERNITY

History, as has been extensively documented, was the great obsession of post-Enlightenment Western Europe. The Enlightenment notion of history was based on three foundations: a sense of anachronism, rules of evidence and causality as a principle of explanation (Burke 1969). By suggesting that things could be 'out of date', such a notion of history divided entire societies into the modern and the traditional through what Johaness Fabian (1983) has called 'the denial of coevalness' to non-Western cultures. As such, of course, these teleological narratives fed directly into the idea of 'progress' on which the project of colonization was based—the whole idea of 'civilizing the natives' of colonized lands.

Educated into the conceptual world of colonial modernity, the native intelligentsia in India too sought to emulate both the rationale as well as the institutions of colonial rule. The inescapable link between the history of Western modernity and the experience of colonization in the non-West, however, made it inevitable that an anticolonial intelligentsia would also contest the universality of the claims made by the Enlightenment, and try to clear a space where it might produce a modernity that would be its own, distinctly *Indian*. Chatterjee describes the distance between the two:

> My argument is that because of the way in which the history of our modernity has been intertwined with the history of colonialism, we have never quite been able to believe that there exists a universal domain of free discourse, unfettered by differences of race and nationality [. . .] It is for this reason that we have tried, for over a hundred years, to take our eyes away from this chimera of universal modernity and clear up a space where we might become the creators of our own modernity. [. . .] Ours is the modernity of the

once-colonised [. . .] Our attitude to modernity, therefore, cannot but be deeply ambiguous [. . .] [T]he uncertainty is because we know that to fashion the forms of our own modernity, we need to have the courage at times to reject the modernities established by others (1995a).

As an exciting body of work has documented, during the nationalist movement efforts to fashion a distinctly *Indian* modernity did, in fact, erupt across the range of cultural forms—in the fields of science, literature, music and the visual arts.[8] The humiliating 'present' of the colonial situation however overlaid all these endeavours with discourses of traditionalism— pictures of a glorious 'past' that would counter the abjectness of subjection.

This leads us, then, to a fundamental difference between the ways in which the 'classical' democracies of Western Europe and the anticolonial nationalisms of Asia and Africa were imagined into existence. As Chatterjee has argued, the most creative results of these anticolonial nationalisms were posited not on identity but on their difference from the modular forms of nations imagined by the West. The objective presence of colonial rule in the domain of the state further meant that, in these anticolonial nationalisms, it was in the 'cultural' rather than the 'political' terrain that the most spectacular acts of nationalist imaginations were articulated. But the dynamics of this entire process, Chatterjee argues, is lost in conventional histories that conceptualize nationalism only as a political movement:

> [In the domain of culture, anticolonial] nationalism launches its most powerful, creative and historically significant project: to fashion a 'modern' culture that is nevertheless not Western. If the nation is an imagined community, then this is where it is brought into being.
>
> [. . .]
>
> The result [of reducing nationalism to a political movement] is that autonomous forms of imagination of the community were, and continue to be, overwhelmed and swamped by the history of the postcolonial state [. . .] If the nation is an imagined community and if nations must also take the form of states, then our theoretical language must allow us to talk about community and state at

the same time. I do not think our present theoretical language allows us to do so (1994a: 6–11).

In the light of Chatterjee's analyses, let us go back to our conceptualization of Hindi as language of the popular. We can now argue that, given the nature of nation-formation in India, it was in this domain of 'culture' (as opposed to 'politics') that the nation was most powerfully imagined into existence. My contention, moreover, is that the decisive shift in both the terms as well as the mode of this popular articulation of 'Indianness', from the 1950s to the 1980s, had to do with both global and national contradictions.

Internationally, the emergence of the post-Fordist model of production and the new globalization of finance has resulted in a profound shift in the very nature of social space. As Foucault writes, 'The present epoch will perhaps be above all the epoch of space. We are in the epoch of simultaneity; [. . .] of the near and far, of the side-by-side, of the dispersed' (1986: 24). The shift this has precipitated in the relationship between the terrains of politics and culture is that the one has now moved into the terrain of the other, i.e. it is in the cultural terrain that political struggles seem to be located.[9] As Fredric Jameson has argued, the new stage of global capitalism also requires a profound retheorization of the public sphere from the earlier base–superstructure model of Marxist theory (1994: 278–95). The new dominance of the media, Jameson observes, has resulted in a situation where the 'market' is so over-saturated by the libidinal excess of the media image that the two have become almost indistinguishable. Socially, this corresponds to the moment of the so-called post-ideological subject. Represented most powerfully through the ideology of 'cynicism', Slavoj Žižek proposes that the present stage of capitalism corresponds to a new mode of ideological interpellation:

> The cynical subject is quite aware of the distance between the ideological mask and social reality. But he none the less still insists on the mask [. . .] It is clear therefore that confronted with such cynical reason, the traditional critique of ideology no longer works [. . .]
>
> But cynical reason, for all its ironic detachment, leaves untouched the fundamental level of ideological fantasy, the level at which ideology structures social reality itself (1989: 28–30).

Given this global context, cultural theorist Vivek Dhareshwar has summarized the major cultural discourses that have emerged within the decolonized world to mediate the modernity of the West: the aesthetic appropriation of modernity as 'modernism' by the nativist bourgeoisie; the programme of 'secular modernization', as envisaged by the Left avant-garde; and 'postmodernism', the 'radical' discourse of the West (1995b: 104–12). While the aesthetic appropriation of modernity, Dhareshwar argues, can conceptualize the subaltern postcolonial only as exotic double, the programme of progressive modernization envisaged by the Left becomes, ironically, that of completing the task of the national bourgeoisie as the Left tries to retain the category of the nation in the face of an aggressive globalization. 'Radical' discourses of the West, on the other hand, attempt merely to appropriate non-Western identities through effete forms of cultural relativism. As Dhareshwar has outlined in a series of programmatic essays, the theoretical–historical impasse which all these scenarios are locked into results from their conceptualization of politics within the idiom of liberal democracy—the language of sovereignty, citizenship and rights. Such an idiom, however, fails to account for the conflicting social idioms that shape postcolonial spaces. As Dhareshwar argues, the project for us, then, in the spirit of Jean-Luc Nancy, is to construct 'our time', where there is a reciprocity between 'our' and 'time':

> If culture is supposed to tell us who we are, politics, one imagines, has the task of telling us what we are and how we are and should relate to others. [. . .] What is involved in the *translation* of political idiom? How to characterise the resulting imbrication? [. . .] Our modernity too has produced thick concepts [. . . W]e will not find them if we look to the 'work' of modernity, but to the figures of its 'unworking', the forms of community that come into being in the very unworking of modernity (1995a: 3).[10]

In a fundamental sense, therefore, we may argue that a *bilinguality* defines the objective situation of the postcolonial world. By bilinguality I invoke not only the multiplicity of languages but also the conflicting conceptual idioms that shape postcolonial spaces—terrains of discourse or circuits of knowledge production that are asymmetrical—circuits that represent impassioned collective desires to translate the modernity imposed by the West into indigenous frames. It is this bilingualism that both the worlds of 'English' and 'Hindi' (or the vernaculars) signify.

RETHINKING THE NATION

In classical rhetoric, a concept-metaphor for which there is no adequate referent is called a catachresis. The nation-state, the most dramatic *aspiration* to modernity, is undoubtedly one such concept-metaphor for which no historically adequate referent can be advanced from postcolonial spaces. Thus, Gayatri Chakravorty Spivak describes the condition of postcoloniality as a 'deconstructive case' (1993a: 281) while Dhareshwar describes it as the 'unworking of modernity' (1995a: 322).

Politically, the 'modernity' promised by the Enlightenment came to be translated into the liberal nation-state in the West. Economically, into a capitalist mode of production. As Foucault's work has most persuasively shown us, the underlying link between the discursive universe signified by the post-Renaissance sense of history, the rationality of the market and the political institutions of liberal democracy was that they were all grounded on principles of enumeration. This preconditional link between 'governmentality' and measurement fundamentally structured notions of identity in the post-despotic state of Western Europe.

Yet, as Sudipta Kaviraj has argued, it is not only the nation that can be 'counted' in this enumerated world. Other communities, based on other principles of enumeration, can also emerge (1992: 1–39). And in the larger politico-cultural attempt to fashion a distinctly Indian modernity, the idiom of liberal democracy was differentially mobilized by a range of social groups as they attempted to imagine forms of community other than the classical nation-state. (We will engage with this point at some length in the following sections.) This is precisely the thrust of an exciting moment of contemporary political theory—it maps these *Eastern* careers of modernity and evolves theoretical languages to account for the paradigmatic forms of community which emerged in most parts of Asia and Africa, drawing on traditional (kinship) idioms to negotiate the governmental practices of the twentieth-century ('developmentalist') nation-state.[11]

With regard to the bilingualism of the postcolonial world, one of the fundamental sources of non-coherence between Enlightenment modernity and lived experience in the non-West is this contradiction between the institutional logic of state structures that define identity in terms of discrete, watertight categories and other notions of identity that are more context-specific and lack such a sense of rigidity. By this I do not imply that the subject-position of modernity in India has so far only been available to speakers of the English language. On the contrary, as Hindi moves confidently into the terrain of 'high culture', it too mobilizes the logic of numbers to redefine notions of community on its own terms. What I mean, rather, is that the conceptual universe symbolized by English as a signifying system cannot account for notions of being ethical and political agents in the world other than in terms of post-Enlightenment Western Europe. And, as will be the major enterprise of this book to demonstrate, the move of Hindi into the status of 'national modern' represents not only a renegotiation of the language-question but also a new conjuncture of the ideological domains English and Hindi have historically represented.

In his theorization of 'ideology', Žižek makes a break from the Althusserian position which defines ideology as 'false consciousness' or illusion (1989: 11–54). For Žižek, fantasy is rather on the side of reality, structuring our social relationships in the 'real'/phenomenological world. The place of ideological interpellation, he argues, is not on the side of knowledge, the 'intimate'/'private' beliefs of subjects, but, rather, on the side of doing, as these beliefs are 'objectively' embodied through social institutions and practices. Žižek argues that there is a double illusion in the historical moment of the 'cynical subject'. Even when we assume an ironic distance from things, we are still doing them. The ideological fantasy is in overlooking this illusion which structures our social reality.

The Symbolic, then, is not simply the place of the external; it is, rather, the place where our most intimate beliefs are embodied. The external state apparatuses are able to interpellate the subject, i.e. law can exist as *law* only insofar as it is experienced or internalized by the subject as such—as a traumatic senseless injunction. Drawing on the Lacanian formula of fantasy, Žižek suggests that just as (in Lacanian logic) the sleeping subject awakens to *escape* the reality of the desire that he encounters in his dream, so also, in the social realm, for Lacan, ideological fantasy does not provide an escape from reality. Rather, it masks the traumatic social antagonism which cannot be symbolized.

Placed vis-à-vis modes of self-formation universalized through Enlightenment rationalism, we may here refer to the principle of enumeration on which the art of governmentality is premised. As representatives of the Enlightenment, the most far-reaching innovation that the British introduced in India was the modern state. In so doing they introduced both a mindset as well as a whole set of institutional structures grounded in the logic of counting. The implication, then, is that the conceptual vocabulary of the state in India could not accommodate the dynamic indeterminacies of social identities that have existed (and continue to exist) in domains outside it.

At the present moment, this instrumental logic of counting is most virulently being mobilized by the Hindutva brigade. In its present guise, the Hindu Right too is trying to deny the heterogeneity that characterizes Hinduism and the many alternative practices of toleration that exist in India. It is, instead, fixing the idea of cultural difference to mobilize the rhetoric of numbers in order to argue for the relative backwardness and/or disadvantage of a particular ethnic community.

While in its spatial logic Hindutva both contradicts as well as complements the logic of transnational capitalism, it is, in keeping with global trends, through the cultural terrain that the Hindutva project has initiated its most sustained onslaught.[12] But this will take us back to the interrelationships noted earlier—among an emergent Hindu neo-nationalism, new technologies of mass culture (such as television and satellite networks) and the new consumerism in India.

THEORIZING MODERNITY

In 1784, Immanuel Kant published a response in the periodical *Berlinische Monatschrift* to the question, 'What is Enlightenment?' which began as follows:

Enlightenment is man's release from self-incurred tutelage. Tutelage is man's inability to make use of his understanding without direction from another. Self-incurred is this tutelage when its cause lies not in lack of reason but in lack of resolution and courage to use it without direction from another [. . .] 'Have courage to use your own reason!' that is the motto of the enlightenment (1963: 3).

According to Kant, to be 'enlightened' is to be self-reliant—to become free from self-imposed dependence on authority figures through the acquisition of knowledge. Modernity, in this sense, was the first social philosophy promising universal self-determination. As Foucault has observed, Kant's text marks the entry into history of a question that has confronted philosophers for the last 200 years—'What does it mean to be "modern"?' For Foucault, the unique aspect of Kant's text was that the latter was theorizing modernity within the conditions of possibility of his age, identifying those features that were most conducive to the pursuit of knowledge:

> It is in the reflection on 'today' as difference in history and as motive for a particular philosophical task that the novelty of the text appears to me to lie. And, by looking at it in this way, it seems to me we may recognise a point of departure: the outline of what one might call the attitude of modernity [. . .] Thinking back on Kant's text, I wonder whether we may not envisage modernity rather *as an attitude* than as a period in history. And by 'attitude', I mean a mode of relating to contemporary reality; a voluntary choice made by certain people; a way, too, of acting and behaving that at one and the same time marks a relation of belonging and presents itself as a task (in Foucault 1984: 38–9; emphasis added).

The 'modern' attitude, Foucault goes on to suggest, is inextricably linked to the desire for social change, 'to imagine it [the present] otherwise than it is, and to transform it not by destroying it but by grasping it in what it is' (ibid.: 41). Having outlined several features of what he calls the 'modern' attitude, Foucault concludes that the ultimate stake in such a rethinking of modernity is to fulfil that dream of the Enlightenment which still eludes us 200 years later—the collective growth of human capabilities. Such a theorization of modernity, in terms of *modes of engagement* with one's present, defines the conceptual ground on which I have tried to locate modernity, in its commonsensical usage, as 'lived experience', in contemporary India. Further, within the institutional site of the university, such an attitude, I would contend, has been most forcefully articulated by that body of work loosely grouped under the rubric of 'Critical Theory'/'Cultural Studies'. It seems appropriate, then, to locate my own concerns within the specific institutional context in which they took shape.

THEORY, CULTURAL STUDIES AND INDIAN FILM STUDIES

In one of his essays, Stuart Hall lucidly traces the intellectual history of the Birmingham Centre (1992: 15–48), the founding of which was undoubtedly a crucial moment for the ways in which a new mode of studying 'culture' emerged in the West in the 1960s. Yet, though drawing on currents that have shaped the contours of the Anglo-American academy over the last half-century or so, the cultural politics of post-Nehruvian India is also shaped by significantly different dynamics. The attempt to locate my research within the new mode of academic practice signified by 'Critical Theory'/'Cultural Studies' is because, as Hall suggests, since its inception Cultural Studies has been the institutional manifestation of a new *kind* of research—a body of work defined by its active political engagement with the contemporary rather than predetermined 'objects' such as institutional affiliation, area of research and/or methodology. The enormously liberating effects of such a broad-based definition is of course that, as a mode of engagement with the present, 'Theory' opens up possibilities for forging alliances among initiatives to produce non-dominating systems of knowledge across a whole range of hitherto isolated or disconnected disciplinary and institutional locations. To locate my research within this broad intellectual terrain is to attempt to forge solidarities with similar initiatives in many other parts of the world.

However, as part of its defining parameters, a 'Critical Theory' approach is one which also tries to be sensitive to the specificity of socio-historical contexts.[13] It might be relevant, then, to trace the intellectual contours of the new mode of studying culture as it emerged in post-Emergency India, the arrival of Theory in the 1980s with which we began our discussion and under whose umbrella the new study of Indian popular cinemas emerged.

In India, this new mode of studying culture can be plotted around the founding of the *Journal of Arts and Ideas* (1981), the publication of feminist historiographies such as those by Kumkum Sangari and Sudesh Vaid (1989) and Susie Tharu and K. Lalita (1991, 1995), the rethinking of nationalist historiography through the work of the Subaltern Studies collective, the interrogation of the politics of 'disciplinary' formations of the Indian university through anthologies such as that by Svati Joshi (1991) and the increasing emphasis on the cultural in influential academic journals such as the *Economic and Political Weekly*. Specifically with reference to Film Studies, mention must be made of the annual conferences at Jadavpur University, Calcutta, as well as the publication of the *Journal of the Moving Image* (since 1999). As evident from the 'founding' texts, the socio-institutional configurations of a new mode of studying culture in India were quite distinct from those that fed into, say, the Birmingham Centre. Nor was the emergence of a new study of culture in India simply an imitation of the disciplinary crisis in the West. Rather, a rethinking of culture here emerged from questions raised by the women's movement, the uprising of Naxalbari,[14] the proletarianization caused by the Green Revolution, a new 'moment' in Dalit (lower-caste) politics—in short, from wide-ranging critiques of Nehruvian paradigms of growth/development. It was at this juncture, amid the enormous intellectual and political upheavals that marked a definitive interrogation of Nehruvian nationalism, that Theory with a capital T arrived on the intellectual scene in India. The new study of popular cinemas also emerged at this point.

Describing a process akin to what she says calls the 'birth of criticism' (as opposed to cinephilia) in Film Studies in Britain in the 1960s, Mulvey (1996) traces the obsession of a whole generation of European intellectuals with the mass-produced cinema of Hollywood—a romance that moved from an entranced fascination with the Hollywood screen to a gradual intellectual distancing from it, one that nevertheless brought its own rewards of intellectual curiosity and pleasure. In this criss-crossing of transatlantic fantasies, Mulvey recounts that, while European intellectuals were initially attracted to Hollywood in a spirit of polemic, as a cultural form that represented the polar opposite of all the weight of tradition/distinction with which the high cultures of painting/literature/music had historically been encrusted, this revaluation of Hollywood was in turn exported back to the American academy, only this time with the trappings of 'French theory'—in the first instance structuralism, then psychoanalysis. However, Mulvey points out, the decisive factor that precipitated this taking of a critical distance from Hollywood was politics—not only the events leading up to 1968 but also Vietnam, coupled with feminism and the growing awareness of the stifling of indigenous Third World and European cinemas under the American export of Hollywood.

The birth of Critical Theory marked a moment of rupture with dominant institutions/traditions of knowledge, even in its European heartlands. Thus the famous 1967 statement from Jean-Luc Godard:

> On our own modest level, we too should try to provoke two or three Vietnams in the bosom of the vast Hollywood–Cinecitta–Mosfilm–Pinewood, etc., empire, and both economically and aesthetically, struggling on two fronts as it were, create cinemas which are national, free, brotherly, comradely and bonded in friendship (cited in Mulvey 1996: 23).

As we trace the arrival of Theory vis-à-vis the study of popular cinemas in India I recall this familiar history because of a problem that subterraneously haunts the new academic study of popular culture—a too-easy polarization between the West/'them' (invariably marked as monolithic and oppressive) and 'us'. In turn, this binary between 'them' and 'us' leads to a problem that I can only mention in passing—of entirely culturalist descriptions of the 'popular' in India in ways which neatly fit the emergent professionalization of this terrain as its radical edges are gradually blunted and a study of Indian popular culture becomes merely the next avenue for upward mobility in an already established academic hierarchy.

To avoid this trap it seems imperative to remind ourselves that as opposed to, say, the knowledge imposed by the colonial government on nineteenth-century Bengal, Theory marked a moment of radical critique of dominant Western intellectual traditions too. Its overlaps and modes of negotiations into the Indian academy have, consequently, generated very different kinds of resonances from those of traditional imperial knowledges. Within Cinema Studies, as M. Madhava Prasad (1997) has thoughtfully noted, the major paradigm shift enabled by the conceptual vocabulary provided by Critical Theory is that the study of Indian cinema has finally broken out of the 'myth'- and 'Indian psyche'-based interpretations that had dominated the field for nearly four decades. The obverse of this process is the reading of popular Indian cinema as one still in a state of not-yet-ness given that the aesthetic of the popular Indian film varies so dramatically from that of Hollywood. The emergence of alternative film practices in the West has a special significance for the new Theory-oriented studies of popular cinema in India because it shows us that the technology of the cinema was in itself 'empty of any cultural content and capable of entering into combinations in which its potential could be realised in [. . .] completely different form(s) [from that of Hollywood]' (ibid.: 2). And, in undoubtedly a very sophisticated analysis of Bombay cinema, Prasad locates the specific nature of the ruling bloc in India—comprising a coalition of the bourgeoisie, the professional classes and the feudal landowning elite— as providing the constitutive ideological ground for the distinctive narrative structure of the classical Bombay film.

The task for the new body of writing on Indian cinema is to evolve a language of talking about films that does not assume the 'Hollywood Mode of Production' as the norm. As Rajadhyaksha remarks in one of his essays, his attempt 'is to try and put together not so much an "Indian" film theory (as against, typically, a "Western" one) but rather the outlines of *a theory of the cinema that can account for the Indian cinema*' (1995).[15] Additionally, in its attempt to construct a new theory of the cinematic institution, this body of work—which takes Bombay, rather than Hollywood, as its entry point—has to renegotiate two major concerns of Film Theory as it currently exists: the concept of 'realism' which has implicitly informed most of the theoretical writing on cinema so far; and, relatedly, the category of the spectator/viewer whom this conventional realist/narrative film addresses. In the following sections, I will lay out some of the major issues that have emerged out of the new dialogue between Bombay and Hollywood. But, for reasons that I hope will become clear, we will take a (somewhat extended) detour at this point. I will first sketch the broad theoretical–intellectual genealogy of the book and then return to the 'realism' question. By approaching questions of re- alism/narrative form in this manner, my aim is to more clearly define my own position vis-à-vis some of the current debates in Film Studies in India.

PSYCHOANALYSIS AND THE 'POSTCOLONIAL MODERN'

What did Australia force Freud to do with his thought? [. . .] If you try to confront another system of thinking or way of being in the world, what does it do to—what does it expose, unsettle, about your own? [. . .] Rather than ask what psychoanalysis might be able to tell us about Australia and its specific crisis of prejudice, my ques- tion is: what can Australia [. . .] tell psychoanalysis, and the forms

of Western thinking it both embodies and queries, about itself?
(Rose 2003: 125)

Sigmund Freud's 'Totem and Taboo', first published in 1913, is infamous
as the text that marks the culmination of his racist arrogance:

> For external as well as internal reasons, I shall select as the basis
> for this comparison the tribes which have been described by an-
> thropologists as the most backward and miserable of savages, the
> aborigines of Australia (1953c: 1).

However, in a painstaking rereading of 'Totem and Taboo', and locating the text at one of the most fragile and poignant moments in the history
of psychoanalysis, Jacqueline Rose asks why Freud used the trope of the
now-notorious 'Australian aborigine'. 'Australia', as Rose points out, was also
the site of the definitive rupture between Freud and Jung. Not only did they
both not go to Australia to the conference to which they had been invited,
they also failed to collaborate with and did not even send each other their
papers. Moreover, while Freud started work on 'Totem and Taboo' in 1911,
Carl Gustav Jung published *Symbols of Transformation* in 1912, in which he
decisively challenged the primacy of incest (and relatedly, of sexuality) in
Freud's framework. 'Australia' thus became the site on which battles over
some of the most fundamental concepts of psychoanalysis were fought (Rose
2003).[16]

My purpose here is to use Rose to address the concern—given recent
social science debates on cultural specificity on the one hand and charges
of ethnocentrism on the other, how does one begin to formulate the whole
question of the 'relevance' of psychoanalysis to the postcolonial world?
However, while it is perhaps no longer very original to say so, it was the
figure of the non-Western 'savage' (the infamous Australian aborigine)
and the figure of the child that came to increasingly haunt Freud's work in
its later years. But these are areas that have hardly got the same attention
as Freud's preoccupation with female sexuality in his later work. The
non-West then, from my perspective, is actually a very relevant site for
raising questions about the unconscious of the classical analytical tradition
itself. (Rose, in fact, evocatively refers to 'Australia' as the 'phantom of
psychoanalysis' [2003: 128].)

The psychoanalytical notion of the sexual drive confounds all popular notions of sexuality. In fact, the crucial point about his 'Three Essays on the Theory of Sexuality' (1905) was that, here, Freud laid out the difference between the psychoanalytical notion of the 'drive' and the biological notion of 'instinct' (see Freud 1953b). As opposed to the biological instinct, the drive does not have a clearly defined aim or objective nor any straightforward notion of satisfaction. Further—and this is the point to which Jacques Lacan makes the most emphatic return—Freud also highlighted the fundamental link between sexuality and the unconscious, repeatedly underlining that the latter was consubstantial to the former. And the most crucial point about the unconscious is that it bears testimony to the fact of repression being a central aspect of universal human existence.

Although Freud identified certain universal features of human life such as the existence of unconscious mental processes, the presence of repression and the importance of sexuality, he was aware that psychoanalysis was not in any way a 'completed' science. On the contrary, it was a science which could only grope its way forward through experience, always incomplete and always ready to modify its theories. And while Frantz Fanon (1965) remains one of the most passionate practitioners of psychoanalysis in the colonial world, there has recently emerged a new body of work on psychoanalysis and postcoloniality, most especially that of Homi K. Bhabha (1994), to which my project is indebted.[17] In terms of the specificity of the analytical tradition per se, the two best-known theorists in India (outside the therapeutic–institutional setting) are Ashis Nandy and Sudhir Kakar. It is beyond the scope of this book to map the fundamental differences of positions on analytical theory between Bhabha on the one hand and Nandy and Kakar on the other. But both Nandy and Kakar, even while they differ significantly between themselves in their assessments of the 'relevance' of psychoanalysis to India (Kakar, of course, operating within an explicitly Ericksonian grid), miss Freud's central discovery—that human subjects are not predetermined entities. Rather, we become human within culture and the unconscious represents precisely the ways in which laws of human culture are acquired (Sircar 2009: 53–78). But, in a more general intellectual sense too, the engagement with Freud and psychoanalysis has a robust tradition in South Asia. South Asian intellectuals, from A. K. Ramanujan (1999) to Gananath Obeyesekere (1999), have used psychoanalysis in their examination of

Indian myths, folktales, kinship structures, etc. Interestingly, a recurrent motif in all these analyses has been the insistence on the different form and resolution of the 'Indian Oedipus complex' as compared to its Western counterpart (Sircar 2009: 53–78).

In her analysis of 'Totem and Taboo', Rose demonstrated that instead of reading the essay as a cardinal text of Western prejudice (as has conventionally been done), it is possible to read it

> [A]s Freud's dissection—albeit tentative and anxious—of authority, one of the texts in which, for all the drive in the opposite direction, he knows the precariousness of his own reason. *This would make the journey of the book not from primitive to civilised, from Australia to Europe, but into the heart of a civilisation that is aware, if only unconsciously, just how shaky it is on the ground* (2003: 147; emphasis added).

The tensions within 'Totem and Taboo' over non-Western belief systems in Freud's engagement with sacrifice and ritual make it just as possible, Rose argues, to see the 'Australian aborigine' or the 'primitive' as someone who has retained a valuable psychic capacity that the 'civilized' West has had to repress at great cost to itself. More importantly, in the equation between aborigine and infant, it is unclear whether Freud proposes a straightforward stagist history—that non-Western societies represent a stage of history or culture that the West has left behind.

One of the most crucial areas where Freud finds in the 'primitive mind' a capacity that the West has lost is the ability of primitive emotion to sustain ambivalence. (The fundamental importance of this emotion to Freud's insights on the nature and formation of collectivities will be discussed later in the chapter.) Rose reminds us that while it would not be until the First World War that Freud would derive the origins of ethical life from the ambivalence of mourning, he was already groping here with notions of belonging and subjectivity quite different from the forms of collective identity through which the West defines itself. Freud's claim to have uncovered the origins of society in the Oedipal struggles of the primitive man can be read, Rose argues, as his conviction that there is something ineradicably violent about the social tie itself. From this perspective, Rose suggests that for Freud—even though he struggled with himself to admit to this—the ability of primitive emotion to sustain ambivalence indicated a capacity to move back and forth across the different strata of the mind that the civilized man had had to repress. The animistic soul could thus show us something about the fundamentally unreasonable nature of law/authority itself.

Placing 'Totem and Taboo' in the context of the historic Freud–Jung rupture (another dissection of authority), Rose further points out that the (mournful) underlying link between authority and identification (with the neurotic) that Freud finally proposed in response to Jung is absolutely central to the analytical project:

> It all depends—the problem we have seen Freud struggling with in 'Totem and Taboo'—on whether you think psychoanalysis is a myth of progress, of civilised advance and advantage, a way of leaving something distasteful (primitive?) behind. One man's privilege is another man's shame. Or to put it in another way, is losing your authority—your distance, your normality, your belief in the logic of your own thought—something to be ashamed of? To whom does the neurosis, and the shame, properly belong? (2003: 139)[18]

I wish to bring Freud (1953c) into conversation with Dipesh Chakrabarty (2001), whose work emerges from a very different theoretical lineage, primarily that of Karl Marx and Martin Heidegger.[19] Putting into perspective the intellectual inheritance of the Subaltern Studies project from which his book emerges, Chakrabarty reminds us that the discipline of Subaltern Studies grew out of a deep sense of unease with the very idea of the 'political' in established traditions of English-language Marxist historiography. Thus, he recalls Ranajit Guha's criticism of Eric Hobsbawm's category of the 'prepolitical' in Guha's landmark book *Elementary Aspects of Peasant Insurgency in Colonial India* (1983a). For Hobsbawm, the world of the peasant and his forms of action mobilized—more often than not—along axes of kinship, religion, caste and involving gods, spirits and supernatural agents were evidence of the prepolitical. For Guha, on the contrary, peasant consciousness in India was categorically *political*. Chakrabarty recounts:

> By explicitly critiquing the idea of peasant consciousness as 'prepolitical', Guha was prepared to suggest that the nature of collective action taken by peasants in modern India was such that it effectively stretched the category of the 'political' far beyond the boundaries assigned to it in European political thought.

[. . .]

South Asian political modernity, Guha argued, brings together two non-commensurable logics of power, both modern. One is the logic of the quasi-liberal legal and institutional frameworks that European rule introduced into the country . . . Braided with this, however, is the logic of another set of relationships . . . that articulate hierarchy through practices of direct and explicit subordination of the less powerful by the more powerful. The first logic is secular [. . .] The second has no necessary secularism about it; it is what continually brings gods and spirits into the domain of the political (2001: 12–14).

Over a series of essays, Chakrabarty then traces some of the socio-intellectual implications of the way these non-commensurable logics structure the very shape and texture of politics and modernity in the postcolonial world. The idea of 'history' was central to Marx's philosophical understanding of 'capital' itself. But, as Chakrabarty reminds us, *two* notions of history are actually at work here. The first history is what Marx calls capital's antecedent 'posited by itself' (History 1). This is the history that is 'established' by capital—the sum of those elements that are the logical structural presuppositions to the reproduction of capitalist relationships. The second is what Marx refers to as another past which is also encountered as an antecedent but which does not have any natural or necessary connection either to capital's life-process or to the past posited by it (History 2). And it is at this interstice—located at the very heart of Marx's idea of capital—that, Chakrabarty suggests, the postcolonial scholar can wrench possibilities of inscribing *difference* in history:

Marx thus writes into the intimate space of capital an element of deep uncertainty. Capital has to encounter in the reproduction of its own life-process relationships that present it with double possibilities. These relationships could be central to capital's self-reproduction, and yet is also possible for them to be oriented to structures that do not contribute to such reproduction. History 2s are thus not pasts separate from capital; they inhere in capital and yet interrupt and punctuate capital's own logic (ibid.: 64).

To read Marx in this way is to account for modes of being human in
the world where the empty homogeneous time of secular history coexists
intimately with the world of gods and spirits. It is to argue for a contemporary that is 'so radically plural that it is not possible for any aspect or element
to claim to represent the whole in any way (even as possible future)' (ibid.:
88), or—to invoke a cardinal principle of the Subaltern Studies initiative—
to account for the *many* distinct idioms of the political in the postcolonial
world. Drawing specifically on Partha Chatterjee's work, we will now carry
this argument a little further, to how we may bring Freud in conversation
with political theory in India today; and, generally, on the ways in which
psychoanalysis, as a conceptual apparatus, can enable us to better understand issues of citizenship especially in the non-classical context of the East.

FREUD IN THE 'HETEROGENEOUS' TIME OF THE *EAST*[20]

In her essay 'Freud in the Tropics' (2003), Rose argues that, contrary to its
popular image, 'Totem and Taboo' is actually a critique of 'Western'
racial/cultural authority. She also points out that as Freud engages with the
emotions and rituals of the Australian aborigine, in 'Totem and Taboo', he
is led to speculate on forms of collective life which are not defined through
lineage and possessive familial continuity. He is convinced, for instance,
that the denial of paternity amongst the Arunta is not simply a matter of
'primitive' ignorance. In fact, biological paternity might be an obstacle to
forms of being and belonging not limited to the here and now. And here,
to make the most explosive point in her essay, Rose cites Australian anthro-
pologist Tony Swain. In his book, *A Place for Strangers: Towards a History of
Australian Aboriginal Being* (1993), Swain hypothesizes that only a driven
people have to mark time:

> [L]inear time was a 'fall' from place. History, associated quintes-
> sentially with the Hebrews, was something which intervened when
> the Israelites lost their place [. . .] From the moment God said to
> Abraham 'Leave your country' instead of their place, the Hebrews
> had history and a promise of land—and *Zakhor*, remembrance
> [. . .] For Aborigines, as indeed it may have been true for the an-
> cient Hebrews, cosmic time emerged with the breaking of a con-
> nection between a land and its people (ibid.: 27).

So it is only when the earth has been plundered by the violence of colonial contact does power come to reside in the sky. And this leads us, in turn, not only to the fact that 'developmental' stories never follow straight lines but also to a 'here and now' that is 'radically plural' (Chakrabarty 2001: 88), to a present where the homogeneous time of secular history coexists seamlessly with the world of gods and spirits.

These ideas of heterogeneous time and the formation of collectivities can be run in two directions. On the one hand, as an example of the interrogation of the homogeneous time of the classical nation-state, one can draw on the idea of the *heterogeneous* time of the postcolonial nation that Partha Chatterjee has been developing in his current work. (Especially interesting is the way he has worked this notion into the idea of the 'political society'—as opposed to 'civil society'—as the representative social formation of postcolonial modernity.) On the other hand, one can read some of Freud's writings on the nature and formation of collectivities (see Freud 1955b). (Along with his notion of the unconscious and infantile sexuality, it was Freud's concept of 'the group' or 'the mass'/'mob'—or his attempt to understand how one changed into the other—that was most unsettling.) In short, this is the conversation that this book will attempt to engage in—between political theory and psychoanalysis—in order to show how the intersection of the two enriches a reading of Indian cinema.

For over a decade now, Partha Chatterjee has debated with Benedict Anderson the ways in which the nation was/is being imagined into existence in the postcolonial worlds of the *East*. I especially draw on two of Chatterjee's essays—'The Nation in Heterogeneous Time' and 'Populations and Political Society' (see Chatterjee 2004a, b)—where he lays out his central propositions:[21]

Citizenship will take on two different forms—the formal and the real. And unlike the old way [. . .] of talking about the rulers and the ruled, I will invite you to think of those who govern and those who are governed [. . .] Democracy today, I will insist, is not government of, by and for the people. Rather it should be seen as the politics of the governed [. . . L]et me begin by posing for you a conflict that lies at the heart of modern politics in most of the world. It is the opposition between the universal ideal of civic nationalism, based on individual freedoms and equal rights irrespective of race, language, or culture, and the particular demands of cultural identity, which call for the differential treatment of particular groups on grounds of vulnerability or backwardness or historical injustice, or indeed for numerous other reasons. This opposition [. . .] is symptomatic of the transition that occurred in modern politics in the course of the twentieth century from a conception of democratic politics grounded in the idea of popular sovereignty to one in which democratic politics is shaped by governmentality (2004a: 4).

Chatterjee then points out that the most significant addition that Anderson (1998) has made to his analysis of nationhood is the attempt to distinguish between nationalism and the politics of ethnicity. He underlines that Anderson achieves this by identifying two kinds of seriality produced by modern imaginings of community—the unbound seriality of the everyday universals of modern social thought (nations, citizens, revolutionaries, intellectuals, etc.) and the bound seriality of governmentality. Anderson hangs his argument about the residual goodness of nationalism and the unrelieved nastiness of ethnic politics on the kind of progressive universalist critical thought characteristic of the Enlightenment that he is keen to preserve. The aspiration here is to affirm an ethical universal that does not deny the variability of human lives but acknowledges them as the ground on which the universal must be established. It is this very universalism, according to Chatterjee, that leads Anderson into a theoretical blind:

> [Anderson] sees the politics of universalism as something that belongs to the very character of time in which we live. He speaks of the 'remarkable planetary spread, not merely of nationalism, but of a profoundly standardized conception of politics [. . .]' Such a conception of politics requires an understanding of the world as *one*, so that a common activity called politics can be seen to be going on *everywhere* [. . . P]olitics, in this sense, inhabits the empty homogeneous time-space of modernity [. . .] I disagree [. . . E]mpty homogeneous time is the time of capital. [. . . I]t is not located anywhere in real space—it is utopian. The real space of modern life consists of heterotopia [. . .] Time here is heterogeneous, unevenly dense [. . .] Politics [. . .] does not mean the same thing to all people (2004: 6–7).

As an example of the tension between the homogeneous time of capital and the heterogeneous time of governmentality that shapes the postcolonial world, Chatterjee cites the contradictions that marked certain moments in the career of B. R. Ambedkar as he struggled to resolve the rival demands of universal citizenship on the one hand and the protection of particularist rights for certain groups on the other. As Chatterjee points out, there is no available historical narrative that can resolve these contradictions. Hence, the present impasse. However, as terms of political justice are invented anew through the contestations between mass democracy and class rule, Chatterjee speculates that the domain of political society will decisively rewrite the language of classical liberalism.

Recalling the split in the domain of politics (in the colonial period) between the realm of the elite and that of the peasantry that informed the early work of the Subaltern Studies collective, Chatterjee emphasizes that political society is a recent formation—the product of the democratic process in India bringing under its influence the lives of subaltern classes and the resulting *new* forms of entanglement of elite and subaltern politics:

> [I] mean by political society and how it works [. . . the] politics emerging out of the developmental policies of government aimed at specific target groups. Many of these [. . .] transgress the strict lines of legality in struggling to live and work [. . .] Yet state agencies and nongovernmental organizations cannot ignore them [. . .] since they are among thousands of similar associations whose very livelihood or habitation involve violation of the law.
>
> These groups on their part accept that their activities are often illegal [. . .] but they make a claim to habitation and livelihood as a matter of right.
>
> [. . .] What happens then is a negotiation of these claims on a political terrain where, on the one hand, governmental agencies have a public obligation to look after the poor and the underprivileged and, on the other, particular population groups receive attention from those agencies according to calculations of political expediency. Groups in political society have to pick their way through this uncertain terrain by making a large array of connections [. . .] They often make instrumental use of the fact that they can vote

[. . .] But [this] is possible only within a field of strategic politics. This is the stuff of democratic politics as it takes place on the ground (ibid.: 40–1).

The real stuff of democracy therefore, in a country like India, is neither the constitutional model of the state nor the domain of the rights-bearing bourgeois individual or citizen of civil society. On the contrary, in postcolonial nation-states, these are both restricted to the small enclave of the cultural elite. The terrain of political society, on the other hand, is the terrain of 'populations', a category that is the target of state policies. 'Populations' are, moreover, empirical and descriptive, and, in describing them, the postcolonial state often continues to use classificatory criteria used by colonial regimes. Thus caste and religion, for example, continue to remain the dominant criteria for identifying communities as objects of state policy in India. Demands that emerge from this terrain are collective or communitarian and crucially involve transformations of property and law within the existing state. However, the collectivities in question here are not 'primordial' and do not seek legitimation on these grounds. Yet, they do seek to invest themselves with moral content. In fact, the collectivities in question here not only may be in implicitly competitive relationships vis-à-vis each other but they also may be imaginatively defined *in opposition* to the community of the nation.

Additionally, while groups in political society only form 'for the moment', as it were, for Chatterjee the distinct character of mobilization of collectivities in this terrain—since roughly the last three decades in India—emerges out of two very specific conditions. One: the rise to dominance of a notion of governmental performance that emphasizes welfare and protection of 'populations' rather than citizens. (Invoking Foucault, Chatterjee calls this the 'pastoral' function of government.) Two: the widening of the arena of political mobilization itself. The resulting historical contradiction of the present is the resistance that the postcolonial elite encounter in their attempts to 'modernize' subaltern subjects into national citizens. However, as the subaltern classes resist (and, in the process, transform) the modernizing project imposed upon them, they also embark on a process of internal transformation.

Chatterjee's explicit debt to Bhabha in his conceptualization of the heterogeneous time of the postcolonial nation makes it especially easy for me to dovetail arguments emerging from political theory into psychoanalysis. But there is, I would argue, another thread one could tease out—that between Chatterjee's idea of the heterogeneous time of the postcolonial modern whose imagined futures (and, of course, possible pasts) might even be radically incommensurable and the psychoanalytical notion of 'development'/sequence that moves in both directions and draws, additionally, on atemporal aspects of personality.[22] And to substantively acknowledge this 'psychoanalytic' debt, let us turn to Freud's writings on the nature and formation of groups, seen through the works of Edward Said[23] and, again, Jacqueline Rose.[24]

Referring to Freud (1953c, 1974), Said proposes that one can reject the 'flawed' historical arguments in both these texts while still accepting Freud's underlying thesis that there is no sociality without violence. For Freud, what a 'people' have in common is a trauma. What unites them most powerfully is what they agree to hate. Said points out that Freud's writing possesses a dimension that also suggests that the act of investigating a trauma psychoanalytically might—far from generating freedom—lead to a very different kind of fragmentation. It might turn out to be devastating, causing identities to flatten, leading to dogmatic coercive faith. This may, in turn, lead (formerly oppressed) people to justify the violence of the state. Freud points out that the most historically attested response to trauma is the repetition of it. In some ways, this is also the most stubborn and self-defeating psychic terrain where a people can be both loving (towards themselves) and lethal (towards others). In a passionate invocation of the situation of the Middle East, Said argues that there can be no progress without a shared recognition of pain; that all critics of Israel (Arab or Jewish) need to hold together in their minds the polar emotions of empathy and rage—however reluctant the first, and however legitimate the second, for the Palestinians. (Needless to say, the importance of sustaining ambivalence that Said invokes here resonates directly with the 'primitive' ambivalence of Freud [1953c].)

Rose carries forward this dialogue with Freud and Said, and points out that Freud was faced with two radically different concepts of nationalism in his time: an expansionist German nationalism; and the nationalism of a dispossessed people. Insisting that Auschwitz should not be monumentalized,

Rose points out that the signifier 'Palestine' was as much a phantom of psychoanalysis as the infamous Australian aborigine. But Rose also traces Freud's writings on the 'group' back to his crucial paper 'On Narcissism' (2007: 62–92; see also Freud 1959), and points out that Freud's discovery that the subject could be her/his own love-object not only challenged his earlier distinction between the self and the other but it also brought him to confront the question: if not for the satisfaction of sexual drives, how and why do we connect to others? Freud's answer: what we most yearn for is to be recognized and acknowledged; that we need others to fashion ourselves. Rose cites Freud on the process of identification: 'Identification [. . .] behaves like a product of the first *oral* stage of the libido organisation in which the coveted, treasured object was incorporated by eating and annihilated in the process' (ibid.: 63).

Identification is ruthless—we devour those we wish to be. It is central to Freud's thinking on the topic that what binds people together, for better or worse, is their commitment to an internal ideal. Further, since we are all narcissists, we will only give up our self-love if there is something or someone we can put in the same place—something that makes us feel good about ourselves. Freud's originality in his thinking on this topic is his insight that even while being part of a group, we feel we are a cut above the rest. Hostility is therefore integral to the very formation of the group. Chillingly, the two groups that are the objects of Freud's analysis are the Army and the Church. So Freud not only places murder at the origin of the group but, by making Moses into an Egyptian (a non-Jew), he also suggests that identity, while necessary, is always provisional. Most importantly, Freud's insights on collectivities pose the question: 'how do you save a people both from the hatred of others *and* from themselves?' (In Rose 2008: 87.)

The point of this extended detour was to map the ways in which Freud and Marx will continually dovetail in my subsequent analyses of Bombay cinema and the Bombay film industry. Such a conversation, I suspect, might provide yet another opening in terms of inscribing the 'Indian point of view' on the institution of cinema. Further, a 'symptom' (in the analytical sense) never has a one-on-one correspondence with the unconscious psychic scars from which it erupts. A dream, as Freud states, 'appears as a reaction to everything that is simultaneously present and active in the sleeping psyche' (1953a: 176). Dream analysis always carries a certain uncertainty—involves a necessary risk. Freud writes: 'Indeed, the dream-thoughts we come upon as we interpret cannot in general but remain without closure, spinning out on all sides into the web-like fabric of our thoughts' (ibid.: 341). Following Freud, I have analysed the emergence of Madhuri Dixit as a Star, for instance, not in the idiom of 'established' Film Theory but as the only 'manifest' symptom of fundamental shifts in Bombay's production base that were precipitated by liberalization, changes which saw *music* emerge as the dominant sector of the film industry. So too with my discussion of the New Indian Man as represented by Aamir Khan—this refiguring of the hero in 1980s' Bombay cinema, in my reading, was a symptom of the tremendous anxiety caused to the traditional middle-class imagination by the new wave of the women's movement. With this broad mapping of the book's intellectual terrain, let us examine the current concerns of Indian Film Theory and the new dialogue on 'realism' and 'narrative form' that has emerged between Film Theory in India and the West.

THE 'REALISM' QUESTION

In our discussions so far, we have noted that modernity, as an idea, has carried very different connotations at different times and places. Emerging with the European Enlightenment and floating as a concept outside its usage in the historical reality of struggle in India, modernity, as a philosophical concept, both precipitated and fossilized changes in complex and unpredictable ways as it interacted with preexisting ideas and institutions in India. We have characterized the resulting situation as the bilingualism of the postcolonial world, a situation where there is a fundamental difference between the conceptual language of the state and its reworking in the terrain of culture. Further, the most crucial marker of difference between the two domains was the way in which the colonial logic of counting and modes of self-definition (on which this logic was premised) were negotiated into idioms that reinforced the socio-political interests of traditional Indian elites. What is more, the nature of the ruling bloc in modern India has been markedly different from that of the West, the nascent Indian bourgeoisie being only one of several partners in the ruling coalition which comprises landlords and professional classes as well. And the question of 'realism' has been a key site in the struggles between these different segments of the Indian ruling bloc in their attempts to achieve hegemonic status. As an aesthetic strategy, realism had performed crucial ideological functions in the ascendancy of the Western bourgeoisie to state power as well. In what follows, I will very briefly retrace some of these connections.

It is roughly about 200 years ago that the term 'modern' first begins to appear as synonymous with 'now'/'the present'. Broadly, the Enlightenment sense of the modern could be mapped along two axes—of time and of space. The decisive shift in notions of time that enabled the Enlightenment sense of the 'now' was the emergence of the secular regimented time of the clock and the calendar as opposed to the mediaeval time of prefiguring and fulfilment—a conception of time whose emergence was coterminous with the decline of the great sacral cultures of Christendom.[25] This change in notions of time was simultaneous with an equally fundamental shift in notions of space when, around the sixteenth century, land/physical space became a commodity that could be bought and sold.[26] These twin phenomena—the emergence of enumerated/economic time and commodified space, signifying labour-market mobility and the emergence of a mercantile economy—in turn fed into the new imagined form of community that emerged contemporaneously in Western Europe—the classical nation-state, a form of community that emerged also as the obverse of the project of colonization.

Importantly, as an aesthetic strategy, realism marked the decisive transition from the sacred to the post-sacred world in the realm of culture. The constitutive link between the new regime of power and emergent discourses on 'art' lay in the crucial ideological function of realism to reproduce the 'free' contracting *individuals* on whose circulation the new state of the West depended. In the cultural terrain, this involved a reconstitution of the social world around the figure of the 'citizen'. As recent debates on the classic realist text of nineteenth-century Western Europe have shown, realism as an aesthetic strategy reproduces this prior 'social contract' along two axes— the legal and the economic. On the one hand, it orders narratives according to possibilities permissible under the Rule of Law.[27] On the other (the economic), it produces an internal unity within the text while generating a tendency for external differentiation. Thus the proliferation of genres in

Hollywood, for example, is dependent on an advanced capitalist mode of production. In contrast, as Prasad has demonstrated, the Bombay industry, historically marked by 'backward' capitalism, has proved resistant to genre formation (1994: 251–60). Given the differential nature of the Indian political formation, where the question of 'representativeness' acquired a completely different hue owing to colonial rule, the aesthetic of Bombay has, therefore, also varied dramatically from Hollywood.

In fact, in the fashioning of a distinctly nationalist modernity in India, the language of liberalism was hitched on to new collective identities such as 'nation'/'region' rather than the autonomous 'individual' who formed the linchpin of the conceptual world of the Western bourgeoisie. Consequently, the aesthetic of realism in India too was transformed into a whole new set of strategies as well as ideological functions in the service of these new socio-political formations. The language of Bombay cinema acquired its distinctive accent from its location at this interstice of the project of translating modernity. The arrival of Independence and the subsequent moment of liberalization saw further negotiations of the Enlightenment notion of the modern in India's political life. As a result, definitions of cinematic realism in Bombay also underwent modifications.

My aim in this book will be to show that the changed relationship between 'English' and 'Hindi' in India in the 1980s provided the constitutive ground for a new hybrid form of commercial cinema that emerged in Bombay at the time, indicative of a distinctly altered location of the film industry vis-à-vis the newly 'liberalizing' Indian nation.[28]

THE STRUCTURE OF THE BOOK

The first chapter is in the nature of a prelude, providing an overview of 'English' in India. The aim here has not been to give a historical account of the disciplinary formation of English Studies. Rather, in keeping with the engagement of the book with the philosophical concept of modernity, it tries to plot the major moments of English, as a signifying system, within the national imaginary—of the aspiration to modernity that English in India signified under colonial rule; the reworking of this modernity in the context of Nehruvian socialism and the subsequent emergence of a 'new' (American) English as a signifier of the free-market internationalism in the

1980s. Consistently associated with a discourse on secularism—a stand-in for humanism and the scientific spirit—I have tried to show that this whole 'structure of feeling' in India has historically carried a de facto marking as upper-caste Hindu.

The second chapter attempts a similar exercise with 'Hindi'. Beginning with the emergence of a new Sanskritized form of the Hindi language, I have tried to show that a new caste–class–regional hegemony was being articulated in the very creation of a new language. Given that vernacular languages were decisively located in the terrain of culture in the politics/culture divide in the history of Indian nation-formation, the modernity signified by this Sanskritized Hindi both complemented and contradicted the modernity signified by English under colonial rule. These overlaps and contradictions can be read as projects to *translate* the modernity imposed by colonial rule into indigenist vocabularies. Assuming distinctive shape as an act of nationalist self-assertion, the contours of the cultural terrain have, since Independence, undergone two decisive mutations: the first represented by 'regionalisms' of the 1950s leading to the formation of linguistic states; and the second, by 'new regionalisms' of the 1980s emerging out of the interactions of global capital with internal contradictions of the post-Nehruvian nation.[29] The changes in the status of Hindi vis-à-vis the two regionalisms has been dramatic. The formations of the linguistic states in the 1950s—and here Tamil Nadu would be the most dramatic example—mobilized explicitly anti-Hindi sentiments. The new regionalisms that emerged in the 1980s, however, fed seamlessly into the overarching Hindu fascism represented by the politics of Hindutva, one that has actively advocated Hindi as 'national language' instead. The new Hindi jockeying for the status of the 'national modern' with American English is one that has emerged through the popular–cultural terrain, especially television.[30] The larger point that these changes gesture towards is that the classical Western nation-state was radically transformed as it was transplanted in the colonies. The internal redrawing of boundaries along linguistic lines in India is testimony to the fact that there were many other competing narratives of community prevalent in the country. Hindi was only *one* among many such conceptual worlds. Moreover, as we shall see in subsequent sections, these competing narratives would find most eloquent expression through the technology of the moving image. Thus, as we locate Bombay cinema within the historical and political conditions of its emergence, it becomes evident that the very institution of cinema was radically transformed both in form and content while taking root in the colonies.

With this background—and given the new equation between English and Hindi since the 1980s—the third chapter attempts a topoanalysis of the 1980s' Hindi/Bombay film industry. Given the changed cultural context signified by the dominance of transnational capital, North American consumer culture and a simultaneous new visibility of Hindi in the public sphere, I have proposed some tentative hypotheses on a new kind of commercial cinema that emerged in Bombay at the time. To anticipate arguments of subsequent sections, given the new technologies of mass culture mediating the process of structural adjustment, I have proposed that there also occurred a realignment of dominance within the different sectors of the Bombay industry. The prominence of the Film Star of the 1950s and 1960s was now replaced by that gained by the music segment. This shift in dominance also saw the related emergence of a new cinematic aesthetic premised on the ordinary.

Paralleling the major moments in the trajectories of English and Hindi, one can also plot three moments in the history of realism in Bombay—realism as it was mediated by the cultural politics of Swadeshi,[31] the symbolic realism of the Nehruvian era[32] and what I have termed as the 'televisual realism' of the 1980s. Drawing on the 'middle cinema'[33] of the 1970s, the new televisually mediated aesthetics of 1980s' *commercial* cinema in Bombay foregrounded the 'ordinary'/'the everyday' as the site of significant action.

Having proposed the emergence of a new cinematic aesthetic in the 1980s, I have also traced the reworking of narrative structure that this new realism precipitated in both Bombay's major 'genres'—the love story and the action film. Keeping in mind Bombay's massive impact on the self-definition of the nation, I have read the love story and the anti-hero film as cinematic negotiations between the 'nation and its fragments'[34]—women and lower castes/classes respectively, the 'others' against whom a 'normative' Indianness has historically been consolidated.

In the light of the structural analysis of the 1980s' Bombay film industry attempted in the third chapter, the fourth and fifth chapters present close readings of representative texts from the love story and the anti-hero genre respectively, *Qayamat Se Qayamat Tak* (From Disaster to Disaster, 1988) and *Tezaab* (Acid, 1988). In the context of the three moments of realism just noted, it is significant that the televisually mediated realism of the 1980s reworked the ideological ground of Swadeshi, its thrust on ordinariness feeding into the whole relaunching of Indianness that marked the Hindutva project. As my close readings of *Qayamat Se Qayamat Tak* and *Tezaab* show, a concern with the 'Indianness' of filmic representations resurfaced in both Bombay's major genres in the 1980s.[35] Further, given the different class segments which were the referents of the love story and the anti-hero film, my readings show that this resurgent concern with Indianness was differentially mediated within discourses that constituted upper- and lower-middle-class subjectivities, respectively.

Given the identification effect with the upper middle class constructed by the 1980s' love story, a milieu in which feminism exerted its maximum pressure in India, the reclaiming of authentic Indianness was displaced onto anxieties over changing forms of 'marriage' and 'family'. But, given the identification effect with the lower middle class constructed by 1980s' action cinema—a milieu in which questions of 'work' and employment came to assume enormous significance—the anxiety over sex and violence mediated the Swadeshi-generated ideological distinction between 'good' and 'bad' capital to argue that 'deserving' and 'meritorious' upper-caste young men were now being 'deprived' of their rightful place within the nation. If we use 'Mandal'[36] and 'Ayodhya'[37] as shorthand terms to indicate the nature of some landmark political initiatives that shaped the times, it does not take too much belabouring of the point to map this overarching generic logic onto the politics of the New Right.

We have noted earlier that modernity functions in this book as a sliding signifier, its connotations changing over time and space. From this perspective, as we trace the ways in which modernity as a concept travelled from Enlightenment Europe to 1980s' Bombay, what becomes obvious is that ideas rarely have unambiguous meanings. As they journey across time and space, they gather significations that do not derive either from a straightforward impulse to dominate (which clearly was the major thrust of the colonial rhetoric in India) or from an equally unproblematic story of resistance (as nationalist historiography would have us believe). Instead, they precipitate changes that are unintended, become eroded by the conditions in which they exist and shift in ways that are discontinuous.

To sum up, then, this book raises some halting speculations on the present, some tentative questions on the very nature of modernity we have inherited as part of our postcolonial legacy. In this broad sweep from the language-question to cinema, from high to popular culture, I draw on that sublime moment of Marxist cultural theory represented by the writings of Antonio Gramsci. His research into the history of culture of the Italian nation led him to analyse a whole range of related questions, what he called 'the connection of problems'—from the education system in Italy to popular romances and the relationship between traditional intellectuals and the masses of Italian people. Such a wide-ranging analysis, Gramsci argued, was warranted on the ground that the proletarian revolution could not but be a total revolution—that the 'objective' conditions necessary for the emergence of a 'national popular' cultural practice required a decisive restructuring of the whole terrain of the social:

> The sum of these problems [of language, territorial unity, religion, etc.] reflects the laborious emergence of the Italian nation, impeded by a balance of internal and international forces. [. . .] The intellectual and leading classes in Italian society have never been aware of the fact that there is a connection between these problems, one of co-ordination and subordination. [. . .] Nobody has ever presented these problems as a coherent and connected whole [. . .] Therefore, they have always been treated in an abstractly cultural and intellectualist form, without a precise historical perspective and hence [. . .] without a solution to them ever emerging. It may well be that nobody has had the courage to pose the question exhaustively because it was feared that vital dangers for the unified life of the nation would immediately result from such a rigorously critical and consequential formulation (1985: 199).

Given the enormity of the task that Gramsci has set us—of the creation of a whole new concept of what it means to be human—my research can, of course, only hope to be one among many similar initiatives in many other parts of the world. Within the specific context of India, too, my research does not have 'solutions' to the theoretical–political impasse in which we, as postcolonials, find ourselves. It draws, instead, on a challenging ongoing debate interrogating modernity in India. The overarching aim of this debate has been to rethink dominant notions of modernity in ways that might question its very logic—to imagine new forms of community where identities do not feed into the relentless logic of measurement on which the liberal nation-state is based,[38] and to create modern knowledges in the Kant–Foucault tradition of our present.

Notes

1 For an early formulation of this, see, among others, the special issue of *Journal of Arts and Ideas* 25–26 (December 1993).

2 My use of the term 'popular' draws on Stuart Hall (1981). Analyses of popular culture on which I have modelled my research would necessarily include classics such as Roland Barthes (1972). In terms of research specifically focusing on interconnections between the emergence of the category of the 'popular' and the nation-state, see Peter Burke (1978).

3 I will elaborate on this later. It might, however, be appropriate to introduce here the fact that the 'language-question' in India has an extremely charged and complicated history. (In fact, the relationship of Hindi as *language* to Bombay cinema is itself full of twists and turns.) But the immediate inspiration for my research is Antonio Gramsci's analysis of the language-question in Italy (1971: 24–63; 90–102). There is another point that this book seeks to make. Given the way in which the Enlightenment notion of the 'modern' was rewritten in the non-West, the technology of the moving image in India too came to be invested with a set of meanings completely different from its European heartland. It became, in effect, a *different* socio-cultural institution from that, say, in the US. Moreover, the language-question in India had particular relevance to this whole process. To understand the differences between the aesthetic strategies adopted by Bombay and Hollywood, for instance, we need to understand the different histories of the popular in these two locales. And as I will show, an analysis of the language-question, or the dichotomy between the world of 'English' and the world of the 'vernaculars' in India, is crucial to an understanding of the aesthetics of Bombay.

4   I will deal with this point in the 'Afterword'. I refer here to the period which, in the history of Indian cinema specifically, has been referred to as the era of its 'Bollywoodization' in recent critical writing (see Rajadhyaksha 2007).

5   According to current statistics on its official website, Doordarshan, the state-owned public television service of India, now covers more than 90.7 per cent of the Indian population. But it was in the 1980s that this growth saw its major spurt. I will elaborate on this point in Chapter 3. But, soon after the introduction of colour in Indian television, the Ministry of Information and Broadcasting proposed an ambitious plan (1984) to extend Doordarshan's coverage significantly (see Joshi 1985).

6   I use this term to refer not only to the expressly articulated political ideology of the Bharatiya Janata Party (BJP) but also to the virulent resurgence of Hindu neo-nationalism that now clearly exceeds organized party politics (and party lines), manifesting itself most lethally in a new fundamentalist 'common sense'.

7   To recap a by-now familiar history, there was an interesting tension in the kind of Hindi that was used in Bombay cinema in the early days ever since the birth of the talkies. But, despite being located in a non-Hindi speaking region (Maharashtra), and in an official climate where Hindi was being increasingly Sanskritized, the decision of the Bombay film industry to use Urdu/Hindustani in the initial days was remarkable. (This has been the object of a series of studies such as those by Amrit Ganghar [1995] and Nasreen Munni Kabir [1999].) Moreover, it was the highly cultivated, poetic Urdu that was used (for the protagonists) in the films of the 1930s and 1940s. Gradually, however, Hindi was purged of its Urdu-ness, and a hybrid Hindi (popularly called 'Bambayya' and used primarily by the then-newly immigrant population of Bombay) made its appearance. It is a certain appropriation of this hybrid Hindi as radical chic in the 1980s and 1990s, for example, that will be the focus of my analysis.

8   See, among others, a selection of essays in *Journal of Arts and Ideas* 14–15 (1987).

9   For a discussion of the new conjuncture of 'politics' and 'culture' that marks the politics of the New Right in the US, see Henry A. Giroux (1993):

> In the current historical conjuncture there is an ongoing attempt by the forces of the new right to replace the practice of substantive democracy with a democracy of images [. . .] The war being waged by the new conservative bloc is not simply over profit or the securing

of traditional forms of authority, it is over the emergence of decentred and oppositional discourses such as feminism, postmodernism
and post colonialism, that have begun to call into question all the
grand narratives of modernism [. . .] and its adamant insistence that
Western culture is synonymous with the very notion of civilisation
[. . .]

The political currency of popular culture is not to be determined
within a binarism that simply reverses its relation to high culture.
The more important task for cultural workers is to reconstruct the
very problematic that informs the high vs. popular cultural distinction in order to understand more specifically how cultural production works within and outside of the margins of power in texts
actively engaged in the production of institutional structures, social
identities and horizons of the possible (ibid.: 37–8).

10 In tune with this continuing interest in developing 'Asian' paradigms/
frameworks for social sciences, see also Vivek Dhareshwar (2010).

11 Partha Chatterjee's work is the foundation on which I have built my analysis of Bombay. I will return to this point in the Afterword, but we must
note here Chatterjee's continuing dialogue with Benedict Anderson and
the way in which he has reworked and developed the passive revolution
argument in the light of the consolidation of a new phase of corporate
capital in India in the 2000s.

12 For an interesting discussion on the spatial strategies of the Hindutva ideology, see Satish Deshpande (1995).

13 For a discussion of the institutional contours of the area as it has emerged
within the American University, see Gayatri Chakravorty Spivak (1993a:
244–55); this is a point she has subsequently elaborated in Spivak (2003).

14 Naxalbari is the name of a village and a development block in northern
West Bengal. Naxalbari became famous for the violent, radical Left, pro-
poor-peasant uprising that began there in the late 1960s with the slogan,
'Land to tiller'. This was also in the aftermath of the split in the Communist Party of India (Marxist) and the formation of the Communist Party of
India (Marxist-Leninist). The movement gained a strong presence among
radical sections of the student movement and found many supporters in
elite colleges of especially Calcutta and Delhi. The movement continues
at present, in various parts of India. These Maoist-Communist groups have
been declared as terrorist organizations under the 1967 Unlawful Activities
(Prevention) Act.

15 The argument has been further developed by Ashish Rajadhyaksha (2009: 3–45). However, framed within the (turbulent Third World) Marxist–internationalist lineage of the 1970s that he refers to (ibid.: 5), and cognizant of the contradictory yet intimate relationship of postcolonial scholarship with 'friendly Western theory' (ibid.), my analysis of Bombay stems specifically from the vantage point offered by psychoanalysis.

16 While Jung has popularly been seen as more sympathetic to India, the context of the Second World War, however, gave his sympathies a rather different colour. Jung's fascination for 'National Socialism' contrasted starkly with Freud's sympathies for the non-Western 'savage'. 'Australia' therefore also became the site for the underlying conflict between the Aryan and the Jew. See also Edward Said (2003) for a brilliant reading of 'Totem and Taboo' and 'Moses and Monotheism'.

17 See, for example, Homi K. Bhabha (1994). In this context, I also want to mention Spivak (1993c, d). Here, Spivak engages with the theorist who has been formative to my own project, especially as she takes up 'a sort-of Derrida' against Jacqueline Rose's 'a sort-of Lacan'. My reading of poststructuralist theory is fairly rudimentary at this point in the book. But as my work progresses, I do hope to be able to engage with Spivak's work more critically.

18 Rose develops these arguments further in her Introduction to Moustafa Safouan (2000). The central questions that the book raises are: what does the process of training-analysis actually involve?; what is the analysed encouraged to identify with and at what cost? For Lacan, according to Moustafa Safouan, all that one learns at the end of the training analysis is the shared ability to mourn (along with the analyst).

19 But in so doing I am aware that this is, in many ways, quite contrary to Dipesh Chakrabarty's own theoretical impulse, which has seen psychoanalysis as the cardinal text of Western prejudice.

20 I owe this phrase to Chatterjee (2004: 7).

21 For a further development of these ideas, see also Chatterjee (2008).

22 Childhood for Freud (unlike Jean Piaget and his 'developmental' psychology) is not a stage that we ever simply outgrow or leave behind—it is something that persists, something that we endlessly rework. Formative to the notions of identity we construct, it also constantly shows us that there is a part of our minds over which we have no control—see especially Freud (1953b). The theorist who has carried Freud's insights furthest in this regard is the child-analyst, Melanie Klein. This conversation—between

Chatterjee's analysis of our 'heterogeneous' present and Kleinian notions of time, sequence and development—is explored in Sircar (2009).

23 I refer here to the reading of Freud's 'Moses and Monotheism' in Said (2003). But the questions of state formation and psychoanalysis resonate equally powerfully in his works as far back as Said (1979).

24 My reference here is to Rose (2007). However, the question of Israel/ Zionism has increasingly been the theme of her work over the last few years—see Rose (2004). In fact, Rose (2005) is a tribute to Said (1979).

25 I refer here, of course, to Anderson (1983).

26 See, among many others, Lennard Davis (1987).

27 For discussions, see Pam Cook (1985: 222–49) and M. Madhava Prasad (1994: 115–31). Where cited, Prasad's dissertation—'The State and Culture: Hindi Cinema in the Passive Revolution'—is henceforth referred to as 'SCH'. See also the introductory essay—'The Literature of the Reform and Nationalist Movements'—in Susie Tharu and K. Lalita (1995) for an extended discussion on the ways in which women in India negotiated the new writer-subjectivities being sculpted by the new aesthetic of realism.

28 While obviously emerging out of vastly different historical trajectories, a parallel development also seems to have happened in Hollywood in the context of the new phase of capitalism. See, among others, Thomas Schatz (1993).

29 It is beyond the scope of this book to trace the formation of three subsequent states—Chattisgarh, Uttarakhand and Jharkhand. Questions of language/dialect (especially vis-à-vis 'standard' Hindi) were raised in the demands for statehood in these regions too. Statehood to the city of Delhi, however, followed a different trajectory. But the language-question has resurfaced with intensity in the new phase of the Telangana agitation and the present uncertainty of the coming into being of India's 30th state.

30 It is useful to underline here the different trajectories that English and Hindi, as signifying systems, have followed in their aspirations to hegemonic status. As a signifying system, Hindi has had its high-cultural component too, as institutionalized in Hindi Literature departments in Indian universities, for example. However, given that the nation-state in India was imagined into existence as an anticolonial gesture, at its originary moments, Hindi lacked the charisma attached to English under colonial rule. For reasons that I will elaborate in the following chapters, English has continued to occupy the high-cultural realm even after Independence. The impact of Hindi's high-cultural component has remained marginal. It is

only as it is articulated through the popular terrain that Hindi is now making a concerted bid for the 'national modern' status on the lines of English.

31 The term roughly translates as 'Indigenism'. Used to describe a major moment in the nationalist struggle, from roughly 1905 to 1908. The period was one of great intellectual and political ferment as Eurocentric modes of looking were critiqued across the range of cultural forms, accompanied by the impetus to recover an ostensibly pristine 'Indian Tradition'. See, among others, Tharu and Lalita (1995: 71–90).

32 I have elaborated this argument later in the book. Here I would merely like to point out that recent debates on Indian cinema have documented that, even in the classic era of nation-building, the differential formation of the Indian nation from that of Western Europe meant that the realism of the classic era of Bombay cinema in the 1950s was *different* from both the classic realist text of nineteenth-century Western Europe as well as its manifestation in the domestic melodrama of 1950s' Hollywood.

33 I owe this term to Prasad (1997) who has pointed out that the emerging dominance of capital in the Indian economy since the late 1960s and early 1970s generated a related thrust towards product-differentiation within the mainstream Bombay industry, which is why that period saw the emergence of three distinct generic tendencies within the overarching genre of the Bombay 'social'—the 'middle-class' cinema, or 'middle cinema', popularly called New Indian Cinema; a new kind of 'political' cinema which Prasad describes as the 'developmentalist aesthetic' of filmmakers such as Shyam Benegal; and a new reformed 'social' which Prasad describes as the 'mass cinema' of the 1970s. We will return to this classification at several points later. Important for our purposes here is that middle cinema marked itself off from mass cinema precisely by playing up certain notions of verisimilitude—low-budget films, the use of deglamorized Stars and social-reform-oriented scripts, etc., to suggest that unlike the melodramatic Bombay commercial, middle cinema was presenting pictures of the 'ordinary'/ 'the everyday' (1997: 162–87). This book is actually a reworking of Prasad (1994). I have referred, at different instances, to both these works by Prasad.

34 I owe this phrase to Chatterjee (1994a).

35 Rajadhyaksha argues that the overall paradigm shift from the 1920s to the 1950s in mainstream Indian cinemas was a concern from 'Indianness' of images on screen to a concern with their 'realism' (1993a: 55–70). The 1980s, then, in interesting ways, bring the two together as a new thrust on *representationalism* is now pressed into the service of *re*-claiming Indianness.

36 A violent upper-caste hysteria erupted in the wake of the Janata Dal government's decision to implement the affirmative action policy of increasing
reservations for 'backward castes' in educational institutions and the public
sector as per the recommendations of the Mandal Commission in August/
September 1990. It led to a nationwide outcry on the 'death of merit' with
several upper-caste students immolating themselves.

37 Hindu fundamentalists have argued that the Indian government has consistently pandered to the interests of the 'minority', i.e. the Muslims, at
the expense of that of the 'majority', i.e. the Hindus. To avenge this deep
historical injustice, the BJP and its allies set as their one-point programme
the destruction of a sixteenth-century mosque in the Northern Indian city
of Ayodhya which, they claimed, had been forcibly built on a temple marking the birthplace of the mythical Hindu king, Ram. The complicity of the
liberal with this New Right was blatant when, in the presence of central
government troops, BJP cadres vandalized and destroyed the mosque on
6 December 1992. In what is popularly believed to be a retaliation, massive
bomb blasts ripped across Bombay in January 1993, supposedly master-
minded by the Dubai-based mafia don Dawood Ibrahim. The events indicate the charged caste and communal tensions within the country today.

38 For a sense of the enormity of this concern at the time, see: 'Secularism,
Modernity and the State', *Economic and Political Weekly* (special issue) 29(28)
(1994).

CHAPTER ONE

'ENGLISH', MODERNITY AND THE LANGUAGE OF NATIONHOOD

How far did they fly? Five and a half thousand as the crow. Or: from Indianness to Englishness, an immeasurable distance (Rushdie 1989: 41).

[I]f, like Derrida and Foucault, you are a scrupulous academic who *is* largely an academic, you stage the crisis relationship between theory and practice in the practice of your theoretical production in various ways instead of legitimizing the polarization between the academy and the real world by disavowing it, and then producing elegant solutions that will never be seriously tested either in large-scale decision-making or among the disenfranchised (Spivak 1993b: 51).

In 1835, Thomas Babington Macaulay recommended to the Governor General in Council that Britain officially support English education and withdraw support to Sanskrit and Arabic/Persian. His hysterical dismissal of the entire body of indigenous learning in these three languages, made in ignorance of both, was enabled by about 100 years of colonial scholarship that legitimized the notion that the peoples and societies of India were inferior and defective versions of their Western European counterparts.

And what about Saladin Chamcha? Eternally haunted by the fear that modernity was something that had already happened somewhere else in the West, in its broadest terms, it is the history of *his* journey that this book tries to narrate, not as an attempt to reclaim lost traditions but as an assertion of what Fanon calls 'national culture' (1990).[1]

Speaking of the difference between dogmatic and critical philosophies, Spivak suggests caution at overhasty notions of 'freedom' and 'liberation'. Our notions of political activism, she argues, derive fundamentally from the bourgeois revolution of 1789—the call for individual rights, psychosexual liberation and constitutional agency. Within the context of the decolonized world, the scenario is further complicated by the fact that these notions are also coded with the legacy of imperialism. But that, she suggests, does not make these claims any less valid, given that they are now being advanced from social spaces for which there have not been any historically adequate referents. Thus, even as the Enlightenment is 'cited', it is reinterpreted as a different scene. By way of a deconstructive theorizing of practice, she argues, such 'misfit' between example and theoretical argument represents not an accusation or failure. Rather, it describes how 'theory brings practice to crisis, and practice norms theory, and deviations constitute a forever precarious norm; everything opened and menaced by the risk of paleonymy' (Spivak 1993b: 37).

Following Spivak, the aim of this chapter is to explore the dynamics of the institutionalization of English in India—to account for the roles it has played in the national imaginary since its introduction in the nineteenth century. I use 'English' here not only as a language but also as a signifier of the conceptual domain of the state, the domain of formal culture, gesturing towards the decisive changes that occurred in the social terrain in the nineteenth century as a result of British colonial intervention. As indicated in Macaulay's Minute, the term 'English Literature' included the entire field of writing—history, moral philosophy, political economy, creative writing, i.e. the entire post-Enlightenment conceptual apparatus introduced in India through colonial rule. What follows, therefore, is not a history of the disciplinary formation of English Studies but an attempt to trace the inter-secting interests of colony and nation as a new discursive world was sought to be transplanted—initially, for the most systematic extraction of land revenues and, later, to convert India into a market for British goods—and as this discursive world was, in turn, negotiated by the indigenous intelligentsia.

In such an analysis of English, of course, I draw on the writings of Gramsci, especially his analysis of the language-question in 1920–30s' Italy. For Gramsci, linguistic relations were not simply traces of 'political' power but were also paradigmatic of the whole range of social forms through which the hegemony of the ruling class was secured and maintained through, for instance, the relationship between high and popular literature or that between philosophy and folklore. Gramsci argues:

> Over the last century a unified culture has in fact been extended, and therefore also a common unified language [. . .] Every time the question of the language surfaces, in one way or another, it means that a series of other problems are coming to the fore: the formation and enlargement of the governing class, the need to establish more intimate and secure relations between the govern-ing groups and the national–popular mass, in other words, to reorganise the cultural hegemony (1985: 184).

Following Gramsci, the aim of this chapter is to analyse the language-question in India and to examine the major moments in the reorganization of cultural hegemony within the nation. As mentioned in the Introduction, my contention is that three major moments can be marked in terms of the changing conceptions of modernity that English in India has signified since its introduction. As a signifying system, English in India under colonial rule promised the modernity embodied by liberal democracy and free-tradism. Given the fact of the colonial condition, however, it was impossible for the liberal ideology, which was ascendant in contemporary England, to fulfil similar functions in India in any substantive manner. Instead, colonial education policies and the conceptual world signified by English became the means for reconstituting pre-existing social structures in ways that would create a new middle class—the class that Macaulay had famously hoped would be 'interpreters between us and the millions whom we govern'

(1957: 729). Of course, Macaulay's theory backfired when this class went on to become the hegemonic group in the struggle for Independence.

Emerging in the contested terrain between the colonial and the indigenous elite, the second moment in the trajectory of English can be located in the context of Nehruvian nationalism. For reasons that I will elaborate later in the chapter, English in India continued to occupy the terrain of high culture even after Independence. The difference was that, under Nehru, the centralizing impulse of the liberal nation-state was reinflected into the idiom of centralized state planning, modelled especially on the Soviet Union. The contradictions that marked the birth of an anticolonial bourgeois democracy, however, meant that socialism under Nehru proved to be little more than populist rhetoric.

The third moment in the trajectory of English in India can be located in the 1980s. Metonymic of the shift of global dominance from the UK to the US, a new 'American English' now emerged as hegemonic within the nation, in tandem with the swamping of the economy by multinational capital and North American consumer culture. As mentioned in the Introduction, this 'new' English was no longer a signifier of high culture in the traditional sense. Instead, the 1980s saw Hindi gain a new sense of cultural capital. My overarching contention is that this realignment of the language-question, indicative of a changed equation between high and popular culture in the 1980s, is symptomatic of the ideological reconfiguring of Indianness in the post-Nehruvian era. Let us begin, however, with the modernity promised by English at its originary moments.

'ENGLISH' AND THE 'DESIRE FOR MODERNITY'

As Joshi has pointed out, the trajectory of the English language in India is, in a fundamental sense, the trajectory of its urban middle class (1991: 1–32) and one that begins in the early nineteenth century. In her influential study, Gauri Viswanathan (1990) has documented the ways in which English Studies in India was integral to the project of colonial rule. English Literature, as a subject of study in the curriculum, was institutionalized in India in the early 1820s, long before it was institutionalized in England. In the Charter Act (1813), Britain had already accepted responsibility towards native education. The Education Act (1835) was important not only because it formally institutionalized a new language, English, as the medium of instruction, but more so because it dramatically reversed Britain's official commitment to religious non-interference. English was now to be used as a tool for the dissemination of moral and religious values. Viswanathan documents how, given the official disavowal of the connection between English and Christianity, a subtle but palpable shift of emphasis in pedagogic values occurred, from the centrality of universal Christian truths to the values and legitimacy of British institutions, law and government. Moreover, in the tensions between the Evangelicals, who saw English as a source of moral regeneration, and the Utilitarians, who saw English as a prerequisite to good governance, English was made to affirm a double stance to both faith and reason, belief and knowledge, intuition and empiricism. Further, both the Orientalists, who advocated education in the vernaculars, and the Anglicists, who advocated education in English, agreed on a common method of governance. A small class was to be co-opted as the conduit for Western thought and ideas—'a class, Indian in blood and colour but English in tastes, opinions, morals and intellect' (see Macaulay 1957). In fact, the Indian university system derives from a theory of culture devised by Thomas Macaulay and James Mill—the Filtration Theory, predicated on the assumption that only the class that had both the requisite economic means and the amount of leisure necessary for an education in English should be encouraged to pursue the same.[2]

While Viswanathan has focused on the policies of the colonial government, a considerable body of work has also documented the reception of these policies on the ground. As this body of work has shown, it is necessary to see the introduction of English in India as an embattled response not only to the tensions between the British Parliament and the East India Company and between the Parliament and the missionaries, but also between the East India Company and the indigenous elite.[3] Influential sections of the Indian intelligentsia made demands and took initiatives to promote English education long before the announcement of official policy. The Hindu College was established in 1817 with English as the medium of instruction. The Calcutta Book Society, also known as the Calcutta School Book Society, was also established in 1817. The Committee on Public Instruction responsible for the 1835 Education Act noted that while the

School Book Society had sold over 30,000 English books in two years, it had hardly sold any books in Sanskrit and Arabic.

Jasodhara Bagchi (1991) analyses the deep ambivalence that characterized the use of English by this indigenous class. She suggests that the active demand for English by the whole spectrum of the indigenous intelligentsia, from the modern to the conservative, cannot simply be read as a model of a comprador culture. Instead, in the ways in which it was eventually institutionalized, English was seen not only in the intuitionist and revelatory terms of nineteenth-century England but also as a means of access to Enlightenment Reason that would be an agent of social transformation for a colonized people. One of the most significant aspects of the philosophical arguments of the Enlightenment introduced in India through English was their ostensibly 'secular' outlook, the idea that the morality/aesthetic being introduced through English represented the triumph of humanism and, therefore, had universal ('human') relevance. It was this association of English with a secular/universalist aesthetic that was then drawn upon by indigenous social reformers, from Raja Rammohun Roy to Ishwarchandra Vidyasagar, to critique religious obscurantism and to fashion a modern Indian identity. In the process, Anglicism also provided the impetus for the efflorescence of a new brand of Orientalism, consolidating an upper-caste Hindu male identity as the normative 'Indian self' (ibid.: 146–59).

Further, the modernity promised by English under colonial rule was defined along two axes—an intellectual adumbration of Enlightenment rationality to be employed for a cultural regeneration; and the development of capitalist industrialization/free-tradism for the development of productive processes on the lines of nineteenth-century England. Politically, English in India under colonial rule came to denote a corpus of attitudes aligned to British liberalism and constitutional governance. These ideological positions would again be reinforced by the nationalist movement, which self-consciously located itself as heir to the social reform movement of the nineteenth century. I will elaborate these ideological interconnections in subsequent sections. But at this point it is important to emphasize the shift that occurred in the process of the institutionalization of English in India—from English as language to English as the discursive universe on which the institutions and apparatuses of the classical liberal nation-state of

Western Europe were grounded. What follows, therefore, is an attempt to trace the multiple ways in which English in India functioned, across a range of discourses, as the signifier of the 'desire for modernity'[4] that was sought to be given concrete shape through the emerging community of the Indian nation.

MODERNITY AND THE ASPIRATION TO NATIONHOOD

A host of colonial writers from William Jones to James Mill had used concepts such as 'Oriental despotism' and the 'Asiatic mode of production' to dismiss pre-existing social structures in India as degenerate and characterized Hindus as slothful and deceitful, incapable of appreciating the idea of liberty. The implicit logic of colonial historiography was, of course, that India's path to progress and development lay in opening her markets to the capitalist bourgeoisie of Western Europe, a process that resulted in massive *de*-industrialization, mass *de*-skilling of labour, growing pressure on land and widespread famines—turning India from one of the richest countries in the world to one of the poorest.

Despite these disastrous consequences, the nationalist intelligentsia endorsed the colonial parameters of modernity—capitalist technology, a liberal democracy with a centralized administrative structure (the bureaucracy) and a centralized legislative system. The only change, articulated most forcefully through the politics of Swadeshi, was the demand for 'Indian domination of Indian markets'. Using Gramsci's notion of a 'passive revolution', Chatterjee has analysed how such a political strategy maximized the interests of a very small minority—the indigenous bourgeoisie defined vis-à-vis both the colonial rulers and the vast subaltern sector consisting of peasants, rural artisans, agricultural labourers, industrial workers, etc. (1986). Similarly, Sumit Sarkar has documented how the Gandhian model of non-violent agitation became acceptable to both the rising Indian urban bourgeoisie as well as the feudal land-owning classes in the face of radical popular movements that would threaten their self-interests if they turned the entire nationalist movement into a violent socialist revolution. At numerous instances, therefore, popular movements were abruptly discontinued by the nationalist leadership for negotiated settlements, the most important of such being the 'transfer of power' in 1947 (see Sarkar 1982, 1985).

Colonial historiography had portrayed British rule as the protagonist of Indian history. Seeking to empty local politics of all significance except its dangers to the colonial state, colonial historiography had seen all forms of mass mobilization as problems of law and order. Nationalist historiography in its turn simply substituted colonial rule with elite Indian personalities such as Gandhi and Nehru as protagonists of Indian history. On numerous occasions, in telling imitation of the colonial rulers, the nationalist leadership attempted to contain radical subaltern movements by defining them as 'lawless' simply because they did not operate within the parameters of the Western legal system, i.e. the system of pleading/providing evidence or other similar requirements of the Western system of constitutional politics. As Tharu and Lalita, among many others, have documented, in the climate of approaching power during the 1930s and 1940s, the Indian National Congress (INC) de-legitimized many popular struggles—which it had earlier tried to orchestrate and support—that did not consider Congress a fitting resolution to their specific problems (1995: 54–64). Effectively, nationalist historiography also reduced Indian history to the 'biography of the Indian state'.[5] Guha remarks:

> What is clearly left out of this un-historical historiography is the
> *politics of the people*. For parallel to the domain of elite politics there
> existed throughout the colonial period another domain of Indian
> politics in which the principal actors were not the dominant groups
> of the indigenous society or the colonial authorities but the subal-
> tern classes and groups constituting the mass of the labouring
> population and the intermediate strata in the town and country—
> that is, the people (1983b: 40).

Working within colonial parameters of modernity, the nationalist leadership sought to recreate India in the image of the classical liberal nation-state. The crux of the issue was, of course, that this modernity could only be obtained through an education in English. As early as 1904, Gopal Krishna Gokhale, as president of the INC, clarified that political rights were being demanded '[. . .] not for the whole population but only such portion of it as has been qualified by education to discharge properly the duties of such associations' (cited in Sarkar 1985: 90).

Further, the very terms in which the national bourgeoisie defined its cultural formation (the idea of a golden Vedic Age) and the periodization of Indian history, where the Muslim interregnum was constituted as inaugurating its process of downfall, were all constituted within the domain of Orientalist scholarship.[6] However, given its historical opposition to colonial rule, nationalist discourse also affirmed possibilities that colonial discourse had denied, even as it adopted colonial modes of thought. Hence, as Chatterjee has shown, unlike the subject of colonialist historiography, the Oriental/Indian as represented in nationalist thought was active, autonomous and sovereign. Nationalist historiography accepted the essentialist distinction between the East and the West as that between the traditional and the modern. But even here, while on the one hand pre-colonial lifestyles were being rejected as obstacles to progress and modernity, on the other certain reconstructed pasts were being valorized as the essence of an 'Indian' identity (Chatterjee 1986).

As mentioned earlier, it was the secular European nation-state that was held up as the norm. The only difference was that while for the colonial rulers 'communalism' was evidence of the fundamental irrationality of Indian society, for the nationalists communalism was important precisely because it was *not* nationalism. As Gyanendra Pandey's (1990) work most persuasively shows, in nationalist historiography communalism became merely a backward-looking/atavistic discourse propped up by the colonial state to bolster its own interests. Nationalism was all that was forward-looking and progressive. The new nationalist history emphasized not only the tolerance and adaptability in Hinduism and Indian culture but also the importance of the great rulers of the state in the realization of the 'Indian dream'. India itself became a metaphysical truth and, by the 1930s, what was being stressed was the critical importance of a leadership that would resurrect this essence of the nation that had continued uncontaminated into the present, despite the fact that outsiders had conquered India again and again.

But such an idea of the nation being above primordial loyalties emerged in India only in the early decades of the twentieth century. The idea of the secular nation here grew in direct response to increasing tensions between religious communities (especially Hindu and Muslim), as well as between the upper and lower castes within the Hindu community. As various depressed castes sought direct negotiations with the colonial state, Gandhi, among others, took up cudgels against the 'sin' of untouchability. Similarly, as demands grew for a more egalitarian participation of women in the social sphere, a new conception of civil society saw the Indian woman as a person upholding the essence of her culture. And, since Orientalist scholarship had defined this essence in largely spiritual and religious terms, freedom for the Indian woman came to be defined, unlike her Western counterpart, not as a demand for equal citizenship but as a freedom from her ego through free submission to the authority of the *shastras* (religious scriptures) and to that of her husband (Chakrabarty 1993; Tharu and Lalita 1995). Similarly, disregarding its own Hindu Brahmanical bias, 'real' nationalism came to be defined as something beyond religion.

To comprehend the present, we must understand the philosophico-political consequences of such constructions of nationhood. As Anderson has brilliantly demonstrated, nations have to be *imagined* into existence (1983). For Anderson, the conditions of possibility for the historical emergence of the nation-state involve the interaction between a system of production (capitalism), a technology of communication (print), and human linguistic diversity. As I have tried to show, English in India under colonial rule emerged as a surcharged signifier around which these inter-actions coalesced.

MODERNITY AND THE *ENUMERATED* NATION

In the Introduction I have mentioned the pre-conditional links between the principles of measurement and the new art of governmentality on which was based the post-despotic state of Western Europe. The endorsement of colonial modernity in the domain of the state meant that the nation-state in India too reinforced the relentless logic of counting. Kaviraj has sketched the cognitive re-mapping that was involved in the transition from *gemein-schaft* to *gessellschaft*—from community in its traditional senses to the community of the nation-state (1992). The conditions of possibility for what Kaviraj has called 'the imaginary institution of India' also revolved crucially around principles of enumeration:

> [E]arlier communities tend to be fuzzy in two ways in which no nation can afford to be. First, they have fuzzy boundaries, because

some collective identities are not territorially based [. . .] Second, part of this fuzziness of social mapping would arise because traditional communities, unlike modern ones, are not enumerated. The most significant implication of this is the following: [s]ince they did not ask how many of them there were in the world, they could not consider what they could wreck upon the world for their collective benefit—through collective action.

[. . .]

The boundaries of nation states cannot afford to be fuzzy in the same way. Indeed the territorial attachment of modern states is sometimes so intense as to be rationally incomprehensible, as evident from the cheerful intensity with which modern nations fight wars for control of uninhabitable land. Second, a parallel principle, the national community, must be enumerated; nations must know how many they are. It is not surprising that in the discourse of Indian nationalism the question of numbers figures so prominently (ibid.: 26).

Kaviraj goes on to suggest that within an anticolonial nationalism such as India's, the logic of numbers was doubly important in calculations of the possibilities or effectiveness of resistance. However, the inevitable by-product of living in such an enumerated world, he adds, is that it is not only the nation but also other communities, based on other interest-actuated decisions of belonging, that can be counted on these principles.

The objective presence of colonial rule meant that the indigenous intelligentsia was largely dysfunctional in the production process, i.e. in no position to actively shape state policy in ways analogous to the capitalist bourgeoisie of nineteenth-century England. Co-opted largely into the lower rungs of official machinery, the new education policies did, however, open for some limited opportunities for upward social mobility. Perceiving the nationalist leadership as upper caste, demands consequently arose from various underprivileged groups for a more egalitarian redistribution of social privileges.[7] Such responses, which demanded English as part of a larger demand for social justice, identified Brahman domination as the key element against which various underprivileged sections had to organize themselves. In this policy of positive discrimination, it was the state's responsibility to equalize educational opportunities so as to prepare and better equip the lowest-ranking castes and tribals for the competitive job market. Demands were also made for reservations in jobs. Perceiving the Congress as a Brahman-dominated organization, such groups preferred direct negotiations with the colonial state instead. However, given the ideology of paternalism that informed the colonial educational agenda—one that meshed neatly with the asymmetries of pre-existing feudal educational ideologies in India—such endeavours remained marginal, while the upper castes monopolized the educational and social opportunities provided by colonial rule (Kumar 1987a: 45–52).

As opposed to these democratizing lower-caste initiatives, a third response to English under colonial rule can also be identified—in the programme of so-called national education where various indigenist alternatives to the colonial education system were proposed as part of a broader current of nationalist self-assertion. Though a range of responses—from Tagore's Santiniketan to Gandhi's *nai taleem* (new/basic education)—can be located within this programme, the Swadeshi movement took on a particularly virulent form in the Hindi-speaking United and Central Provinces. Drawing on the conceptual framework of Orientalist scholarship, Swadeshi endorsed the idea that India's cultural essence lay in a Hindu past. The role of resurrecting this past had been assigned to Hindi not only by the United Provinces literati but also by the two major social reform movements which had arisen in the nineteenth century—the Arya Samaj (Association of Aryans) and the Brahmo Samaj (Association of Brahmos, a 'modernized' form of Hinduism). As we will see in the next chapter, the Arya Samaj was one of the major organizations through which a new Sanskritized version of Hindi would be created and propagated. Running schools would also be a major part of the Arya Samaj's social reform programme. Textbooks would be produced and syllabi codified, reinforcing revivalist notions of Indian history. Similar associations would also be formed for the promotion of this new Hindi. In 1905, the Benares Hindu University was set up, the only university to be set up entirely through indigenous funding. Such initiatives would arise as a new 'Hinduism' was sought to be created which would not only transcend caste barriers but also incorporate the various heterodox sects, including Jains and Buddhists. At stake in the forging of such a unified Hindu community[8] was greater access to socio-economic privileges under the colonial system of proportional representation.

It is necessary, I believe, to delineate the complex conjunctures of linguistic and political debates in India to emphasize that though inevitably influenced by theoretical debates within the Anglo-American academy, my work derives from, and is a response to, a different set of historical pressures.[9] My work foregrounds the fact that, for the postcolonial, to speak in the imperial tongue is to call forth a problem of identity.[10] As Satish Deshpande reminds us, the politics of the language-question in India erupts directly out of the historical contradictions that mark the coming into being of an *anticolonial* nation:

> [C]ontemporary social theory reminds us that nations inhabit a space that is simultaneously abstract (imagined, mental) and concrete (physical, geographical) [. . .] However, contemporary social theory also reminds us that both space and nation are implicated in power relations. The production of a sense of nation-ness clearly involves ideological and material contests. In a [post-]colonial context, this includes both the dimension of nationalism as anti-imperialism, as well as the different possible nationalisms, each with its own equations vis-à-vis various regions, classes or ethnic groups within the proto-nation. The idea of the nation can thus be suitably inflected [by different emergent proto-nationalisms] to facilitate its use as a weapon in a broader social struggle for hegemony (1995: 3220).

Using 'English' as a shorthand term for the new conceptual vocabulary of the colonial state, the volatile politics of the language-question can be read as metonymic of how different kinds of communities attempted to mobilize the logic of numbers to claim the benefits of institutional structures put in place by colonial rule.

ENGLISH AND THE SECULAR AESTHETIC OF THE 1950s

The work of recent scholars such as Etienne Balibar, Pierre Macherey and Benedict Anderson have shown us the crucial role played by 'national languages' in the consolidation of bourgeois hegemony in the classical democracies of Western Europe. Similarly, as one analyses the role of English in India, it becomes evident that its influence went far beyond the introduction of a language to a whole new corpus of ideas on 'textuality', 'the aesthetic' and 'literary text' that were integral to the very conception of civil society introduced by colonial rule.

As Joshi has pointed out, the colonial intervention in education actually started much before the 1835 Education Act (1991: 1–31). The earliest colonial interventions, in fact, were in the form of efforts to reconstitute the vernaculars. Through efforts of members of the Asiatic Society (est. 1784), the scholarship that emerged out of the Fort William College (est. 1800) and the activities of missionaries who translated the Bible into the indigenous languages as well as produced textbooks and dictionaries in them, it was in the vernaculars that colonial ideologies of culture and literature were first developed. The grammars of these languages were reconstituted in terms of European grammatical categories, and Sanskritized versions of indigenous languages were produced. Pecuniary inducements were also given for the creation of original works in the vernaculars. As Tharu and Lalita argue, the new genres that arose in the vernaculars can be seen as responses to the new writer-subjectivities that were thus being created (1991: 160–80). According to Charles Trevelyan:

> This diversity among languages is one of the greatest existing obstacles to the improvement of India. But when English shall everywhere be established as the language of education, when the vernacular literature shall everywhere be formed from materials drawn from this source, recast in the same mould, with a common science, a common standard of taste, a common nomenclature, the national languages as well as the national character will be consolidated. We shall leave a united and enlightened *nation* where we found a people broken into sections [. . .] and depressed by literary systems, designed much more with a view to check the progress, than to promote the advance, of the human mind (cited in Tharu 1991: 166).

Thus, English decisively constituted 'national' languages and literatures for the Indian intelligentsia in ways that still inform our critical and academic practices.[11] Fuelled by the initial need to gain access to indigenous systems of land holdings, the colonial impulse fed, in enormously complex ways, into a new education system, a centralized system of law and administration—in short, to a complete redefinition of 'legitimate knowledge'.

The changed significations accruing to English in the Nehruvian era, then, have to be seen in terms of both continuities and contradictions.[12] Nationalist discourse in India endorsed fundamentally the parameters of Enlightenment modernity. The continuities in nationalist thought for over a century lay in the fact that, in both its liberal as well as its socialist moulds, the nationalist leadership assumed that modernity meant an emulation of parameters set by the West.

My argument in this section is indebted to Chatterjee's (1986) pioneering analysis of the different 'moments' of Indian nationalist thought, from Bankimchandra Chattopadhyay to Jawaharlal Nehru. Given the objective presence of colonial rule, Chatterjee has argued that the anticolonial nationalist bourgeoisie in India adopted what Gramsci called the strategy of a 'passive revolution' to establish their position in state power. In a passive revolution, the emerging ruling coalitions first seize control of the institutional apparatuses of the state and then attempt to reform civil society in accordance with the cultural logic of statehood, i.e. reconstitute the terrain of the social around the figure of the citizen-subject. This is in opposition to classical bourgeois democracies, as in Western Europe for instance, where the bourgeoisie first establish their hegemony in civil society and then seize control of state apparatuses. Chatterjee argues that the imperative informing Indian nationalist discourse at its 'mature' moment—i.e. the moment of 'arrival' of Independence—was to reconstitute Indian nationalism as state ideology. The objective presence of colonial rule meant that the impetus at this mature moment was to reconstitute Indian nationalism as a mass movement that would lead, firstly, to the seizure of control of the institutional apparatuses of the colonial state *and then* to a reformation of civil society under the directing influence of the national state.

> [The Nehruvian reconstruction of nationalist thought represents] the final, fully mature stage of the development of nationalism in India—its moment of arrival. It was a reconstruction whose specific form was to situate nationalism within the domain of a *state ideology*. Given the historical constraints placed upon the Indian bourgeoisie

within the colonial social formation, its intellectual-moral leadership could never be firmly established in the domain of civil
society. Of historical necessity its revolution had to be passive. The
specific ideological form of the passive revolution in India was an
etatisme, explicitly recognising a central autonomous and directing
role of the state and legitimising it by a specifically nationalist marriage between the ideas of progress and social justice (ibid.: 132).

One of the most effective arguments for the introduction of English in
India was that the cultural values being introduced through it were nonde-
nominational or secular, i.e. they had universal relevance. To relate this to
the language-question within Nehruvian nationalism, Chatterjee has
pointed out that, in reworking the Orientalist thematic of an essential
distinction between the East and the West, historical time itself becomes
episodic:

> Every civilisation, it is now argued, has its periods of growth and
> periods of decay. There are no essential or organic, or insuperable
> connections between them [. . .] Further, the cultural values, or the
> 'spirit' which go with a particular sort of growth are capable of
> being extracted from their particular civilisational context and
> made universal historical values [. . . P]ast and present can be sep-
> arated out of the histories of particular nations and represented
> as the universal 'spirit of the age'. That determined the norm ac-
> cording to which particular nations could be shown to be advanced
> or backward, and the particular stage of that cycle explained in
> terms of specific conjunctural factors (ibid.: 137).

Chatterjee proposes that for Nehru, the distinctive twentieth-century
'spirit of the age' meant, above all, giving primacy to the economic sphere
in all social questions. Given the logic of progressive etatization, or the
gradual extension of the state into increasing areas of social life, however,
the emphasis on the economic translated not into a fundamental critique
of the nature of property but also became technical problems to be solved
by experts/planners and heavy industrialization; a technicist utopianism
proposed in lieu of a political resolution of the contradictions of class–caste–
region–gender. Socialism for Nehru was merely a matter of distributing
production evenly. And within such a reconstruction of nationalism, English

became the signifier of all the democratic aspirations represented by the birth of the national state, a space where a universal aesthetic would be forged that would be above sectarian loyalties of caste–region–religion—a stand-in for a socialist internationalism.[13] Thus, in his *Discovery of India*, Nehru not only writes approvingly of the efforts of social reformers like Raja Rammohun Roy who were instrumental in starting English-medium colleges, but also expresses his indebtedness to the missionaries who, he argues, have contributed greatly to the 'development' of indigenous languages by standardizing orthography, compiling dictionaries and so on.

> English education brought a widening of the Indian horizon, an admiration of English literature and institutions, a [much-needed] revolt against some customs and aspects of Indian life and a growing demand for political reform (Nehru 1946: 319).

This equation—of English with a secular-universalist aesthetic—was made from the point of view of the coalition that assumed power at Independence. As we shall see in the next chapter, this equation appeared to be very problematic from a whole range of other social positions.

These contradictions in Nehruvian nationalism, emerging from its endorsement of universalizing narratives, point to a much deeper theoretical complicity between liberal and leftist models of social analysis, given that the basic unit of currency in both is the *individual*. As Susie Tharu and Tejaswini Niranjana point out:

> The notion of the 'human' as it appears in political theory and more importantly in humanist common-sense is inextricable from what has been called the metaphysics of substance. Framed by this metaphysics, the human appears as a substantive base that precedes and somehow remains prior to and outside of structuring of gender, class, caste or community [. . .] Humanist Marxism offers a critique of the class investments of liberal individualism, but preserves the normative idea of a human essence [. . .] It is not difficult to see that these theories, and their politico-legal derivatives, actually produce what they claim to recognize [. . .] Thus produced, this human subject, on whom the whole question of 'rights' is predicated, is imaged as the citizen subject and the political subject. This imaging (a) articulate[s] gender, caste and community (and

initially even class) only in the realm of the social (b) mark[s] these
as incidental attributes of a human self and (c) render[s] invisible
the historical and social/cultural structuring of the subject of
politics (1996: 235–6).

However, as Tharu and Lalita have documented, the debates shaping
curricula of the Indian universities as well as the literary movements in the
1950s were all informed by this very impulse to consolidate a citizen-self
that would be simultaneously Indian as well as universal. But, given the
social construction of secularism, a new critical pedagogy and a high-
modernist aesthetic slipped in effortlessly to consolidate a male upper-
caste Hindu self as the normative, secular Indian subject (see Tharu and
Lalita 1993). And, as will become evident in the next chapter, the implicit
social markers of this desire to construct an Indian as well as universal
nation/culture would also inform the troubled status of Hindi as 'official
language' of Indian democracy in the 1950s and 1960s.

EDUCATION POLICIES AND THE NEHRUVIAN NATIONAL IMAGINARY

The internal contradictions of the Nehruvian ruling bloc, comprising a
coalition of feudal, capitalist and techno-managerial groups, meant that socialism in India was more rhetoric than commitment to egalitarianism. With
regard to the language-question, the first fact of significance has to do with
the status accorded to India's regional languages in the 1950s. Though
coded as a gesture towards decentralization, the linguistic reorganization
of the states in 1956 was, in fact, a response to the growing influence of a
stratum of rich farmers and an emerging regional bourgeoisie. Thus, the
regional languages in the 1950s were assigned a purely 'cultural' agenda.
Politically, such regional articulation, even when positioned explicitly in
opposition to Hindi (as in the case of Tamil Nadu, for instance), did not
challenge the fundamental tenet of Nehruvian nationalism—of centralized
planning. Instead, as Shalini Advani corroborates through a rereading of
Education Commission reports and the Indian government's publishing
ventures such as school textbooks published by the National Council for
Educational Research and Training (NCERT), the underlying ideological
impulse here is to tie up *both* the rural–urban gap and the regional differences into a homogenized national culture:

India's diversity is acknowledged but only to be superimposed onto the larger trope of unity—via myth, symbols such as the flag and history such as the freedom struggle and nationalist leaders [. . .] Similarly, the superiority of rural India is celebrated, but so is modern, industrialised India, the two aspects appearing in uneasy juxtaposition. Thus the farmer is important in the discourse of the nation, but it is only the rich, independent farmer and not the agricultural worker or the poor peasant [. . . E]conomic disparity is glossed over by the suggestion that wealth is irrelevant to true happiness

[. . .] The acknowledgement of the presence of different social groups does not bring the student any closer to the reality they inhabit, only deepening the gulf between dominant and the subject worlds (1996: 2081).[14]

These contradictions within the Nehruvian ruling coalition are evident in the first educational plan of 1949 in which the Education Commission formulated a two-pronged strategy. At the lowest level, education was to be organized to meet the urgent need for technicians who would ensure a continuous flow of skilled labour for the modern industries. At the higher level, a liberal education was to be organized in English to yield a class that would uphold the new democracy. As analysed by Gramsci, the educational scene in India in the 1950s had striking parallels with that of 1920–30s' Italy:

The tendency today is to abolish every type of schooling that is 'disinterested' (not serving any immediate interest) or 'formative' —keeping at most only a small-scale version to serve a tiny elite of ladies and gentlemen who do not have to worry about assuring themselves of a future career [. . .] The multiplication of types of vocational schools tends to perpetuate traditional social differences; but since, within these differences, it tends to encourage social diversification it gives the impression of being democratic in tendency [. . .] But democracy, by definition, cannot mean merely that an unskilled worker can become skilled. It must mean that every 'citizen' can 'govern' and that society places him, even if only abstractly, in a general condition to achieve this (1971: 27).

Similarly, historian Damodar Dharmananda Kosambi[15] has argued that the Nehruvian paradigms of national development also left out the vast majority of the Indian people. No consistent effort was made to impart mass literacy or to build a credible base for the expansion of elementary education. But given that free and compulsory elementary education for all was a Directive Principle of the Constitution, the Government could not openly abandon this rhetoric. It therefore accepted a subtle change in the role education was to play. As Kumar (1987a) has pointed out, the Constitutional position on 'equal opportunities' did not contradict the view common among the propertied classes, especially the urban bourgeoisie, that a select few institutions should deal only with 'meritorious' students. From the beginning of the nineteenth century itself, wealthy Indians had started investing in educational institutions. A qualitative change in the role of capital came with the founding of the Doon School in 1935. Modelled on the public school system in Britain, it marked the beginning of a process whereby other similar schools would also be established in Gwalior, Lovedale and Sanawar. Though, in theory, these schools claimed to be accessible to all, in practice, the fee-paying capacity of the parent became the crucial factor. This condition was later complicated by the system of government scholarships for the *poor* meritorious students. The whole idea of a secular meritocracy thus served as a pedagogical device to uphold claims to equality within an exclusive structure. To go back to Gramsci, 'merit' occludes not only the distinction among classes in *economic* terms but also the whole struggle around what Pierre Bourdieu has described as 'taste'/ 'cultural distinction' (1984). As Gramsci notes:

> In a whole series of families, especially in the intellectual strata,
> the children find in their family life a perpetuation, a prolongation
> and completion of school life [. . . Similarly,] city children, by the
> very fact of living in a city have already absorbed by the age of six
> a quantity of notions and attitudes which make their school careers
> easier, more profitable and more rapid (1971: 30–1).

Forty years later, in the New Education Policy formulated in 1986, such a rationale was to be institutionalized as state policy in India with the setting up of the Navodaya Schools in select districts, with the specific aim of imparting an education, on the Public School model, to 'meritorious' students from rural areas. Therefore, the discourse on 'secular merit' does not signify a democratizing initiative. Rather, given the social construction of secularism in India, it signifies social privilege, functioning as a marker of cultural distinction.[16]

We have noted earlier the symbiosis of English with orthodox Hindu hierarchies in the colonial era. Within the educational scene of the 1950s, the discourse on 'secular merit' signified by English led to a situation where, as Kaviraj sarcastically notes, 'only those people who [were] unable to speak any Indian language [were] seen as the real repositories of Indian nationalism' (1990: 75).' The parallels with the situation in the 1980–90s are too obvious to draw. It was precisely this discourse on 'secular merit' and 'excellence' that was invoked by upper-caste students protesting the increase of reservations for 'backward castes' in educational institutions and the public sector after the Mandal Commission recommendations.

'AMERICAN ENGLISH' AND 1980s' CONSUMER CULTURE

Although the beginning of English can be located in the colonial period, its continuance has to be located within today's politics. In the Nehruvian era, English was privileged in order to hold the nation together. Today, the logic of its continuance derives from the politics of free-market internationalism, a perspective of 'development' which fetishizes scientific and technical information. The hegemony of the US has also meant that American (rather than the 'Queen's') English has emerged as the norm under the newly undertaken project of 'structural adjustment'. Prasad neatly sums up the changing roles of English over the last 150 years:

> What English Studies, with its humanist agenda, taught us was English as the language of the *ancien regime* [. . .] It taught us obedience, reverence for those who are better than us, and other feudal virtues [. . .] I]ts 'enemies[s]', the rival 'native' language(s) with a will to demystify English [were] perhaps less determining for the fortunes of English than the rapid transformation of English into a technology. I use the term technology in a general sense, to mean the reduction of the language to a code, similar to, say, a computer language. These two challenges derive from the two great transfers of power that took place at the same time: the transfer of power to the Indian

ruling class: a political event; and the transfer of power to America: primarily a military and economic event. Today the dynamic initiated by the former finds itself on the margins while the onward march of the latter continues unobstructed (1995).

Within the educational sphere, these 'objective' contradictions have resulted in an overall decline in the rate of literacy in the country. The expansion of higher education has been at the expense of the primary sector. While in 1947 there were 19 universities within the country, there are now 140. But this expansion has occurred in a highly chaotic manner and largely as result of political manoeuvring. As Alok Rai (1991) notes, this chaotic expansion has most adversely affected the humanities disciplines. Whereas the study of sciences needs a certain infrastructure, even if minimal, enrolment in Literature or Philosophy, represents zero marginal cost. Therefore, there has been a flood of enrolment in the humanities with completely inadequate infrastructural facilities. To this has been added a pattern of examination that actively discourages alternative readings of pedagogic practices. Rajeswari Sunder Rajan observes that there has been, in the recent context, a narrowing down of the concept of the university itself. As research, specialization and development-oriented studies have grown in importance, technology, medicine, economics, statistics and so on have moved *out* of the ambit of the university. The university, as a consequence, has shrunk to being the location of only undergraduate and postgraduate courses in the sciences and the arts (see Rajan 1992: 7–29).

The obverse of this process is the growing demand for functional goal-directed teaching of the English language. Institutes offering crash courses in 'spoken English' have mushroomed over the past decade for a variety of reasons, most significantly to feed the booming outsourcing or call-centre industry. However, as Prasad has argued, the decline of *humanist* English Studies does not reflect a decline of English. Instead, it signals the transition to a new phase of capitalism, one that no longer banks on the traditional mystique of language. He describes this new phase of capitalism as a period of generalized translatability, a phase where capitalism can be taught without the aid of the English language, through a training in consumerism instead. This new phase of capitalism, where English can now be taught as a 'native language' in India, has seen a parallel move by Hindi to 'national' status as well as a new ideological axis along which the regional languages have now taken position. The linguistic states created in 1956 not only institutionalized new hierarchies among languages but also suppressed existing pluralities of cultural traditions of the different regions (Joshi 1991: 1–31). Transnational capitalism is now further appropriating each of the regional languages in its own image. Increasingly, regional-language-based agitations are being linked to right-wing politics—their chauvinistic 'sons-of-the-soil' arguments feeding into the overarching Hindu fascism of the Sangh Parivar. Moreover, the Hindu political machine has been advocating Hindi as national language as part of its larger move to reclaim a Hindu/ Indian culture.

But even as Hindi moves in to share national status with English, the latter continues to be the language of law as well as that of the growing private sector, business management, technology (especially computer science), advertising and, as Srilata Krishnan (1996b) describes it, of the most coveted thing—a university degree from the US. The continued availability of subsidized books in English—through subsidy schemes such as the PL 480 with the US or the ELBS with the UK—makes it even more difficult for their Indian counterparts to compete, given the already existing consensus on the superiority of the Western article.

The radical conceptual break marked by the Enlightenment was its critique of the Church and the triumph of humanism. Claiming the universal relevance of Enlightenment humanism, English was institutionalized in India to cloak over the brute economic and political calculations of colonial rule. In the process, the colonial rhetoric intersected with pre-existing feudal hierarchies and helped consolidate a new Hindu Orientalist classicism. The secular aesthetic promised by English has had specific caste–regional markers in India. Within the etatizing impulse of Nehruvian nationalism, the secularism associated with English was renotated into the language of centralized state planning, science and technology. While framed within the ideology of distributive justice, the caste–class composition of the Nehruvian ruling bloc precluded any substantive moves towards democratization. Over the last two decades or so, the new conjuncture of global capital with caste–region–religious contradictions of the *post*-Nehruvian era is again invoking the discourse on 'secular merit' to delegitimize the interrogations that the Nehruvian state had come under. As will be the focus of the next chapter, the modernity promised by English in India has been reclaimed, contested and reworked from a whole range of social positions. But given the integral association of English with successive ruling blocs, these *other* notions of modernity have found articulation in domains *outside* that of the state. It is precisely this contradiction between the two conceptual domains that we have described as the framing bilinguality of the postcolonial world.

This book analyses the language-question in India to map the ways in which notions of modernity have journeyed through cultural spaces, keeping in mind Spivak's distinction between dogmatic and critical philosophies with which we began this chapter. A critical philosophy, she suggests, is one that is conscious of the limits of its knowledge. There are no ready-made scripts with which we can replace, in a single stroke, the epistemological and political impasse of 200 years. Instead, Spivak ends only by suggesting caution at what one cannot *not* want. As 'scrupulous academics', she argues, the best one can hope to do is to critically analyse the present and 'leave it to the people' (1993b: 25–52). In historicizing the trajectory of English in India, I have tried to follow a similar gesture—not proposing 'solutions' to the socio-political impasse generated by encrusted colonial modes of thought or education; but merely the hope that, since the nation at its birth was pregnant with *many* possibilities, we have not yet exhausted our capacities to dream up democratic futures.

Notes

1   Describing the three phases in the creation of a 'national culture', Frantz Fanon says that in the final phase, the native intellectual of the colonized country, instead of trying to bring back to life abandoned traditions, will immerse himself in popular struggles for freedom which these countries are carrying on (1990: 166–99).

2   For a useful documentation of these debates, see Eric Stokes (1959).

3   For excellent documentations, see Ania Loomba (1989), Svati Joshi (1991) and Rajeswari Sunder Rajan (1992).

4   I owe this phrase to M. Madhava Prasad (1993).

5 I owe this phrase to Gyanendra Pandey (1990).

6 For a succinct formulation, see Ronald Inden (1986: 401–46).

7 For a scathing renunciation of Gandhian nationalism, see B. R. Ambedkar (1967). More recent Dalit critiques of the dominant ideology in India include Gail Omvedt (1996) and Kancha Ilaiah (1996).

8 For an analysis of the construction of the new Hindu identity, see, among others, Romila Thapar (1989: 209–31).

9 It might be useful, then, to briefly lay out the theoretical distance between the study of India's culture as I have undertaken here and the politics of what has been institutionalized in the Anglo-American academy as Literary Theory. Aijaz Ahmad notes that the historical shift from 'criticism' to 'Theory' in the metropolitan academy occurred in the 1960s. With this shift of terminology, he points out that 'literature' has undergone both a deflation and an aggrandisement (1991: 206–63). On the one hand, literature has become just one discourse among others, but on the other hand there has also been a much more persuasive displacement which argues that there is *nothing* outside language and representation. Everything becomes, in a sense, 'literature'. Much of the writing that emerges from this position, since it also valorizes indeterminacy and deferral, neutralizes the politically charged moment of social transition by relocating change everywhere. Alternatively, the death of stable subject-positions is taken to be the death of politics as such.

   This is not to discount the fact that radical strains of post-structuralist discourse have forced the metropolitan academy to face issues of gender, race and empire as never before. But, as Kumkum Sangari warns, to believe that a decentring of unitary discourses is equal to a critique of colonialism and its accoutrements is to disregard the different historical formations of subjectivities (1987: 157–87). One could cite as an example Frederic Jameson's influential 'Postmodernism, or, The Cultural Logic of Late Capitalism' as symptomatic of the problems inherent in globalizing Eurocentric epistemologies (1993: 62–92). Drawing on the periodization provided by Ernest Mandel, Jameson proposes that capitalism has now entered a third (multinational) phase. Multinational capitalism, he argues, generates a decentred global network in which processes of *reproduction,* rather than the industrial production of classical capitalism, predominate. It also creates its own cultural space—postmodernism. In keeping with the decentred world of the new communication networks and technologies, postmodern cultural production also generates a decentred subject. The subsequent breakdown of distinctions between 'inside'/'outside', Jameson argues, results in specific features of postmodern art—a quality of depth-lessness, the waning of 'personal' style, a certain concept of 'pastness' in which an aesthetic style displaces an active sense of history. The distinctive feature of postmodern art for Jameson is, therefore, pastiche—a parody without a norm. In such a context, Jameson proposes that a cognitive mapping of this decentred cultural space can be a gesture towards radical politics.

But, as Martin Jay and Jane Flax remark, there are several problems with the mapping Jameson proposes (1993). By assuming the determina-tion of the cultural by the economic, in the last instance, Jameson is unable to account for the theoretical interventions that have demonstrated that history has no such singular logic. Issues of gender and racial domination are as global and durable as economic ones. Jameson's periodization, moreover, assumes an evolutionary and teleological view of history that excludes the possibility of temporal discontinuities and radical ruptures.

More fundamentally, as Simon During observes, Jameson's concept of postmodernism is constructed in terms that necessitate the conceptual annihilation of the postcolonial condition (1993). In the tradition of Marx and Lenin, Jameson argues that progressive aspects of the new phase of capitalism lie in its internationalism. The strongest enemies of this inter-nationalism, then, appear to be the postcolonial nationalisms that have emerged in the decolonized world. However, as Geeta Kapur (1991) warns, it is precisely in the context of the new free-market internationalism that it is imperative for hitherto marginalized societies to *retain* the category of the nation. The cultural logic of late capitalism is to ethnicize these so-cieties into myriads of tribal/local units and then appropriate them as signs of cultural difference. These marginalized cultures are then valorized as the ground of truth/authenticity. The allocation of 'radical' status to post-colonial cultures however proceeds from a viewpoint of the cosmopolitan centre—one that sees them as marginal and *therefore* oppositional/radical. In contrast, Kapur argues that the nation is *not* a devolving concept. Na-tional units, having emerged through collective struggles, suggest larger solidarities. Being an expressly political category, the nation also suggests that cultural practices within its territories be interpreted according to their own criteria, rather than some hypothetical absolute into which West-ern European societies may have developed. Moreover, the category of the nation, in calling forth a certain history, also actively militates against the postmodernist pastiche in which an aesthetic style stands in for the past. For large parts of the globe, where the effects of this past are palpably visible, such a denial of history can only serve to de-politicize the desire for social change (see ibid.).

However, Ahmad argues that the appropriative tendency, which views cultural products of the whole world though Western European frames, is evident in the way in which Third World literature has been 'profession-alized' in the metropolitan academy (1991). He points out that the terms under which this new area was constituted derive from the pressures that the Euro-American academy has had to respond to over the last three decades. A significant result of this process was that the issue of literary representation of colony and empire was posed from the beginning, not from Marxist positions, but in response to nationalist pressures, so that the subsequent theorizing of the subject, even when undertaken by Marx-ists, proceeded from an already existing nationalist premise. The same period also saw the arrival of a new political theory, the Three Worlds theory. Though initially used as synonymous with the Non-Aligned Move-ment, i.e. as a real alternative to the inexorable logic of the cold war, the term has, since then, undergone a sea change of meaning as evident by its conceptualization by theorists of even such radical persuasion as Jameson. His by-now notorious 'Third World Literature in the Era of Multinational Capitalism' can be read as a continuation of his cognitive mapping of post-modern culture (1989). The politico-historical consequences of his theo-rization of the Third World can, at best, be described as disturbing. Jameson defines the First and Second Worlds in terms of their modes of production capitalism and socialism respectively. The Third World, a vast and historically differentiated part of the globe, is homogenized as 'coun-tries which have suffered colonialism and imperialism'. Jameson, however, is not alone in maintaining this position. Even such a path-breaking work as Edward Said's *Orientalism* (1978), while it shows that particular kinds of 'legitimate' knowledge are impositions, is unable to account for the fact that discursive configurations are always produced in a mesh of collusion and contradiction between the colonizer and the colonized. A fundamental problem with an exclusive emphasis on the colonial encounter is that the political category that necessarily follows is that of the nation. But, as a growing body of scholarship has shown, when we look into the project of the Indian nationalist movement at its various regional sites, for example, the focus on the colonial gets dispersed over other concerns. The nation is reconfigured beyond the colonial experience to other social structures; other formations of gender and religious communities. As Tanika Sarkar notes in a different context, it is striking that it is only 'Third World histories' that are made to seem so flat and monochromatic, capable of being read off from a single perspective (1993). By positing a single binary opposition between colonialism and nationalism, such a historiography reaffirms the mastery of Western knowledge-systems, since both complicity and resistance equally and exclusively shape themselves around a colonial agenda and remain eternally parasitic upon it. It also gives colonial discourse—itself an undifferentiated, unhistoricized, stereotyped construct— the power of completely eradicating all other histories.

Instead, as has been persuasively demonstrated, while acknowledging the relation of dominance between the West and the non-West, one has to locate the currency of the category of the nation as also emerging from specific social pressures *there*. This involves a sense of bilinguality defined not only in terms of linguistic competence but, as my thesis tries to argue, to account for the *conflicting* social idioms that shape the postcolonial world.

10 Among others, we may usefully recall here Ngugu Thiongo (1986), or efforts of Caribbean postcolonial intellectuals such as Edward Kumau Brathwaite and Derek Walcott, to create a national language in the context of present-day West Indies.

11 For example, the first printing press in India was established in 1778. It was used, for the first time, to print Nathaniel Brassey Halhed's *Bengali Grammar* (1778). The Serampore Mission Press (est. 1800) also produced books in languages such as Bengali, Tamil, Telugu, Marathi and Oriya. But, as Joshi (1991: 1–31) argues, while the printing press made literary texts available to a much greater number of people, it also displaced existing modes of oral transmission and excluded the vast illiterate majority from its consumption. Moreover, the new aesthetic that valorized individual subjectivity could neither accommodate creative forms of other social formations nor capture the differential nature of their art. Further, the system of printed textbooks also gave rise to what Krishna Kumar has called 'textbook culture', where the printed text became the authoritative sense of knowledge. The centrality of the textbook, in turn, changed the entire nature of the educational institution by introducing a new educational apparatus, an agency of prescribing authorities, fixed syllabi and an examination based on prescribed textbooks. Not only did the colonial education system introduce a new bureaucratic apparatus, it also discredited indigenous knowledge—sciences, crafts or arts—and prevented its inclusion in the syllabi (see Kumar 1987a, 1991).

12 See, among others, Robin Blackburn (1975), Francine R. Frankel (1978) and Achin Vanaik (1990), for comprehensive analyses of the socio-political

contradictions that mark post-Independence India. I have mentioned earlier that nationalist historiography endorsed the ideological biases of colonial rationality while substituting British Rule with elite Indian personalities as protagonists of Indian history. The implicit logic of nationalist historiography, therefore, was to formulate the termination of British rule also as the resolution of all India's internal contradictions. But as recent studies have shown, three main kinds of internal contradictions have emerged in the post-Independence period. The first has to do with the differential formation of the Indian bourgeoisie. Unlike its Western counterpart, owing to the historical circumstances of its growth, this class in India primarily consists of professional and techno-managerial classes. This non-industrial petty-bourgeois class is also highly vocal in politics and tends to form the bulk of membership of all political parties. It has also increased enormously in both size *and* influence in the post-Nehruvian era. This petty-bourgeois view of socialism, for example, has resulted in massive state investment in largely unplanned and wasteful public sector enterprises as well as all the paraphernalia of the state machinery and the bureaucracy.

Further, we find a critical antagonism developing between regional and national capital over the last three decades. Commerce in colonial India had resulted in the creation of an indigenous capitalist class in coastal centres such as Bombay and Calcutta. This had lead, at the time of Independence, to the creation of a highly concentrated private sector. This 'big' bourgeoisie still controls 47 per cent of all non-government companies. However, since Independence, a large number of bourgeois entrepreneurs have emerged whose activities are confined to small regions. They have naturally resented the monopolistic tendencies of the big bourgeoisie. As I will elaborate in the next chapter, in the 1950–60s, the antagonism between regional and national capital produced violent struggles for the creation of linguistic states.

The third, and related, antagonism has emerged largely as a by-product of the much touted 'Green Revolution' which has actually made land distribution even more unequal. The *internal* contradictions of the coalition that assumed state power lead to the creation of a regionally conscious group of capitalist farmers. Given the nature of politics initiated by Indira Gandhi, this has been accompanied, since the 1960s, by the systematic destruction of all the procedural norms and institutional apparatuses of bourgeois democracy and the insertion of feudal forms of power and patronage into bourgeois state apparatuses (Kaviraj 1988).

To this was added the wastage due to conspicuous consumption, which heightened dramatically since the early 1980s, with Indira Gandhi starting the aggressive drive towards 'liberalization'. Andre Gunder Frank's (1970) analysis is applicable here. Frank suggests that postcolonial societies are integrated into the capitalist world order as 'satellites' to the metropoles, fostering a dependent form of industrialization. The Third World nations essentially supply raw materials and cheap labour for the consumer goods industries of the West. Within the national context, this means that the state *diverts* demands from more important domestic needs such as generation of employment or expansion of public services to create a model for a type of consumption that will stimulate demands for Western European consumer goods, and consequently, galvanize Western European economy (ibid.: 4–17). With the delicensing of crucial sectors such as finance and heavy industry in the early 1990s, along with the endorsement of the 1991 Dunkel Draft, India's subservience to the IMF–World Bank combine seemed complete.

13 Thus, for instance, Robert D. King (1997) argues that it was Nehru's cosmopolitanism that was at the root of his reluctance to the linguistic reorganization of states in 1956—a cosmopolitanism without which the nation would have simply been overwhelmed by the primordial loyalties of caste and region.

14 The immediate reference that comes to mind in this context is, of course, Louis Althusser on the school as the major ideological apparatus of the bourgeois state (1971). With regard to theorizations of radical pedagogy, one could, for effective contrast, juxtapose publications of the NCERT to Paulo Freire (1990).

15 Damodar Dharmananda Kosambi's critique of Nehru has now almost attained cult status; see, specifically, Kosambi (1957).

16 Tracing the trajectory of 'secularism' in the West, Tharu and Lalita recall a similar history of exclusiveness there, too:

> The history of secularism in its Occidental homeland is similarly battle-scarred. The white, Protestant, bourgeois male was set up as the norm and his interests entrenched through a brutal process of exploitation (at home and in the colonies) and ruthless homogenization (millions were massacred, their cultures destroyed, their systems of knowledge delegitimated) (1995: 71).

CHAPTER TWO

'HINDI': TRANSLATING NATIONHOOD AS *INDIAN*

Where the mind is without fear and the head is held high [. . .]
Into that heaven of freedom, my Father, let my country awake
(Tagore 1912: 26).

On 2 October 1994, in the southern Indian state of Karnataka, a new item
was introduced in the regular telecasting schedule of the national network—a 10-minute news bulletin in Urdu. Identified immediately by the
local unit of the Bharatiya Janata Party (BJP) as another instance of 'ap-
peasement of minorities', i.e. Muslims, it lead to widespread rioting and
arson. In many ways, this very 'trivial' incident underlined the fact that our
present seems a bizarre caricature of the India that, according to Nehru,
had finally kept its 'tryst with destiny' on 15 August 1947. As a weary and
fragmented nation looks back at that optimistic past, the inevitable question
haunts it at every turn—'Where did we go wrong?' And, as it gropes for
answers, it becomes increasingly evident that the nation needs to rethink
the very image of modernity on which it had sought to fashion itself.

In the previous chapter I tried to sketch the historically changing notions of modernity that English has signified in India. Based on the classical nation-state of nineteenth-century Europe, modernity translated broadly into the principles of liberal democracy and capitalist industrialization. Efforts to emulate Enlightenment notions of modernity has had its inevitable consequence—Indian nationalism now sees itself as having failed to live up to 'universal' standards. But the problem, as we are just beginning to understand, has not been with the object under scrutiny but in the measuring sticks themselves. As Nicholas B. Dirks argues:

> In freeing history from its modernised modalities, we need to treat the past neither as nostalgia nor as anecdote, and we are not forced to choose between fiction and fact. All our histories must be decolonised, and if in this process the modern takes another mortal blow history will not take flight [. . .] For as long as history is genuinely political, there will be ruptures aplenty. [. . . As Walter] Benjamin went on to observe, 'Only that historian will have the gift of fanning the spark of hope in the past who is firmly convinced that *even the dead* will not be safe from the enemy if he wins' (1990: 31).

Following the line of enquiry opened by theorists such as Chatterjee, I have argued that a fundamental bilingualism defines the objective situation of the postcolonial world. By bilingualism I refer not to the fact of multilingual cultural contexts or the process of interlingual transfers but to the conflicting conceptual–political idioms that shape postcolonial spaces. As I try in this chapter to locate Hindi within the politico-cultural imaginary of India, the asymmetry that emerges is not merely one between a metropolitan language and an indigenous one. Rather, it refers to the entire problematic underwritten by Western philosophical notions of reality, representation and knowledge that brought into being hegemonic versions of the colonized and participated in the fixing of colonized cultures in ways that continue to be operative in the postcolonial context.

The nation-state was considered to be Western Europe's most magnificent gift to the rest of the world. Educated into the world of colonial modernity, the Indian intelligentsia reinflected the idiom of liberalism into vocabularies of pre-existing feudal ideologies in the country. Thus, English was institutionalized in nineteenth-century India in ways that would uphold orthodox Hindu social hierarchies. However, as Chatterjee has shown, the objective presence of colonial rule in the domain of the state meant that, within the anticolonial nationalisms of Asia and Africa, the most inventive efforts to rework the modernity of the West into indigenous frames were located in spheres outside the terrain of politics. I will call this project one of *'translating* modernity'—this effort to recast the discursive world of the Enlightenment into non-Western idioms. As Chatterjee has described, this was a project that involved fashioning cultures that would be modern while simultaneously retaining markers of distinct national identities. The point that cannot be overemphasized is that the parameters according to which such national cultures were sought to be fashioned emerged in direct polemic with the parameters of modernity institutionalized by colonial rule in the domain of the state or the conceptual world signified by English.

As mentioned in the Introduction, I have used 'Hindi' to signify the conceptual idiom of the 'popular'.[1] Paralleling the three moments that I traced in the career of English in India, I shall mark three moments in the history of Hindi as well. If we use nation-state as a shorthand term for the modernity promised in India by English, then the first moment in the trajectory of Hindi would be when the centralizing impulse of the nation began to be reinflected at different *regional* sites in the late nineteenth century. Empowered by Orientalist constructions which equated the Indian nation with a specifically North Indian, upper-caste Hindu identity, one such 'region'—the United Provinces or the Hindi heartland—would subsequently emerge as hegemonic in nationalist constructions of Indianness. Consequently, the hegemony of the Hindi language would also be contested, from the early twentieth century itself, by regions of both the South and the North East that were marginalized within this conception of being Indian.[2] Not surprisingly, anti-Hindi regional movements would often be mobilized in the direction of lower-caste politics.

While formulated within a refurbished caste system, the Gandhian intervention then provided the first historical opening for a range of identities to be accommodated within the idea of the Indian nation. For the Indian nation to be imagined into existence, it was objectively necessary that alliances (however fragile) be forged across the range of social boundaries. Within the framework of Nehruvian nationalism—in what constitutes the second moment in the trajectory of Hindi—these alliances would be given official endorsement in the form of the reorganization of the nation into linguistic states/regions in 1956, ostensibly as a gesture towards federalism. The troubled status of Hindi as 'official language' of the Indian democracy is an indicator of the fact that such federalism was never properly implemented.[3]

The third moment in the trajectory of Hindi can be located at what we have described in the previous chapter as the new English–Hindi conjuncture of the 1980s. The interaction of global capital with the internal contradictions of the post-Nehruvian era of Indian political life has seen Hindi move in to share with English the status of the national modern. Further, the cultural neo-nationalism in 1980s' India—represented most dangerously by Hindutva—is directly linked to the needs of multinational capital that has been replacing regional markets with a national market. The crucial difference, of course, is that the new nation—as opposed to the sovereign nation-state imagined by liberalism—is merely a unit of administrative convenience for transnational corporations. Consequently, the 1980s saw a new pan-indigenism displace the earlier specificity of regional identities in India and, relatedly, the emergence of a changed equation between Hindi and the various regional languages. As opposed to the anti-Hindi sentiments expressed by several of the regional movements of the 1950s, the chauvinism of 1980s' regionalism now feeds into the logic of a resurgent Hindu fundamentalism, one that actively advocates Hindi as national language. My contention is that it is this third moment, which has seen the emergence of Hindi as the new lingua franca, that provides the conditions of possibility for the 'new' Bombay commercial cinema of the 1980s. By tracing the changing status of Hindi within the national imaginary, my aim is to show the ways in which official discourses of nationhood were translated by ideologies and institutions in the domain of the popular. The following chapters will place into this larger picture some general readings of contemporary Bombay film industry.

The construction of Hindi as national language was promoted from a range of ideological positions, the common ground between which dramatically diverse and opposing initiatives was that they were all advocating indigenist alternatives to the classical nation-state. Or, to frame it differently, they all represented attempts to translate European notions of nationhood into distinctively Indian dialects. Predictably, therefore, they confronted, in a number of ways, both the advocacy of the English language as well as the modernity that English represented.

Our complicity with the West exists at multiple levels. Given the new translatability of North American consumer culture, it is no longer possible to assume that we can break free of the chains that bind us to English and go back to a 'pure' national language, i.e. Hindi. Nevertheless, as we attempt to forge a politics that mobilizes narratives of community and selfhood other than those historically promised by English in India, it seems appropriate to begin by reclaiming the exclusions on which Left liberal notions of modernity were premised. It is with this larger aim that the following sections will trace the modernity that Hindi signifies.

THE NATIONAL EPISTEME

As opposed to the 'history of ideas', which he describes as the discipline of 'beginnings and ends', Foucault proposes the concept of archaeology as a form of analysis that does away with obsessions of traditional historiography such as genesis, continuity and totalization. Discussing his methodological approach to the 'positivities' that have been the focus of his work, Foucault goes on to outline the form of analysis enabled by an archaeological history:

> Such an analysis sets out [. . .] to outline the history of the sciences on the basis of a description of discursive practices; to define how, in accordance with which regularity and as a result of which modifications, it was able to give rise to the processes of epistemologization [. . .] The analysis of discursive formations, of positivities, and knowledge in their relations with epistemological figures and with the sciences is what has been called, to distinguish it from other possible forms of the history of the sciences, the analysis of the *episteme*. This episteme may be suspected of being something like a world-view, a slice of history common to all branches of knowledge, [. . .] a certain structure of thought that men of a particular period cannot escape . . . (1972: 190–1).

Placed in the context of the language-question, the episteme structuring discourses of the late-nineteenth- and early-twentieth-century India was undoubtedly that of the nation and implicitly of the modernity that the classical nation-state signified. I have cited Chatterjee's work on the 'politics'–'culture' divide in the history of nation-formation in India, as well as the crucial importance of the *cultural* terrain in the anticolonial nationalisms of Asia and Africa as a privileged site in which was articulated their difference from the modular forms of Western nation-states. Decisively located in the terrain of culture, the refashioning of indigenous languages emerged as one of the primary acts of nationalist self-assertion in India. And yet, underlying the creation of a new Sanskritized Hindi language was also the attempt to translate the idiom of liberal democracy so as to construct a specifically upper-caste North Indian Hindu self as the normative Indian citizen. This project, however, was deeply fissured as indexed by the simultaneous emergence of the many vernaculars and their related articulation of many regional identities.

Prasad has pointed out in a series of writings (1995, 1999) that the classical nation-state emerged out of a specific combination of territorial and linguistic factors in the West, factors unlikely to be reproduced elsewhere in pure form. As evident from the contests over national language in India, for instance, the imposition of this European script on social spaces dramatically different from nineteenth-century Europe accounts for the highly volatile political formations that have come to characterize the Global South.

In the Introduction I have discussed Chatterjee's proposition that Foucault's thesis on the new governmentalized form of state power—one radiating from innumerable nodes in the social body rather any one privileged source—holds only in those cases where this state power could fulfil one fundamental criterion—that of representativeness. In a similar vein, Kaviraj observes that since there did not exist any 'individualistic' conception of society in India prior to colonial rule, the language of liberalism was given an entirely new inflection within the discourse of Indian nationalism:

> The liberal argument that the rationality of man must be construed to mean that each human being is the best judge of his own interest and therefore deserved the right to individual autonomy was simply transferred, to the considerable embarrassment of utilitarian theorists, to the national community [. . .] (and meant) primarily

the collective freedom of the Indian people from British rule [. . .] (1992: 24)

The implications of such a translation were enormous and we will discuss it at length in the next chapter when we analyse the ways in which the aesthetic of realism was mediated by Bombay cinema. Here, we need to underline Kaviraj's suggestion that it was the Indian nation—a new collective self, rather than specific individuals—that had now won freedom. However, this Indian nation was also in close competition with other collective identities—the many regional ones. This becomes evident from the fact that within a decade of Independence, the Union had to be redrawn along regional–linguistic lines. At the heart of this process was the whole question of making the socio-political structures of the *postcolonial* state more representative. And it is this critical intersection of the language-question with the exigencies of representative democracy in India and the non-West that this chapter attempts to explore. Prasad has coined the term 'cine-politics' to describe the unique and intimate nature of the link between politics and popular cinema that seems to exist in India, especially in South India (1999: 13–28). In commonsensical usage, Prasad points out, the link between cinema and politics is defined in most parts of the world in terms of some variant of 'communication theory', either that of cinema as transmitting messages which influence the masses or of Stars cashing in on their charisma in an already well-demarcated arena of electoral politics. Prasad argues against both:

> Cine-politics is not about the infusion of star charisma into elec-
> toral politics, nor about the use of cinema to disseminate party
> slogans. It is a distinct form of political engagement that emerged
> in some of the linguistically defined states of southern India at a
> certain historical juncture where the Indian nationalism's ideolog-
> ical suturing could not take care of the gaps in the symbolic chain.
> A set of contingent factors led to a situation where cinema, a form
> of entertainment that was then learning to speak, came to be
> chosen as the site of a strong political investment [. . .] (ibid.: 25).

Analysing the dramatic political effect to which popular cinemas in South India have been put, Prasad points out that a series of momentous events occurred almost simultaneously—the end of colonial rule, the rise of the talkies, the linguistic reorganization of states as well as the dissolution of the Madras Presidency. Prasad notes that this peculiar conjunction of events—where several linguistic nationalisms which had no legitimate grounds of political expression were in competition with a principle of federalism that was attempting to construct a non-linguistic pan-Indian identity—gave rise to a situation in which the popular regional-language cinemas of South India emerged as a 'shadow structure of political representation, a political "supplement" in the Derridean sense' (ibid.). Thus, a unique nature of the Star system arose where the top South Indian male Stars were seen as representatives, par excellence, of their respective *linguistic* communities.

In a finely nuanced argument, Prasad draws on Spivak's reading of the distinction between the two overlapping meanings of 'representation' in Marx (1898)—aesthetic and political—to suggest that the phenomenal popularity of the top South Indian male leads of the 1950s may be attributed to a political situation quite similar to that of eighteenth-century France. In the absence of modes of political representation based on calculations of class interests alone, Louis Bonaparte of France had come to be recognized by the French peasants as speaking 'in their name'. Similarly, audiences of South India recognized their Stars as speaking 'in their name', as their 'representatives' within the newly emerging national Indian cultural and political space. (On the other hand, a *regional* Hindi identity could never emerge because the identity of this linguistic community was fully merged with that of the Indian nation.) This particular aesthetic and political configuration of events derives from the specific history of the emergence of the Indian film industry as an act of nationalist self-assertion in the Swadeshi era. It was imperative, given the political context of the 1910–20s, that not only ownership but also the product itself—i.e. the images produced—be marked as distinctly Indian. Thus the famous origin myth of Indian cinema where Dadasaheb Phalke dreamt not only of setting up an Indian film industry but also of seeing specifically Indian images on screen. Prasad goes on to argue:

> Phalke's story [. . .] is indicative of the primacy that the screen, as the site of production of images, has had in the Indian imagining of a cinematic culture [. . .] The screen here has the status of one

of those neutral spaces whose very existence compels all nations to relocate themselves in them [. . .] This sense of 'our images, their spaces', with its attendant connotation of acts of self-alienation that transport us into modernity, has been a discernible feature of popular cinema in India [. . .] It is [similarly] as 'our representative' in the space of Indian nationalism that the hero [of the South] must function, serving as a linking figure through whom the otherwise unfamiliar thematics of a pan-Indian identity take on a more friendly appearance [. . .] [T]hese stars are not invested with any separatist longings, rather they have tended to function as figures of conciliation between the local and the pan-Indian nationalisms (1999: 26).

While Prasad's formulation is undoubtedly the most sophisticated one, a new body of work is now emerging, especially on popular cinemas of South India, which strongly foreground these connections between the language-question and cinema in the formation of regional and national identities.[4] To relate this discussion to the larger aim of this chapter, the language-question in India shows us that the attempts to indigenize the liberal nation-state meant, in effect, giving it *radically new* institutional and political forms. The translation of modernity into non-Western idioms therefore involved crucial redefinitions. Chatterjee remarks vis-à-vis the whole range of institutions through which new knowledge began to emerge in colonial Bengal:

We are forced to recognise, first, that following its [i.e. modern Western knowledge's] implantation in a different if not entirely alien field, the new discursive formation will open itself to intrusions by various elements in the pre-existing linguistic or intellectual practices of the country [. . .] These 'prior' knowledges are not those whose elements may have gone into the formation of the discipline (such as, let us say, the Greek sciences or medieval scholasticism). These are 'prior' knowledges that belong, so to speak, to an anachronistic present, knowledges that one would have assumed had been overtaken by the process of history or scientific progress, except for the fact that they now have to be encountered horizontally, as adjacent formations that must be engaged in the process of translation (1995b: 23).

THE RISE OF THE VERNACULAR: THEORIZING THE REGION

We have discussed in the preceding chapter that the impact of English in India went much beyond the introduction of a language to that of a new education system (based on textbooks and examinations), a new vocabulary of literary judgement and a new set of political institutions—the whole discursive universe which ideologically reproduced the ethic of individualism, the linchpin of liberal philosophy. Already in 1838, writing in support of the Filtration Theory advocated by Macaulay, Trevelyan was arguing for the need to create 'vernacular' literatures. As a consequence of liberal education in English, he foresaw the creation of a Westernized intellectual elite who would begin to also write in their own languages. Such a reconstitution of indigenous languages was thought necessary because the colonial educationists all agreed that their existing forms did not suit the requirements of a liberal curriculum. For example, one of the persistent objections to the use of local languages for administrative purposes was that they had no 'standard' forms. Thus, the Sadar Court of Bengal in 1837 pointed out that Bengali was unfit to be a court language owing to its multiplicity of dialects. Similarly, the Sadar Court of the North Western Provinces decided that Hindustani had a great variety of dialects, sometimes even differing within a single district, and hence it was unsuitable as a court language (King 1994: 55). The implications of such official positions are evident in the scholarship that emerged out of the Asiatic Society and Fort William College. They also came to be dispersed over increasingly large sections of Indian society through pamphlets, journals and the whole new set of literary–critical apparatuses made possible by the introduction of the printing press—a crucial accessory of the 'modernization' inaugurated by English. Thus, dictionaries of indigenous languages were compiled, orthographies standardized and pecuniary inducements given for creative writing modelled on Western European genres. Added to these subtler efforts was, of course, the brute fact of political power; and the possibilities this generated for introducing social change through legislation. For instance, the Woods Despatch of 1854 emphatically advocated a reconstitution of the vernaculars and gave a major impetus to the establishment of educational institutions in vernacular languages.

However as argued earlier, the new aesthetic and political vocabulary that English signified cannot be seen solely as a matter of colonial imposition.

The participants in this process were also the indigenous elite who re-inflected the idiom of liberalism to reinforce traditional social hierarchies. In fact, in a striking convergence of colonialist and elite–nationalist inter-ests, the indigenous elite often actually demanded a reconstitution of the vernaculars as an anticolonial gesture.[5] On the one hand, colonial educa-tionists sought to standardize indigenous languages to aid a centralized legal system to fulfil the colonial need to gain access to land revenues. On the other, the traditional Indian elite endorsed the colonial impulse to reinforce existing feudal hierarchies by translating liberalism into existing feudal idioms. Consequently, literary societies in vernacular languages sprang up all across the country. These literary societies were closely asso-ciated, right from their inception, with different forms of regional articula-tion. This was because, as Shivarama Padikkal points out, the creation of vernaculars was integral to the newly emerging regional identities—a project which was exactly contemporaneous with the emergence of a new nation:

> Another important element of nationalism [. . . was] the fashioning
> of the vernacular languages and the creation of identities of lin-
> guistic regions. Because of its caste system and other hierarchies,
> India had always had many languages. With the creation of the
> modern educated class, the dialect spoken by it in a particular
> region became the 'standard' form. Being economically and
> socially powerful, this class achieved a convergence of dialects
> through the print medium, shaped a 'new' language which now
> acquired the status of the '*vernacular*' to articulate its political
> ambitions [. . .] Language-centred regionalism and the concept of
> the nation that transcends linguistic divisions emerge as comple-
> mentary notions. This is the unique feature of Indian nationalism,
> which stands at the conjuncture of English—which provided 'mod-
> ern' knowledge and the vernaculars—which recast this knowledge
> into regional forms (1993: 225–6).

Thus, in Maharashtra, the Literary Society was to include political figures of national stature such as M. G. Ranade, G. H. Deshmukh and Jyotiba Phule. The Arya Samaj was formed in 1875. One of its major activ-ities was the propagation of Hindi throughout North India. As a reaction, the Muhammadan Anglo-Oriental College was also founded in the same

year, with Urdu as its medium of instruction. The Nagari Pracharani Sabha
of Benares (Society for the Promotion of Nagari)—the most important vol-
untary organization for the promotion of the new Hindi—was founded in
1893. While the demands of the Sabha for a 'standard' Hindi coincided
with the demands for a Hindu nation, there also emerged simultaneous
demands for linguistic states, associated with the different dialects out of
which the new Hindi was sought to be created. Associated with Bhojpuri
were demands for the creation of Bhojpur, with Maithili the demand for a
Maithili state. The Rajasthani movement voiced a demand for Rajasthan,
the Pahari movement for Himachal Pradesh and the Akali movement for
Punjab.

Similar demands were also raised in other parts of the country. The
Gujarat Vernacular Society was established in 1840. Among its members
the most prominent would undoubtedly be Gandhi himself. In fact, it was
in his address to the Gujarat Educational Conference that Gandhi was to
put forward his ideas on national language and promote Hindustani for
the same. In the same vein, the Andhra Mahasabha (Andhra Society) was
established in 1913. The language-question was an integral part of the
Vishala Andhra (Greater Andhra) movement, whereby the Telugu-speaking
people demanded the creation of the state of Andhra Pradesh, autonomous
of 'Tamil domination' in the Madras Presidency. It was as a result of the
Andhradesa (Andhra country) movement that the demand for a linguistic
reorganization of states made its first appearance in the 1917 Calcutta session of the INC. The Kannada Sahitya Parishad (Kannada Literary Society,
est. 1915), too, demanded the creation of the state of Karnataka, while the
Kerala Sahitya Parishad (Kerala Literary Society) called for the creation of
Aikya Kerala (United Kerala). The point that needs to be reiterated is that
these demands for linguistic states were voiced especially by upper-caste
land-owning groups who formed the traditional intellectual stratum of each
region (Karat 1973; Handa 1983).

I have discussed in the Introduction the grounding of the liberal
nation-state on principles of enumeration. Framing the emergence of the
vernaculars within the cognitive re-mapping that occurred in the transition
from 'fuzzy' communities of pre-colonial times to the enumerated community of the nation-state in India, Kaviraj has argued that the 'region' was a

crucial discursive concept in enabling the transition from *gemeinschaft* to *gesellschaft* (1992). The Indian nation was historically imaged into existence as an anticolonial gesture. Yet, for a specifically 'nationalist' consciousness to emerge, an already existing profound sense of historical pessimism had to be overcome. An anticolonial structure of feeling was primarily a negative consciousness—a resentment towards rule by alien people. For this to turn into historical optimism, for the possibility of challenging colonial rule to be conceived, a new sense of collective self had to be imagined into existence, a new 'we' that was qualitatively different from the 'we' of earlier, more 'organic', communities. And, in this transition from pre-colonial communities to the new community of the nation, the emergence of the region as a concept proved crucial.

Aided by the new possibilities of standardization of languages, dialects of traditional feudal elites became the vernaculars of each new region, marginalizing dialects of the lower classes. However, not only were these new regional identities based on territory, but the new sense of 'collective selves' that arose was also based on clearly defined principles of enumeration. Although more culturally homogeneous than the nation, these two principles—of territoriality and enumeration—would subsequently be extended in the historical construction of an Indian identity.

While work on the differential formation of regional languages is just emerging, it is clear that, by the early twentieth century itself, the narrative of nationhood was being emphatically rewritten at several regional sites, each with its distinct caste–linguistic configuration. The significant difference was that while in most of these linguistic regions the idiom of liberalism was used to prop up traditional feudal hierarchies, there were also some in which regional identities came to be linked to democratizing lower-caste/class political initiatives. To this effect, for instance, the South Indian Liberation Federation, or the Justice Party, was founded in 1916. Similarly, in 1926, Periyar E. V. Ramaswamy Naicker launched the Self-Respect Movement, a radical lower-caste movement aimed at reclaiming a non-Brahman Dravidian identity. Consequently, the Self-Respecters protested the provision of the 1935 Government of India Act making Hindi a compulsory subject in all provincial schools. In 1939, Periyar issued the call for a separate Tamil country and, in 1944, the energies of the Justice Party fed into the founding of the Dravida Munnetra Kazhagam (DMK) as the main political party aimed at the creation of the state (or country) of Tamil Nadu (see Irschick 1969).

HINDI AND THE POLITICS OF INDIGENISM

The emergence of a new Sanskritized form of the Hindi language from roughly the middle of the nineteenth century has to be placed within this contested terrain, as many different proto-nationalisms sought to stake their claims to the 'national modern' status. Recent studies analysing the nature and role of this new Hindi include those by Jyotindra Dasgupta (1970), Paul Brass (1974), S. Dwivedi (1981), Amrit Rai (1984) and Christopher R. King (1994).

Rai contends that before the decline of Mughal rule, a common language, Hindi/Hindavi, united the linguistic (and by implication, the cultural) traditions of both Hindus and Muslims in the Indian subcontinent. In different parts of the subcontinent, this common language was also given specific regional flavours, such as the Dakkani language that developed in Central India (the Deccan). However, two distinct languages, Hindi and Urdu, were created out of that one language through a conscious process of Sanskritization and Persianization, respectively. The earliest attempts to consciously create two languages out of one, with explicit religious overtones, however, go back to efforts of Orientalist scholars as early as John Gilchrist of the late eighteenth century. A whole stream of scholars, from Herbert Risley to George Grierson, advocated 'Hinduwee for the Hindus and Arabic and Persian for the Musalmaans', instead of the common language, Hindustani, for both (Pradhan 1985: 180–1). Similarly, the curriculum at Fort William College included instruction not only in English but also in Arabic, Persian, Sanskrit as well as vernacular languages such as Tamil, Telugu, Kannada, Marathi and Bengali. However, though these efforts, along with the establishment of a bifurcated vernacular education system, had already created the potential for differentiation between Hindi and Urdu, it must be noted that no systematized Hindi movement existed till about the 1860s.

Further, there were fluctuations in colonial policy, often giving rise to extremely confusing situations where adjacent administrative units would have different official languages. Moreover, in the early decades of colonial rule, British policy seems to have actually favoured Urdu (i.e. Hindustani in the Persian script) rather than Hindi (i.e. Hindustani in the Devanagari script) as official language. Consequently, in 1830, it was Hindustani in the Persian script that became the official vernacular while Hindustani in the Devanagari script failed to reach a similar status. Similarly, Urdu became the official medium of transaction in the North Western Provinces in 1835, and that of Punjab in the 1840s.[6] But the most significant implication of these colonial policies was that in much of early-nineteenth-century North India both Muslims and Hindus were familiar with Urdu.

But, of course, neither Urdu nor Hindi compared favourably with English. Till the early twentieth century, there was little initiative by the indigenous elite to establish institutions of higher education using the vernaculars as medium of instruction. In fact, only two such institutions existed—the Anglo-Oriental College of Aligarh, with Urdu as medium of instruction, and the Central Hindu College of Benares, offering Hindi, along with Sanskrit and English.

However, government colleges offering education in the vernaculars were more numerous. The Benares Sanskrit College was started in 1772, the Agra College in 1823, the Roorki College in 1847 and the Bareilly College in 1887. At this point a basic contradiction in government policy became evident. Hindi was recognized as medium of instruction in both primary and secondary schools. It was already being taught in 1815. However, in the early decades of the nineteenth century, there was a tendency for the colonial state to prefer Urdu to Hindi in matters of official transaction. This contradiction was effectively exploited by advocates of the Hindi movement in subsequent decades. They argued that since the government had established Hindi schools in every village there was no rationale in prohibiting its use for official and administrative purposes. And, as a result of hectic campaigning, by the end of the nineteenth century, Hindi did replace Urdu as the official language in most parts of North India (King 1994: 53–79).

Yet, the growing dominance of Hindi was not simply a linguistic issue. As Brass (1974), among others, has argued, the Hindi movement formed part of a much broader process of heightening communal awareness in pre-Independence India. It has to be seen, therefore, as overlapping with other expressions of Hindu nationalism such as the Dayanand Saraswati-led 'Cow

Protection' movement, Bal Gangadhar Tilak's revival of Hindu festivals and so on. As mentioned earlier, the overlap in the imaginations of Orientalist and elite nationalist thought/discourse subsequently led to the equation of a specific region with that of the Indian nation.

Moreover, even within the Hindi movement, the emergence of Devanagari script as the dominant mode was not a natural conclusion. Matters of dialect, script and style generated considerable controversy. As King documents, in the early nineteenth century, it was Kaithi—rather than the Devanagari script—that was better established in North India. Consequently, castes within the Hindu community that advocated Urdu included principally the Kayasthas and the Kshatriyas. Kayasthas, who had historically been court scribes, were the most numerous. But while Kaithi had strong associations with business and trading classes, Devanagari had strong links with the Brahmans. Such a structure was also reflected in the enrolment patterns of indigenous schools. While Muslims and Kayasthas dominated Persian schools, non-Kayastha Hindus such as Brahmans and Rajputs dominated Hindi schools. What is of significance, then, is that the Hindi movement lead to a distinct realignment of caste dominance *within* the Hindu community itself (King 1994: 65–79).

In the 1860s—about the time the Hindi movement began to take shape as a systematic campaign—debates on the official language for the North Western Frontier Provinces began to occupy a prominent place in the vernacular press.[7] The provincial government received a series of memoranda between 1868 and 1873, urging the introduction of Hindi as the official language of India. The Arya Samaj directed all its members to learn either Sanskrit or Hindi. So did the Hindu Samaj (the Hindu Society, est. 1880), under the leadership of Madan Mohan Malaviya, a prominent member of the INC. The Satya Dharmavolambini Sabha (Society for Preserving the True Religion, est. 1878), the Aligarh Bhasha Samaj (Aligarh Vernacular Language Society, est. 1881) and the Devanagari Pracharani Sabha (Society for the Promotion of Devanagari, est. 1882) also advocated the promotion of Hindi.

But the foremost organization of the Hindi movement was the Nagari Pracharani Sabha of Benares (est. 1893). In its efforts to revive Hindi, the Sabha searched for old manuscripts, founded a library, started publishing textbooks, patronized original creative work, published a scholarly journal and actively aided the establishment of Hindi as a legitimate discipline of study. These parameters of legitimacy were, of course, modelled on English. While in the initial years the Sabha's efforts lay in pressurizing the government into using Hindi along with Urdu, over the years its tone became increasingly strident. Thus, by 1897–98, all those who opposed Devanagari were being castigated in the annual report of the Sabha as 'bigots'. And, as a result of relentless campaigning, in April 1900, the lieutenant governor of the North Western Frontier Provinces issued a resolution giving Devanagari equal status as Urdu (King 1994: 126–72; Pradhan 1985: 156–213; Misra 1979).

The Sabha's most enduring contribution to the Hindi movement took the form of the Hindi Sahitya Sammelan (Hindi Literature Conference, est. 1910). At different points, the Sammelan would include people of the stature of Jawaharlal Nehru, Rajendra Prasad and M. K. Gandhi. But given the climate of increasing Hindu–Muslim tensions, the Sammelan's views on Indian history, too, became blatantly fundamentalist. Thus, in its 1947 annual session its president, Mahapandit Rahul, proclaimed:

> What is Urdu after all? Is it not the Indian pillar of victory of Arab *jehadis* [i.e. religious crusaders]? Was not filling the language with Arabic words in the place of national vocabulary the sowing of the seeds of *durrastriyata* [anti-nationalism]? [. . .] Whatever Islam might have said, the Musalmaans have refused to be a part of the country's stream of life [. . .] (cited in Pradhan 1985: 187).

Therefore, when in 1947 the United Provinces adopted Hindi in the Devanagari script as official language, there had already been an entire history of debate and differentiation. And, contrary to what the New Right of the 1980s would have us believe, the construction of the new 'Hindu' identity—in which the Hindi movement played such a prominent part—had entailed a deliberate and violent 'othering' of Islam.

THE LANGUAGE-QUESTION AND NEHRUVIAN NATIONALISM

I have argued in the previous chapter that the contradictions that underwrote Nehruvian socialism derived not only from the theoretical complicity of traditional Marxist theory with universalizing narratives of liberal philosophy but also from the internal contradictions of the coalition that assumed power at Independence. These contradictions underwrote the first education policy of independent India and identified a certain kind of elitism as the obverse of the 'inclusiveness' of Nehruvian nationalism. Deshpande observes:

> Nehruvian nationalism was not really well thought-out but represented rather a negative category. Insofar as its positive ideals had not been indigenised enough and had their roots in the model of a secular–modern nation, this concept of secularism could only exist in the newly created national sphere: it did not strike roots at the regional level [. . .]

> The Nehruvian era created and privileged a pan-Indian elite that could, by and large, afford to cut loose its regional moorings. Not only did this elite seem to be 'placeless', it also appeared to be 'caste-less' and 'class-less': a truly secular, modern elite. This elite spoke in the modernist idiom of secular nationalism, scientific technology and economic development: by adopting this idiom, the elite was to render invisible its own ascriptive markers (1995: 3222–3).

Here it is important to reiterate that vis-à-vis the language-question in the configuration of the Indian modern, English has been a marker of social privilege rather than of democratic politics. However, the citizen, from its very inception, has been a utopian figure. The year 1789, as Balibar argues, marks the moment of this historic rupture—when a new conception of the 'subject' is inaugurated. Suspended between the individual and the collective, the public and the private spheres, Balibar argues that the 'citizen-subject', as a concept, is one which is theoretically unstable—a concept that cannot be reduced to fixed institutional boundaries; a concept that *always exceeds the act of its enunciation* (1991).[8]

With regard to the trajectory of nation-formation in India, the Gandhian intervention provided the first historical possibility for the incorporation of the masses of the Indian people, most notably its peasantry, into the framework of a nationalist politics. As Chattterjee has argued, while the final effectivity of Gandhism lay in the appropriation of the subaltern classes into the logic of a passive revolution, the utopianism inherent in categories such as citizen-subject, however, has meant that the 'message of the Mahatma' was often translated, at different moments, into aspirations that went well beyond the confines of a bourgeois political order.[9] Let us then use Chatterjee himself to situate Gandhism in relation to the Utopia signified by the new nation here:

> Thomas More has been read as the author of a text that laid the moral foundations of the political demands of a rising bourgeoisie [. . .] He has also been regarded as the progenitor of utopian socialism [. . .] It is not surprising, therefore, that in the unresolved class struggles within the social formation of contemporary India, oppositional movements can still claim their moral legitimacy from the message of Mahatma (1986: 124).

Placed in relation to the language-question, the contests over India's national language can therefore be read as the ways in which *different* sections of the Indian people, differentially constituted by factors of class–caste–region, have sought to claim the nation as their own. By this I do not intend to homogenize the socio-political demands of the different peoples of the country. As mentioned earlier, some of these demands were explicitly formulated against the upper-caste Hindu hegemony of the INC. But without glossing over these differences, the Gandhian intervention provided the crucial crossover point from where a range of identities would necessarily have to be accommodated within the conception of the Indian nation.

These differential claims to nationhood and citizenship would then be the 'others' in polemic with which the national language policy was evolved. Taking the final form of the 1963 Official Language Act, its main provisions were:

(a) Hindi (in Devanagari script) was to be the *official* rather than the *national* language of India.

(b) English was to be retained for a period of 15 years from the date of implementation of the Constitution, i.e. 1950.

(c) The claims of the regional languages were to be upheld through Schedule VIII.

However, the hierarchy among English, Hindi and regional languages envisaged by the bill directly resonated with the caste–regional composition of the Nehruvian ruling coalition. Consequently, it faced violent opposition from the states of both the South and the North East. (Based on a theory of neutrality and equal handicaps, the southern states, for instance, have consistently preferred English as the national language instead.) Things came to a head when, during an All India Radio broadcast on 26 January 1965, the then home minister, Gulzarilal Nanda, declared, 'Hindi will take its [i.e. English's] place as the official language of the Union from today.' The broadcast was met with violent protests all across the country. M. S. S. Pandian analyses the significance of the language riots as they erupted in Tamil Nadu:

> [Their] demand, though confined to the issue of the official language of the Indian Union, involved an alternative way of imagining the nation. They desired a nation which would not erase the cultural particularities of the different people who constitute the nation, but would accommodate and foster such differences (1994).

Thus, the agitations against Hindi in Tamil Nadu were consciously launched on 25 January, a day *before* the Republic Day celebrations, because they did not want to dishonour the Republic. In fact, the slogan of the protesters was, 'Down with Hindi—Long Live the Republic.' Moreover, the agitators sought the status of official language not only for Tamil but also for all the other 14 languages of the Indian Union. Consequently, they received support from West Bengal, Andhra Pradesh and Mysore as well.

Given the composition of the Nehruvian ruling bloc, the Central government had buckled under the pressures applied by the emerging regional bourgeoisie after Independence. By 1952, the linguistic state of Andhra Pradesh had already been created. A year later, the government was compelled to form the States Reorganization Committee, which recommended the formation of the linguistic states of Kerala, Karnataka, Tamil Nadu, Hyderabad, Rajasthan, Uttar Pradesh, Madhya Pradesh, Bihar, Orissa, West Bengal, Maharashtra and Jammu and Kashmir. These linguistic states provided the regional bourgeoisie, especially the section of the rural rich they represent, the base to consolidate their political power. In fact, they not only marginalized the different linguistic traditions existing within a geographical region but, by conceptualizing the region primarily through the cultural–linguistic domain, they also glossed over contradictions of caste, class, religion and gender within linguistic communities (Joshi 1991: 1–31). Further, given the wide dissension to the 1963 Official Language Act, especially with reference to the proposed changeover from English to Hindi, the many different claims to the Indian nation had to be given statutory form of the 1967 Official Language (Amendment) Act. The main feature of the amended act was that English, which in 1950 had been unanimously sought to be removed, was now retained as 'associate official language' for an indefinite period.

Though the amended act assured that Hindi would not be imposed except by consensus, steps have consistently been taken to ensure its progressive use in administration. Hindi Advisory Committees have been set up in several key ministries with the Central Hindi Committee (est. 1967) at the apex. Clear directives have been issued to ensure that both Hindi and English are used in government orders, notifications, regulations and parliamentary papers. Instructions have also been given to ensure the progressive use of Hindi in the public sector undertakings of the central government, and workshops to train staff in Hindi have been organized. Ministries have been asked to spend at least 25 per cent of their library grants for the purchase of Hindi books. Finally, implementation of these programmes is to be monitored through quarterly progress reports by the Official Language Implementation Committees (see Dwivedi 1981: 117–55).

In order to allay the perception that North India had been given undue advantage, the Three Language Formula was incorporated into the National Policy on Education in 1968. It was based on the assumption that if students from South India had to work extra hard to learn Hindi, those from the North should also learn a regional language. The resolution thus provided that every school-going child should learn (a) the mother tongue, (b) one of the international languages, presumably English, and (c) Hindi. In effect, this meant that while students from the South would learn Hindi in addition to their respective regional languages, Hindi-speaking students would learn a language apart from their mother tongue. However the Three Language Formula has never been properly implemented in the Hindi-speaking states where most often Sanskrit is taught in place of a regional language. Consequently, in the non-Hindi states, there has been consistent opposition to the hierarchy proposed between English, Hindi and regional languages.

More importantly, for our purposes, the Three Language Formula signifies that under the guise of accommodating differences, the normative
citizen-subject envisaged by the Indian state seeks to homogenize differences among regions into an essentialist Indian self. The year 1977 saw the
first ever non-Congress government at the centre. The Janata Dal government, formed by a coalition of the Left and the Right, was plagued during
its two-year tenure by charges of attempting to impose Hindi on non-Hindi
states on the one hand and of going soft on the language issue on the other.
Such a perception was also reinforced by contradictions within the Janata
Dal's policies and statements. For example, while the home minister categorically stated that the Janata Dal government would not impose Hindi
on any other Indian language, the minister for external affairs chose to
address the United Nations in Hindi. These inconsistencies were effectively
exploited by the Congress (I) in the 1979 elections, and in 1980—in an
instance of a grotesque historical irony—Indira Gandhi returned to power
at the centre, championed as the saviour of the underprivileged, in this
case, the *southern* states.

THE NEW ENGLISH–HINDI CONJUNCTURE

Since 1980, as part of their larger effort to play the Hindu card, successive
central governments have pushed for Hindi with increasing vigour. In the
Nehruvian model of nation-building, the regional state was set up as the
category that would mediate between the Imaginary and Symbolic levels of
the self-formation of the normative Indian citizen-subject. At a basic level,
this involved some sensitivity to the regional aspects of self-formation. As
Kaviraj has analysed, this was in tandem with the nature of the ruling coalition of the Nehruvian era, where the INC relied heavily on support from
regional leaders. A significant feature of the Indira Gandhi interregnum
was the qualitative change effected in the nature of politics in India. The
personality cult that Mrs Gandhi developed, Kaviraj suggests, was based on
a systematic erosion of political discourse and a reliance on populist rhetoric to establish 'direct' contact with the masses. Such a centralization of
power also resulted in an erosion of regional concerns. Consequently, the
changed terrain of politics of the post-Nehruvian era saw the emergence
of a different nature of regionalism in the 1980s (Kaviraj 1988). As opposed

to, say, the Dravidian movement of the 1950s, language movements in the 1980s were increasingly used in the service of chauvinistic, right-wing 'sons-of-the-soil' ideologies. These right-wing ideologies have, moreover, been the obverse of the new ideology of globalization that has seen the dominance of a new American English.

In Chapter One, I have discussed Prasad's argument that the new phase of capitalism marks a period of generalized translatability so that capitalism can now be taught in India without the aid of the English language. In relation to the regional languages, we can recall in this context Hollywood's bid for global markets through the dubbing of English-language films into Tamil, Hindi, Telugu and so on. Prasad suggests:

> The political project of modernity [. . .] has been overtaken by a new order where the logic of 'economic representation' wields a structuring influence of a magnitude which the world has not seen after the demise of classical European imperialism. [. . . T]he expanding presence of English-as-technoculture may have rendered obsolete the very project of translating the modern as a mode of achievement of modernity (1995).

In this new context, where capitalism no longer depends on the traditional mystique of the English, a range of television channels from Cartoon Network to the History Channel has started dubbing their regular telecasts in Hindi. Similarly, the idiosyncrasies of 'Indian English' are now creatively exploited on Indian channels such as Channel V and MTV. English is thus no longer symbolic of high culture in the traditional sense. Hindi, on the other hand, far from being the adversary of English—as was conceptualized by Gandhi—is now actively mediating the logic of consumer capitalism for non-English-speaking audiences. Along with this, a refurbished image of a Hindu Brahmanical past has also seen its growth. Television serials such as *Ramayana* (1987–88) and *Mahabharata* (1988–90) have created telecasting history. Stars from these tele-serials have been elected as members of parliament—having contested elections under both Congress and BJP banners. The liberal stream of Indian politics has meshed this in neatly with the politics of Hindutva.

The 1994 riots in Bangalore erupted in response to the introduction of an Urdu newscast. As Janaki Nair (1994) has argued, these riots testify to the collaboration between a resurgent Kannada chauvinism and the fascism of the Sangh Parivar (the Hindu political machine). The already existing anti-Muslim sentiments were easily tapped by the Shakti Kendra (The Source of Strength), the Karnataka Yuvajana Parishad (Society for Kannada Youth) and the Hindu Jagaran Vedike (Society for Hindu Awakening). Nair points out that the Kannada movement, in its latest phase, is directed against other subaltern communities in the city (as was also evident from the ire against the migrant Tamil population during the recent dispute over the sharing of Cauvery river water between Karnataka and Tamil Nadu). In Bangalore, the centre of multinational capital in India where English is most explicitly the language of economic and social power, the English-speaking elites continue to be comfortably ensconced in their positions of privilege. Riots do not happen in *their* territories (ibid.).

There are, thus, two issues that emerge as the kernel of our discussion: first, the transformations that occurred as the institutions of liberalism were relocated in the colonies; and second, the ways in which these colonial institutions were subsequently forced to respond to the democratic aspirations of the whole range of people that came together to form India. The key thrust of the process was to make the institutions of the new postcolonial state more representative—a process that gave completely new shape to the institutions of democratic liberalism as they had been conceived in their European heartland. The reorganization of regional units along linguistic lines therefore assumes enormous importance from this fact—that a fundamental bilingualism, the world of English and the world of the vernaculars, structures the historical reality of the postcolonial world.

In this background, the realignment of the language-question in the 1980s is indicative of a major trend in the contemporary political universe of the Indian nation as it moves progressively away from pluralist conception of nationhood. At this crucial crossover stage, while there are no privileged points for the unleashing of a socialist politics, questions of language and the identities they have historically conferred seem as legitimate a site as any from which to begin the urgent task of trying to imagine new ways of being together.

Notes

1 This is not to suggest that the terrain outside that of the state is homogeneous. In fact, the aim of this chapter is to outline the major contests that have shaped the contours of the cultural terrain over the last century and a half. The point I hope to bring out through this somewhat amorphous term is that 'popular' has been defined in a wide variety of ways by cultural/ political theorists of different ideological persuasions. However, as Tharu and Lalita point out vis-à-vis the constitution of the different 'Indian literatures', the new conceptual vocabulary signified by English also shaped the contours of the non-formal domain in decisive ways (1991: 160–80).

2 The most obvious parallel of the North–South divide within the Indian nation is, of course, Gramsci's famous analysis of the 'Southern question' in Italy, as representing a similar North–South divide within the Italian nation. This argument being the thrust of my thesis, I will return to it at several points in the subsequent chapters. Here, it is perhaps enough to highlight that the emergence of Hindi as dominant language and Bombay as dominant film industry within India immediately signifies a whole range of *other* histories that have been suppressed in the construction of a normative Indianness.

3 Despite their individual spheres of autonomy as demarcated in the 'Union List' and the 'State List' respectively, Articles 352–55 of the Constitution of India—giving the president the authority to declare a state of Emergency and the Centre unlimited autonomy—already belie any substantive decentralization of power.

4 Among others, see M. S. S. Pandian (1992). The workshops on 'Tamil Cinema: History, Culture, Theory', organized by the Madras Institute of Development Studies, Chennai (1997) and 'Telugu Cinema: History, Culture, Theory', organized by Anveshi and Centre for the Study of Culture and Society, Hyderabad (1999) have also brought forward new work being done in this area.

5 For the ways in which a new Kannada literati reinflected the literary– critical apparatuses of English, see Tejaswini Niranjana (1993). For a similar analysis of Telugu, see P. Sudhir (1993: 334–7). Although any number of 'empiricist' literary studies of Hindi literature currently exist, critical interrogation of its conceptual vocabularies, periodization and so on are almost non-existent. For an analysis of the emergence of 'New Critical' vocabularies in Hindi in the 1950s, see Tharu and Lalita (1995: 70–9).

6   A point needs to be made here regarding the identification of Hindi with Devanagari and Urdu with the Persian scripts. Technically, both Hindi and Urdu can be written in either. In the early decades of the nineteenth century there was, in fact, no exclusive connection between script and language and authors drew freely on both.

7   As Anderson's thesis on the role of print technology in the ideological creation of nationhood has demonstrated, the growth of the vernacular press in India was also hugely influential in the construction of 'standardized' forms of indigenous languages. For a useful introduction, see Madan Gopal (1990). Although work on the vernacular press is only just beginning, *Economic and Political Weekly* has also done a region-wise study of the Indian press, beginning January 1997. With specific reference to Hindi, mention must be also made of journals such as *Sanskriti* and *Abhyudaya*, which played major roles in the Hindi movement. Unfortunately, limitations of time made it impossible for me to research the emergence of this aspect of the 'new' Hindi more systematically. See also in this regard Avinash Kumar (1999), for a discussion of the modes in which Hindi periodicals in the early decades of the century construct notions of 'community'/'tradition'/'Indian history' and so on.

8   For an excellent selection of essays debating the genealogy of the 'subject', see Eduardo Cadava, Peter Connor and Jean-Luc Nancy (1991). Especially relevant to the discussion here is Mikkel Borch Jacobsen (1991) and Vincent Descombe (1991) for the limits of 'subjectivity' as conceived of by post-Descartian philosophy.

9   For a documentation, see Shahid Amin (1983).

CHAPTER THREE
STARS AND SIGNS OF BOMBAY

The images and stories of popular cinema can function like collective mnemic symbols, and allow 'ordinary people', us, to stop and wonder or weep, desire or shudder, momentarily touching 'unspeakable' but shared psychic structures [. . .] The events of social and political history erupt into representations, [. . .] scars of social or psychic disorders and of the repressed in history that create violence, despair, racism and sexual oppression (Mulvey 1994).

In the last two chapters we have discussed how English and Hindi, as signifying systems, have conveyed—at times overlapping, but at several instances also dramatically different—notions of modernity in India. These overlaps and differences symptomize the specific nature of state formation in India: the attempts of an anticolonial bourgeoisie to reinflect the idiom of liberalism into the (post)colonial context adopting, in a manner similar to that described by Gramsci, a 'war of position' to consolidate its hegemony (1971: 108). Consequently, the sculpting of a national identity has involved a suppression of the many identities and histories of its peoples in order to set up a normative Indianness that is patriarchal, North Indian, Hindu and upper caste. The significance of this normative Indianness lies, of course, in the fact that the governmentalized society that Foucault has described as having emerged with the post-despotic State of Western Europe was similarly premised on a qualitative change in the nature of state power itself—a change from a rule by despotic law to a rule by regulatory apparatuses, *the rule of the norm* (ibid.: 133–59).

However, as the intense career of the language-question makes evident, from the early decades of the twentieth century, the concept of the nation-state in the subcontinent was being internally contested along multiple lines of region, religion, caste, class and gender. The related contests over national language are indicative of the fact that the postcolonial state was marked by both an unmistakable 'derivativeness'—in the sense in which Chatterjee (1986) has used it—as well as a profound ethical–political *difference* from the classical nation-state as analysed by Foucault. The normative Indianness that successive ruling elites sought to fashion was consequently, continually and violently contested from a range of social and ideological positions. The career of modernity in the East has not only followed a very different track from that of the West but it has also seen the rise of social and political institutions very different from their 'classical' forms. Further, two major 'moments' of such a rewriting of the language of liberalism have emerged in the post-Independence era of Indian political life—in the 1950s, when classical liberal–democratic concepts and institutions were reinflected within the discourse of Nehruvian socialism, and then in the 1980s, as Nehruvian paradigms of Indianness were reconfigured at the intersection of multinational capital with the internal contradictions of the preceding era.

In this light, this chapter will now make a further theoretical move—it will attempt to trace the ways in which the 'Hindiness' that acquired dominance in the linguistic sphere from roughly the middle of the nineteenth century was configured in the realm of the visual popular. Political institutions of the West assumed entirely different forms while being transplanted in the East, energized by different strategies and aspirations from those of their Western homelands. Consequently, the moving image in the East took on entirely different forms from that in the West, determined by the specific intellectual and political histories of the postcolonial world. The critical intersections between the language-question and popular cinema derives from a situation where the national identity was only one among many emergent regional identities—identities which had no institutionally validated forms of expression within the parameters of a principle of federalism that was trying to establish a *non*-linguistic Indianness. In such a context, the different regional cinemas, especially those of South India, emerged as shadow-structures to the world of organized electoral politics. Moreover, one of the crucial markers of such contests over India's political structure—contests which were also manifest in the intense battles over its 'national language'—was that moment in Indian cinema from when the idea of a national/pan-Indian identity began to be increasingly replaced by communities/identities with very specific 'regional' connotations in the different 'regional' cinemas. This idea effectively compartmentalized the nation into its several linguistic pockets.[1] In keeping with the focus of the book, I will now show that the changed conception of Indianness in the 1980s—one that has led to a decisive realignment of the language-question —has also seen a reworking of the vocabulary of the visual popular.

WAYS OF SEEING: 'REALISM' AND STATE FORMATION IN INDIA

In its broadest sense this book is about the way concepts travel. It attempts to trace the journey of the philosophical concept of modernity that emerged with the Enlightenment in Europe—how, travelling through space and time, this concept reached the non-West through the project of colonization and how, in its new tropical setting, it changed radically in complexion. In effect, this meant that the classical social and political institutions of the West acquired very different contours as they were relocated in the colonies.

In fact, the primary ideological thrust of the nationalist movement in the Indian subcontinent was to fashion a *non*-Western modernity for India. One of the most significant differences between the philosophical idioms of Enlightenment Europe and their translation within vernacular discourses in India emerged from the fact that the language of liberalism—in the absence of any notion of individualistic society—was transferred, almost directly, to new collective identities such as the nation and the region. While work on this area is still very new, it has categorically demonstrated that the paradigmatic forms of community that emerged in the East mobilized very different social idioms and were premised on very different notions of selfhood from the discrete, *enumerable* identities of classical liberalism. The role of Bombay cinema in this whole process was crucial. Emerging as the emblematic popular cultural form of the nation, it became the major conduit through which the translation of the language of liberalism was effected. Thus, Bombay cinema articulated an aesthetic and a narrative form dramatically different from that of Hollywood.

It is here that the question of 'realism' arises. We have noted in the Introduction that the key ideological function of realism, as an aesthetic strategy in the West, was to reproduce the free contracting individuals on whose circulation the liberal nation-state depended. The emergence of the classic realist text in the nineteenth century was thus emblematic, in a profound socio-political sense, of the ascendancy of the bourgeoisie to state power. In cinematic terms the equivalent of the realist text is the classical narrative film of Hollywood, which emerged around the 1920s. It is also the marked difference of Bombay's aesthetic idiom from this Hollywood mode of storytelling which has generally caused it to be read as an 'inferior' kind of cinema.

Given the focus of this book, I can only summarize briefly some issues raised by the Theory-oriented studies of Indian popular cinemas in their engagement with these questions. Special mention must be made here of two contemporary theorists, Ashish Rajadhyaksha and M. Madhava Prasad, who have both analysed the narrative strategies through which the Hollywood film produces its reality-effect, especially the orchestration of the different 'looks' associated with classical Hollywood cinema.[2]

Chatterjee (1998b) has suggested that in the terrain of the 'popular', the paradigmatic social institutions that emerged in postcolonial spaces were ones which mobilized *collective* identities, as opposed to the normative individual citizen-subject created by socio-political institutions of the 'official' terrain. Drawing on Chatterjee, Rajadhyaksha has tried to understand why cinema, as a social institution, has occupied such a central place in the revolutionary imagination in India. To do so, he has drawn attention to the fact that the difference between the 'looks' of the 'actual' and the 'inscribed' viewer has hitherto been ignored by film theory.

Film theory has usually assumed an unproblematic equivalence between the looks of the actual viewer (who sits in front of the screen in the theatre) and the inscribed spectator (who identifies with the narrator or the dominant point of view of the film). But in doing so, as Rajadhyaksha has pointed out, one has overlooked the enormous gulf represented by the apparatus of cinema itself—i.e. the differences among the look of the actual/real viewer (which is identical to that of the camera looking at the pro-filmic reality), the undisciplined 'outside' and the look of the 'inscribed' spectator of the film (with the untamed reality now framed, edited and mixed with a soundtrack). But it is precisely here, in this transformation from an actual to a spectacularized or empowered viewer, i.e. in this basic transition from pro-filmic reality to framed image that all actual viewers must assimilate for themselves, that cinema performs the democratic function of modernity.

Given that the prerequisites of citizenship are available only to a tiny elite, Chatterjee has argued that the terrain outside these small enclaves in the postcolonial world is a terrain inhabited not by citizens but by 'populations'—a concept that is 'descriptive and empirical, [but unlike the citizen,] not normative' (1997: 31). The significance of the concept of 'population', however, is that it makes available to the state large communities of people who occupy social spaces outside the world of the normative citizen. The right to be counted as beneficiaries of state policies is one such basic democratic right of this terrain. There is a vital difference between the conceptual vocabulary of classical civil society and that of this 'other' terrain. In the former, the discourse of rights is premised on the figure of the bourgeois individual. In the latter, demands are formulated—and state apparatuses negotiated with—on behalf of collective identities.

Extrapolating from Chatterjee, Rajadhyaksha has suggested that, in relation to cinema, it is in the founding ideological contract that must be established between the spectator(s) in the cinema hall and the subject-position constructed by the narrative that the basic right of a population to be counted is performed. The tension Rajadhyaksha is drawing our attention to is the one between frame and image or narrative. While the dominant point of view of the classical narrative tells the spectacularized viewer how to look, coaches him into the protocols of citizenship by guiding him to identify with the gaze of the normative individual, there has to be a prior assertion—an acknowledgement by the apparatus of cinema itself of the look of a collective of actual viewers. This privileging of the frame, Rajadhyaksha points out, is usually done in the first few critical shots of a film, for instance, in the credits. The initial acknowledgement of actual viewers by the frame or the cinematic apparatus is, then, a prerequisite for the subsequent identification of the spectacularized viewer with the narrative of the film. The function of the narrator, or the dominant point of view, of the realist text is precisely to effect this relay from frame to narrative. So, whenever cinema moves too far from realism, the narrator-function also becomes diffuse or unrecognizable in its classic form. Insofar as popular Bombay cinema is so dramatically different from its realist Hollywood counterpart, 'the interpellative machinery [of cinema] incorporat[es] paradigms from democratic functioning—democratic in the sense in which Chatterjee uses the word' (Rajadhyaksha 1996; see also Rajadhyaksha 2009).

The implications of Rajadhyaksha's formulation are yet to be worked out. But Prasad has similarly raised important questions regarding the connections between 'realism' as an aesthetic strategy and the nature of state formation in the postcolonial world. He argues that Bombay's cinematic aesthetic so obviously violates the 'unauthorized scopophilia' of Hollywood realism because of the feudal nature of the political context from which Bombay cinema emerges. The frontality of image in the Bombay 'social' resembles instead, for Prasad, the traditional Hindu religious practice of *darshana* where a resplendent feudal spectacle is displayed (or displays itself) to the public. The most significant difference between the realist aesthetic of Hollywood and this feudal spectacle of the Bombay film is that the axis of identification for the audience in the latter case is not one based on resemblance but on *difference*. According to Prasad, this structure of 'spectation' derives from the fact that the assumed spectator of the Bombay film is not the normative citizen-subject of the West but belongs to a class that subservient to a feudal aristocracy (1998: 56–86).[3]

We will return to these arguments later. Here I wish to underline that, given the redefinition of modernity in the East, aesthetic practices in India adopted strategies markedly different from the realism of nineteenth-century Europe. The aesthetic of Bombay cinema emerged from the contradictions that marked the birth of an anticolonial bourgeois democracy. Consequently, in the first 'moment' in the aesthetic trajectory of Bombay, located during the Swadeshi period, the major impetus was to conceptualize iconographies and narrative strategies that would recode an imported technology (of the moving image) as well as an imported aesthetic (realism) as *Indian* (Kapur 1987; Rajadhyaksha 1987).

Articulated most eloquently through what Rajadhyaksha has called the 'epic melodramas' of the 1950s, the contests over cultural hegemony that shaped the contours of the new postcolonial state were mediated through that large paradigm shift whereby the Swadeshi concern over Indianness of filmic representations was replaced by a new concern over their realism (1993a: 55–70). The changed nature of regionalisms in the 1980s—one concomitant with a reconstitution of the ruling bloc at the level of the Central government—witnessed a whole *re*-launching of Indianness by the politics of Hindutva.[4] In this context, there emerged a new cinematic realism in 1980s' Bombay, one different from the realism of the 1950s. In the analysis of the Bombay industry that follows, realism therefore functions as a shifting signifier, marking the major moments in the reorganization of cultural hegemony within the nation and, relatedly, the changing conception of what it means to be Indian.

SWADESHI AND THE ARTICULATION OF A 'NATIONALIST REALISM'

Let us begin, then, with the Swadeshi era. The economic enterprise of Swadeshi was to bring a nationalistic consciousness to the marketplace. In the process, it invested a range of articles, from common salt to cloth, with intense ideological charge (Deshpande 1993: 5–36). Commodities effectively became mnemonic aids for imagining the spatial boundaries of the nation. Broadly, however, by constructing an ideological distinction between a 'good'(/nationalistic) and a 'bad'(/foreign) capital, the politics of Swadeshi worked not so much as a critique of industrial capitalism but provided the indigenous bourgeoisie its first major opportunity to capture an all-India market. This was done by harnessing the new technologies of mass production into an ostensible effort to regenerate a national Indian culture. Cinema was, of course, only one among many such technologies imported through such ideological justification.

Phalke's desire to portray Indian images on screen, therefore, resonated deeply with the spirit of his age. As he wrote: 'While the life of Christ
was rolling fast before my eyes I was mentally visualizing the gods Shri
Krishna, Shri Ramachandra, their Gokul and Ayodhya. [. . .] Could we, the
sons of India, ever be able to see Indian images on the screen?' (Cited in
Rajadhyaksha 1987: 48.) The critique of modernity generated by Swadeshi
in the realms of both elite nationalist and popular arts resulted in a critique
of regimented secular–economic time, of the laws of perspective and of
symmetry—in short, the entire conceptual world of post-Enlightenment
Europe.

The articulation of nationhood within the world of mass-produced
popular imagery in India, therefore, produced strategies of thinking the
nation that were very different from those of the West.[5] As Christopher
Pinney observes of the chromolithographs of Nathwada, '[i]n this popular
Indian domain, time was still messianic, scripts had fetishistic power and
kings were—in many cases—at the centre of the moral and ritual universe'
(1995). The presence of the mythological/mythical as opposed to the secular/
rational in many forms of mass-produced popular arts must be seen as part
of a larger cultural effort to construct a distinctly *Indian* modernity. Pinney,
in fact, cites a whole range of mass-produced popular arts in which a realist
framing is represented as part of the coercive paraphernalia of the colonial
state including modes of communication (e.g. the telephone) and systems
of temporal regularity (e.g. the clock and the calendar). Now, realism was
also a borrowed tool. So, it too could only enter as a subterfuge—not by
performing its classic function of making things legitimate but as a means
of shoring up a reconstructed Indian tradition. The iconographies and
narrative strategies mobilized by this earliest genre of Indian cinema, the
'mythological', similarly emerged out of this effort to re-designate a technology imported from the West as a nationalist art practice (Rajadhyaksha
1987: 49–64).

Hence, while endorsing the institutional and discursive universe of
colonial modernity, the nationalist bourgeoisie sought to recode it as Indian.
This process of ideological recoding did not involve merely a change of
terminology. Instead, institutions grounded in Enlightenment rationality
were themselves transformed in the process of altering pre-existing intellectual and aesthetic traditions.

THE 'SYMBOLIC REALISM'[6] OF THE 1950s

The contradictions within the ruling coalition of the Nehruvian era emerged from the fact that a passive revolution, by its very nature, prevents an anti-colonial bourgeoisie from mounting a frontal attack either on the structures of the colonial state or on traditional/feudal elites.[7] As has been argued, socialism in India under Nehru was little more than populist rhetoric—a protective shield for the development of indigenous capitalism rather than a commitment to egalitarianism (see, among others, Kaviraj 1988). With regard to cinema, this meant that the new technology of the mass produc-tion of images had to consciously disavow the nature of economic and social relations on which it was based through invocations of (cultural) tradition-alism. As Prasad has documented, while registering the contemporary in diverse ways, a feudal ideology provided the constitutive ground for the emblematic narrative structure of 1950s/1960s Bombay cinema.[8]

However, from the late nineteenth century onwards, as new technolo-gies of mass production were institutionalized and tastes of the local audiences had themselves changed, there had also been the growing dominance of a three-dimensional mass-realist style. The institutionaliza-tion of Eurocentric modes of looking was, of course, symptomatic of the reconstitution of the commonsense of the local elite, thus the importance of 'education' in the colonial administrative agenda. In cinema, this resulted in the static icon of the earlier mythological being gradually replaced with a narrative structure, constructing a dominant narrative point of view and also placing the spectator as the transcendent viewing subject. As Rajad-hyaksha has argued, the cinematic–technological equivalent of the modern, the cultural corollary of the Nehruvian impetus to modernize the nation through heavy industry and a planned economy, referred to the changed function that realism was now called on to perform—'making a reference to something like "the dominant political issues of the day", that was less a shoring up of the fiction (as in Phalke), [. . .] and more a "making familiar" and thus also a "making legitimate"' (1993a: 67). Of course, this new function of realism emerged not only as the nationalist aesthetic was relieved of the burden of defining itself in relation to colonial rule but also out of the internal contests over definitions of Indianness that erupted with Independence.

These internal contests can be mapped through the contestatory trajectories of the indigenist modernism pioneered, for example, by Satyajit Ray; the 'socialist realism' of the documentary wing of the Films Division; and the 'realism' pioneered by the Left avant-garde as represented by the Indian People's Theatre Association. The internal contests over representations of Indian reality were then assimilated at a secondary level by the commercial cinemas through a new cinematic vocabulary in which reference to the contemporary was made through certain objectified values or symbols that functioned as stand-ins for the nation. 'In the process,' Rajadhyaksha says, 'the nation itself emerges as a voyeuristic space, often representing either a legitimacy that could be acquired or other kinds of wish-fulfilling desires such as freedom/salvation/change' (ibid.).

While drawing on the aesthetic–political vocabulary of the West, the trajectory of melodrama in Bombay derived also from the specific contradictions that marked the coming into being of an anticolonial bourgeois democracy. As Ashish Rajadhyaksha and Paul Willeman point out, the ideological function of melodrama in Indian cinemas was to recast the aesthetic–social idiom of Anglo-America into an indigenous frame:

> Defined in the Indian context mainly as a 'musical dramatic' narrative in accordance with its original generic meaning [. . .] Melodrama drew on the same sources as, e.g., the mythological but functioned as the aesthetic regime accompanying the socio-economic transition from feudal-artisanal to industrial ones, both formally and in content matter [. . .I]t recomposed traditional narrative idioms and themes, drawing on Western narrative forms and similarly negotiating modernization tensions (1994: 137).

BOMBAY'S HETEROGENEOUS MODE OF PRODUCTION

Independence marked the advent of a decisively new from of cinematic practice in Bombay. While Swadeshi had generated the impulse, the intervening years of the Second World War had seen the indigenous bourgeoisie acquire an all-India character. Economically, this process was simultaneous with the collapse of the early studios and the decisive entry of speculative finance into the film industry.

Studios such as Metro-Goldwyn-Mayer, Universal and Paramount in 1920–30s' Hollywood had been centres for the mass production of films in ways analogous to automobiles. Opposed to this 'vertically integrated mode of production' of the major American studios, the Bombay industry adopted a 'heterogeneous mode of manufacture' in which several prefabricated segments were assembled under the directing influence of a financier.[9] The entry of speculative finance in 1940s' Bombay manifested itself in the phenomenon of freelancing, thus eroding the authority of the producer–director of the earlier studio era. There emerged, instead, a host of financiers who owned neither production infrastructure nor personnel, but hired both. As a result, as opposed to the camera that had been its most visible symbol, the Star now emerged as the most recognizable icon of Bombay cinema.

In the context of Swadeshi, both the technology (that of the moving image) and the capital invested in filmmaking had sought cultural legitimation through the act of representing 'Indian images'. In the large paradigm shift signified by the emergence of the melodrama in the 1950s, the connection between the nature of capital invested and the nature of film produced was also reconfigured. There emerged a distinction between the 'good capital' of the mainstream Gandhian–Nehruite pan-Indian bourgeoisie that pioneered the apolitical 'All India Film' and the 'bad capital' of speculative financiers who have been consistently charged with vulgar sensationalism and the resultant lowering of audience tastes (Rajadhyaksha 1993a: 55–70). Subsequently, while the 'formula' of the All India Film was replicated in the different regional cinemas, the internal contests over nationalist constructions of Indianness also saw, especially in South India, melodramas that radically critiqued hegemonic conceptions of being Indian.

Beginning as a regional centre, the emergence of Bombay as a national phenomenon was crucially dependent on the transistor revolution. Analysing the politics of genre formation, Prasad has suggested that, as opposed to Hollywood, the prevalence of music in the Bombay 'social' points to the continued reliance of the Indian film industry here on the resources of other popular cultural forms such as the theatre—a feature contingent on the nature of capitalism in the country. Making a distinction between genres that can be identified at the level of the signifier and those that can be identified at the level of the signified, Prasad argues that the Hollywood 'musical' (a signifier-identified genre) served to clear the ground for other signified-identified genres. But, in India, the nature of the Nehruvian coalition meant that the overarching Bombay 'social', till the 1950–60s, combined the aesthetics of the signifier with that of the signified (Prasad 1994: 251–60). The political upheavals of the Indira Gandhi era then saw a rupture of this feudal form and the emergence of art, middle and mass cinemas.

I wish to focus on the moment of 'liberalization' marked by what Prasad has called the 'disaggregation of the Nehruvian consensus' (ibid.) and the emergence of capital dominance. As the liberalization process consolidated itself in the 1980s, there was a congealing of the 1970s' middle and mass cinemas into a hybrid form—a new commercial cinema that staked its credentials primarily on a renewed thrust on representationalism. This new aesthetic emerged as television took over the cultural–educational functions assigned to the Film Finance Corporation in the 1960–70s. While rendering the feudal form obsolete, the political upheavals of the Indira Gandhi era did not completely transform the mode of production of the Bombay industry. My contention is that while continuing to function within conditions of backward capitalism, the process of globalization precipitated a re-alignment of dominance within the different segments of the Bombay film as a mass-produced commodity. The earlier prominence of the Star, for instance, was now displaced by the prominence of music in the industry.

STARS AS SIGNS: OF FLOATING ECONOMIES AND 'ORDINARINESS'

We have cited on several occasions Prasad's thesis on the ways in which the ideological contradictions of the Nehruvian ruling bloc were inscribed not only in the narrative strategies of the Bombay film but also structured its Star system (ibid.: 131–7, 247–51). Prasad has also proposed that Star images in 1950s' Bombay drew on feudal Hindu notions of iconicity. The 'glamour' of Star images, manifested in the noble, aristocratic upper-caste (physical) appearance of the Star, replicated an overarching feudal ideology. This glamour of the Star was indistinguishable from the innate glamour of the feudal spectacle. While melodrama prevailed in North

America for over two centuries, Bombay cinema compressed it into a few decades (ibid.: 130–7). And this, Prasad notes, was due to the specific nature of state formation in India. He also demonstrates the striking formal similarities of the 1950s' Bombay social with the stage melodramas of nineteenth-century America, as opposed to the more 'democratic' manifestations of melodrama in the family romance of 1950s' Hollywood. In the feudal melodrama of North America, the actions of the 'noble' subject would be replicated by lesser characters such as servants or slaves, thereby making the subject's actions exemplary or sublime from an everyday point of reference.

Such a feudal relationship of subservience and apprenticeship, Prasad observes, was directly replicated in the Star system of regional cinemas of, for instance, South India in the purported devotion or loyalty of some 'character-actors' to Stars such as Raj Kumar. The feudal notion of Star as God is dramatically evident here—the relationship between Star and character-actor being explicitly modelled on that between Lord Rama and his disciple (the monkey-god) Hanuman. While not so explicit, the cult identities of Bombay's Stars such as Raj Kapoor and Nargis (e.g. their high-profile connections, their status as 'national ambassadors' and their sensational love affair) did seek to invest Star images in Bombay with a magnificence consciously distanced from the possibility of the 'everyday'.[10]

Ideologically, such a notion of glamour was the opposite of that mobilized through the Star system of Hollywood. As Richard Dyer has argued, the element of the exotic or glamorous in Hollywood Star images advertised the ostensible 'openness' of a democracy that militates against feudal or aristocratic privilege—as paradoxical reinforcements of the 'ordinariness' of Hollywood Stars. This paradox between extravagant lifestyles and ordinariness is reconciled through an ideology which suggests that 'human' qualities exist independent of material circumstances. Stars are constructed as 'typical' of the American people who have had lucky breaks—it can happen to anyone. Fundamentally, such a notion of glamour serves to reinforce the myth that the class system does not operate in America. It is a system that recognizes only talent and hard work (Dyer 1986: 38–51).

In a striking departure from the 1950s' tradition, Star images of 1980s' Bombay, too, play up a certain notion of the ordinary. Underlying this change are the kaleidoscopic shifts that have marked the nation's new modernizing agenda. My contention is that the new ordinariness of Bombay's Star images is not just symptomatic of structural changes in the industry's production base. It also needs to be seen more broadly in terms of the film industry's response to new technologies of mass culture that have rendered obsolete both the twin poles within which cinema, as technology and cultural form, was institutionalized—the space of the nation and the economy of a 'national market'.

The cultural corollary of the liberalization process has been the television/video boom.[11] By the mid-1970s, the developmentalist role that Nehruvian policies had assigned to Bombay cinema had already run into many contradictions. A decisive shift happened in governmental priorities in the 1980s with large-scale import of television sets and VCRs, the change to colour telecasting in 1982 and the Special Extension Plan (1984), along with a host of other initiatives. The change in the government's agenda was, moreover, directly determined by the demands of transnational capital. As Rajadhyaksha suggests, the technologies of television and video do not require the political centralization that is provided by the nation-state, and hence they are compatible with the economic redefinition of the market. Instead of economic centralization, the 1980s saw the centralization of cultural production, determined by the new kinds of consumerism made possible by television (see Rajadhyaksha 1987: 1–5).

Television's rise to prominence within the cultural space of the nation has been synonymous with a new dominance of the Hindi language. Television has been the most important state apparatus for the nationalization of the Hindi language over the last two decades. The rising dominance of Hindi has seen the parallel growth of cultural neo-nationalism in India— its most virulent expression being the Hindutva project. The mega-serials that decisively marked the coming of age for TV as a cultural phenomenon —Hum Log (We the People, 1984–85), Buniyaad (Foundation, 1986–88), Ramayana (1987–88) and Mahabharata (1988–90)—all located the essence of the nation within a reconstructed North Indian, patriarchal, Hindu upper-caste social tradition (see Rajagopal 2001). The subsequent emergence of Star TV, MTV and Channel V—and the new translatability of capitalist culture—has further seen Hindi jockeying with English for the status of the national modern.

However, as a cultural form, television's rise to prominence has also affected the Bombay film industry at the fundamental level—that of form. Independence had marked the advent of a form of cinematic practice premised on the Star. The subsequent transformation of Bombay cinema into a pan-Indian phenomenon had been crucially dependent on the transistor revolution. In his classic analysis of the nature of television as technology and cultural form, Raymond Williams notes that the distinctive characteristic of both radio and television is that they developed their networks of broadcasting and transmission before their actual content or information came into being. This, Williams suggests, was because these technologies 'originated' in the War years. He goes on to analyse the direct and indirect connections of the broadcasting and telecommunications networks of the UK with military intelligence and the business conglomerates of the new industrial core (1990: 7–44). Inherent in both these technologies is the contradiction between the nation-state as a tightly defined geopolitical unit and communication networks whose centrifugal tendencies run counter to such economic and spatial centralization. This relates to a tendency noted by Marx himself, in the nature of movement of capital:

> The more developed the capital [. . .] the more extensive the market over which it circulates, which forms the spatial orbit of its circulation, [and] the more does it strive simultaneously for an even greater extension of the market and for greater annihilation of space with time. [. . .]
>
> Capital drives beyond national barriers and prejudices as much as beyond [. . .] encrusted satisfactions of present needs, and reproductions of old ways of life. [. . .] But from the fact that capital posits every such limit as its barrier and hence gets ideally beyond it, it does not by any means follow that it has really overcome it, and since every barrier contradicts its character, its production moves in contradictions which are constantly overcome just as constantly posited (cited in Chakrabarty 1992a: 58–9).

The larger contradiction that the technologies of TV and video enact is that between the citizen, the normative subject of nationalist discourse, and the new figure of the consumer for whom the nation is no longer the most meaningful category of self-description. As the economy, in the global context of transnational capital, emerges as a floating signifier, this is also the primary objective contradiction shaping contemporary India. Yet, capital exists in history, and one of the contradictions of 'capital in history' is that we are citizens and consumers at the same time (ibid.: 48–65). In the following sections, it is this collusive relationship between citizenship and consumerism that I will trace through the 'ordinariness' of the new Star images of 1980s' Bombay.

MUSIC, 'TELEVISUAL REALISM' AND THE NEW STAR IMAGES OF 1980s' BOMBAY

Liberalization made it more viable for local manufacturers to import components necessary for the indigenous manufacture of cassettes.[12] A thriving pirate industry and an overall lowering of production costs subsequently saw the emergence of a host of companies—Venus, Tips and T-Series— which priced their cassettes at rates affordable to lower-income groups. The more successful of these companies further diversified not only into the manufacture of video cassettes but also set up their own film-production units, reversing the earlier trend of production companies marketing their music. Beginning as a music company, Venus, for instance, diversified into film production. It has set up the 'United Seven' banner which produced mega-hits like *Khiladi* (The Player, 1993), *Baazigar* (Gambler, 1993) and *Main Khiladi Tu Anari* (The Innocent and the Experienced, 1995). Similarly, Time Audio produced *Vijaypath* (The Path of Victory, 1994), while Weston presented *Yeh Dillagi* (The Joke, 1994). The growing dominance of music, in fact, became self-evident in the 1990s with leading industrial houses such as the R. P. Goenka group even presenting films such as Aditya Chopra's *Dilwaale Dulhaniya Le Jayenge* (True Love Wins the Bride, 1995), but also diversifying into the manufacture of music cassettes in conjunction with HMV. The new cultural prominence of television has also given a major boost to Bombay's music sector through the sheer number of film-music-based programmes on TV—*Chitrahaar, Superhit Muqabla, Philips Top 10, Videocon Dhun Dhamaka, All The Best, Close-up Antakshari* and *Meri Awaaz Suno*, etc. (These developments then become even more obvious in the 1990–2000s with shows such as Sony TV's *Indian Idol*.)

Further, the explosion of the cassette industry meant that, increasingly, the pre-release publicity of films came to rest on its music, through sale of audio cassettes or television-based music programmes. While the Bombay industry had always produced the 'hit' song, the music segment now gained near-total autonomy. Already in the 1960s, demands by film producers as well as playback singers such as Lata Mangeshkar that All India Radio give credit to films and playback singers in its broadcasts of film music represented tendencies of the music sector of Bombay for 'relative autonomy' from a purely filmic encasing. The setting up in the mid-1950s of a commercial broadcasting station by Sri Lanka—airing programmes such as *Binaca Geet Mala* that had completely blanketed the nation within two years of its inception—not only pressurized All India Radio to reverse its earlier policy banning the transmission of film songs, but, in fact, to launch its own commercial channel, Vividh Bharati. Decades on, the cassette and television boom precipitated by liberalization in the 1980s not only made music the 'dominant' segment of the Bombay film, but created a cultural space for the music sector which is completely autonomous of any filmic encasing.

Thus there emerged, for the first time in India, a whole extra-cinematic realm of indigenous pop music mediating the MTV phenomenon for the non-English-speaking Indian audiences. Beginning with Nazia Hassan's *Disco Deewane* (Disco Music Lovers), India saw the subsequent emergence of 'pop stars' for the first time—Remo Fernandes, Alisha Chenoy, Sharon Prabhakar, Baba Sehgal and many others.[13] This was simultaneous with the new cult status of music directors such as Anu Malik and A. R. Rahman as well as choreographers such as Saroj Khan and Farah Khan. Consequently, as music emerged as the dominant segment of the Bombay film, the earlier prominence of the Star was displaced or sidelined. In fact, many of the major 1980s' Stars (like Madhuri Dixit) made their claims to Star status primarily through the space opened by the new dominance of music.

Consequently, within the larger cultural space, Star value was now being displaced onto the new pop stars who cultivated images on the lines of earlier film actors and actresses. The obverse of the pop-star phenomenon was the emergence of various kinds of 'ethnic chic' in music from the 'folk' to the 'classical', marketed for the upwardly mobile urban listenership by companies like Music Today, meshing in neatly with the rediscovery of 'Indian tradition' across the range of cultural forms. Thus, Music Today, a subsidiary of the Aroon Purie Group that also publishes the influential and popular *India Today* magazine, released the *Music of the Seasons* series, the *Maestro's Choice* series and *Soundscapes* (featuring the most famous classical musicians of India including Ravi Shankar, Bhimsen Joshi and Zakir Hussain) while also releasing albums such as *The Folk Music of Rajasthan*.

Therefore, the changed nature of Bombay's Star images of the 1980s, emphasizing the ordinariness of its new Stars, has to be placed vis-à-vis the new technologies of mass culture that challenged the Bombay film's role as the pre-eminent host of the musical spectacle. This does not mean that Bombay no longer invoked the Star as a marketing strategy for product differentiation. On the contrary, with the emergence of film magazines such as *G*, the 1980s actually saw a proliferation of popular journalism selling Star lives to a highly cine-literate audience. However, the fragmentation in the industry's production base as a result of the TV/cassette boom (and the consequent pressures for novelty that this generated) reduced the life span of individual actors at the box office. Thus, the love-story genre in the 1980s introduced a new lead pair in each of its box office hits from *Love Story* (1981) to *Qayamat Se Qayamat Tak*. Similarly, the anti-hero genre also introduced a string of new Stars, including Anil Kapoor, Sunny Deol, Sanjay Dutt and Nana Patekar, as opposed to the 1970s, which had been solely dominated by Amitabh Bachchan.

More significantly, the emergence of new technologies of mass culture gave rise to a different image of the Star. As opposed to the feudal glamour of Raj Kapoor or Nargis, the media consistently highlighted a certain (urban, upper-class/caste) 'ordinariness' in its portrayal of 1980s' Stars such as Aamir Khan and Madhuri Dixit. Further, the emphasis on the ordinary translated not only into the literal introduction of actors and actresses without prior screen histories but also into a new cinematic aesthetic that foregrounded the 'everyday' as the site of significant action. This aesthetic, as noted earlier, emerged in the context of the decisive cultural dominance of television. As major sources of financial investment were now routed into TV, the economic base of the film industry was completely eroded. It was now flooded with all kinds of crude entrepreneurial capital—including that from smuggling of goods—evoking once again the Swadeshi-generated 'good' capital/'bad' capital distinction.[14] Classified as 'private sector' by the state, the mainstream Bombay film industry had historically been excluded from most kinds of governmental support. To this had been added the steadily increasing prices of raw stock and filmmaking equipment, most of which is still imported. The emergence of a thriving pirate video industry, curbed only partially by the 1984 Copyright Act 1984, and extremely high entertainment taxes, had affected box office collections even further.

To offset some of these longstanding demands and problems, Sushma Swaraj, the then Union Minister for Information and Broadcasting, announced at a national conference on 'Challenges Before Indian Cinema' (Bombay, 10 May 1998), that the government of India had decided to accord 'industry status' to the business of filmmaking. Among a slew of financial and regulatory concessions that accompanied this policy shift— reductions in import duties on cinematographic film and equipment, exemption on export profits and various other tax incentives—the most significant was the Industrial Development Bank Act (2000), which made it possible for filmmakers to operate in a 'clean' and 'legitimate' fashion, as opposed to the mix of personal funds, money borrowed from individuals at exorbitant interest rates (in some cases, from the underworld), and minimum guarantee payments advanced by distributors, all of which had thus far characterized film-financing in Bombay.

This significant reorientation of policy has since been accompanied by an aggressive new role that the state has imagined for itself in relation to the culture industry in general. Beginning with the late 1990s, the state has actively sought to articulate a vision of a 'corporatized' film industry in India that would resemble Hollywood in terms of technological, economic, business, and regulatory practices. This is part of a broader 'creative industries' policy framework that the successive governments have been encouraging, with the help of consultancy firms like McKinsey and Pricewaterhouse Coopers. The film industry has been brought under the purview of the Federation of Indian Chambers of Commerce and Industry (FICCI) and made part of a larger FICCI Entertainment Committee, which consists of leading players from film, television, cable, radio, music, animation and the live entertainment sectors.

In addition to facilitating a policy framework for the 'growth and development' of the film industry, the FICCI Entertainment Committee has also been organizing an annual convention called 'FRAMES', which attempts to bring the film industry in contact with prominent Non-Resident Indian venture capitalists, influential diasporic filmmakers, media producers and executives (such as Ashok Amritraj of Hyde Park Entertainment), the IT sector in India and abroad as well as representatives and executives from transnational media corporations such as Sony and Warner Brothers, along with global consultancy firms and financial institutions. The whole thrust of these measures, in sync with the larger liberalization project, has been to debate how the Bombay film industry can shed its image as a dysfunctional 'national' cinema and re-imagine itself as 'Bollywood Inc.'. However, the limited 'success' of the global entertainment conglomerates in the Indian market, the arrest of underworld don Abu Salem in 2005 and the continuing influence of feudal modes of production in the film industry have also provoked intense discussion as to why the 'corporatization' of Bombay has not quite followed the script that was envisaged for it.[15]

Moreover, liberalization has coded television most strongly with the promise of access to the global modern in the cultural sphere, complementing the claims of structural adjustment in the economic. In this process of 'access to the latest', the availability of certain consumer goods—especially in the fashion industry—is coded by the neo-nationalist bourgeoisie as evidence of India's taking world centre stage. Access to commodities is equated with access to technology—a stand-in for a technicist utopianism. Moreover, this promise of 'access to the latest' comes coded most dramatically through the television news or the 'live' telecast, where events from across the world are delivered or reported to the home even as they occur.[16] Television thus seems to fulfil the ultimate promise of instant access to the world. Given, moreover, that televisual representations are coded as 'objective'/'true', cinema becomes the 'fictional'/'exaggerated' social technology by default. And this is especially the case with the mainstream cinema of Bombay.

As Prasad has pointed out, there was an overall thrust on representationalism in all the segments of the Bombay industry in the 1970s—a registering of the changed social context where the 'splendour' of the feudal aristocracy was no longer a viable narrative possibility. Prasad describes the realisms of the art, middle and mass cinemas as 'developmentalist realism', the realism of identification and the aesthetics of counter-identification, respectively (1994: 247–51). The new configuration of 1980s' Bombay was therefore one where the general accent on representationalism of the 1970s was reinforced by the documentary-style truth-effect promised by television as well as the simultaneous movement of 1970s' middle cinema on centre stage.

The crossover of a number of directors from the 'art' to the 'commercial' industry in the 1980–90s underlines the point. While 'art directors' such as Shyam Benegal and Sayeed Mirza moved directly into television, others such as Govind Nihalani made 'commercials' like *Vijeta* (The Victorious, 1982), while Ketan Mehta made *Hero Hiralal* (1988) and Kundan Shah made *Kabhi Haan Kabhi Naa* (Yes and No, 1993). A similar move also occurred in the Tamil and Telugu cinemas. Further, these art directors have been credited with infusing a new sense of verisimilitude into the different commercial industries into which they moved. The new representationalism informed the 'hybrid' commercial cinemas of the 1980–90s at the level of editing, shot composition, camera work, acting styles, etc. As Vivek Dhareshwar and Tejaswini Niranjana (1996) have proposed, the 'achievement' of these new directors is that they combined the naturalism of 1970s' middle cinema with the song-dance-entertainer of the 1950s into a new Bombay aesthetic. The changed nature of Bombay's Star images in the 1980s, highlighting the ordinariness of its new Stars, thus points to the ways in which the Star persona emerged as a crucial mediating category between the structural changes precipitated by liberalization and the film industry's bid for survival in the changed cultural space.

SEEING ROMANCE POLITICALLY: BOMBAY'S 'RURAL BELLE'

We have just discussed that the reworking of Bombay's Star images in the 1980s was contingent on the emergence of a changed nature of realism— a new 'televisually mediated realism' that came into being simultaneously with a new dominance of the music sector of the industry. My contention is that the changing nature of realism in Bombay can be used as signposts to mark the major shifts in definitions of Indianness over the twentieth century. From this perspective, an analysis of Bombay's genre system can be used to trace the ways in which a normative 'Indianness' has been consolidated vis-à-vis the 'others' of the nation. In the changed socio-political conjuncture signified by the new realism of the 1980s, this normative 'Indianness' was re-articulated through a marginalization of the democratizing critiques of Nehruvian nationalism that emerged in the 1960–70s.

On an average, the commercial industry in the 1980s produced about 130 films annually. Of these, roughly only nine per cent were commercially successful. The love-story and the anti-hero genres, however, consistently produced at least one major hit each year, right through the decade. In what follows, I will now map the changes in narrative structure at the generic level precipitated by the changes in the production base discussed in the last section. Necessarily, due to the specific logic of genre formation in Bombay, the trajectories of both romance as well as action cinema follow neither the clear-cut pattern of differentiation of Hollywood nor trajectories of movement identical to their Hollywood counterparts. What I wish to trace instead are the ways in which, beginning as tendencies within the umbrella genre of the 'social', the love story and the anti-hero film emerged as the strongest genres in 1980s' Bombay.

Looking back, we can see that melodrama emerged as the emblematic mode narrativizing the bourgeoisie's ascendancy to political power in nineteenth-century Western Europe—a process that required the creation of a civil society based on a demarcation between 'the public' and 'the private'. The new realm of 'the private' was constructed around 'the couple' constituted by the nuclear family. In a 'peripheral' country such as India, where the nuclear family is set up as the utopian promise of the modernizing nation, the problems in couple-formation are compounded by the nature of state power on which the notion of the private is grounded. The ruling bloc in India has historically consisted of a coalition of pre-capitalist, capitalist and techno-managerial groups. Given the persistence of pre-capitalist enclaves in its social formation, the dominant textual form of the Bombay film had to incorporate the couple into the authority of the feudal joint family. The political upheavals of the 1960–70s saw a change in the feudal form of the 1950s' Bombay film. The 1980s had seen the 1970s' middle cinema expand to capture a commercial market. Consequently, a 'new' love story emerged in the mainstream industry in the 1980s. I wish to place these new notions of 'romance' in Bombay vis-à-vis the new conjuncture of consumer capital and Hindu neo-nationalism of the 1980–90s.

In his classic thesis, *The Origin of the Family, Private Property and the State* (1902), Friedrich Engels characterizes the nuclear family as the primary social institution that reproduces the sexual inequalities on which capitalism, as an economic and political system, is premised. Complicating this thesis considerably, Foucault has argued that the nuclear family not only marked a new ordering of sexual practices into the general currency of profit and productivity that marked the bourgeois enterprise, but it also signified a change in the nature of power itself—a new form of power that was at the same time individualizing as well as totalizing in nature. This new nature of power marks the birth of the governmentalized society of Western Europe (see Foucault 1990, 1991). The analysis of sexuality, Foucault further suggests, gains its enormous significance from the fact that the new discourses on sex are located at this historico-political juncture—as a means of access both to the individual body as well as to the body of the species. Thus, Foucault documents that an increase in the scope of Christian confessions (from 'immoral' acts to 'transgressive' thoughts and desires), for example, was concomitant with the birth of the sciences of demography, eugenics, economics and a whole new range of discursive positions, which attempted to 'manage' the sexuality of a population not on the basis of ethics/morality but from the point of rational governance. This historic shift, from a society governed by despotic law to a society governed by the rule of the norm, was moreover effected by creating sexual 'others'—women, children and people following all those modes of sexual practices that now became classified as 'perversities'.

While realism is ideologically geared to reproduce 'free' contracting individuals, as a narrative form, melodrama foregrounds the fact that women (as well as other subaltern groups) were not signatories to the fictive social contract that marked the formation of the post-despotic state of Western Europe.[17] Consequently, the entire range of narratives (literary/cinematic) that can be placed under the umbrella term 'melodrama' display certain broad structural similarities—the negotiation of social conflicts through the institution of the family and the equation of social with sexual identity; in short, the definitive split between law and (feminine) desire that marks post-Enlightenment notions of modernity.

According to Kaviraj, all nationalist movements construct the nation-state, a product of modernity, as an ancient community that was lost, and has to be regained—to steal what Marx calls 'the poetry of primordiality' (cited in Kaviraj 1992: 21) from pre-modern social forms. This is necessary not only because of the contractual nature of the nation-state but also because its formation often requires sacrifices which most people would be unlikely to make if they calculated their actions on a pure cost-benefit account (ibid.). In India, the paradoxical pressures of externality and the desire to emulate the modernity introduced through colonial rule necessitated not only that the nation-state be set up to reclaim an ancient 'Indian tradition' but also charged discourses on traditionalism (vis-à-vis peasants, lower castes and women) with a distinctive anti-West stance. The different discourses on Indian tradition caused an ideological overspill which was then reworked into some of Bombay cinema's most enduring motifs. One such motif—articulated through Bombay's love-story genre as one of the most popular tropes of the national imaginary—is that of the 'rural belle',[18] explored through mega-hit films like *Achhut Kanya* (The Untouchable Woman, 1936), *Barsaat* (Rain, 1949), *Madhumati* (1958), *Junglee* (The Uncivilized, 1961) and *Kashmir Ki Kali* (The Belle of Kashmir, 1964).[19]

While Swadeshi generated the impulse for charging 'the countryside'/ 'the folk'/'women' as repositories of Indian tradition and as sites opposed to Westernization, discourses of Nehruvian nationalism reframed this Indian/Western opposition around notions of the secular modern—a modernity whereby the new nation would leave behind all practices placed under 'bad tradition' (casteism, communalism, etc.) and join the other free nations of the world.[20] A series of recent articles have debated the semiotic prohibitions that marked the transition to modernity in India.[21] Reworking the Swadeshi-generated Indian/Western opposition, they have suggested that the ideological imperative of the Nehruvian era was to select the best from tradition even as the nation raced towards an industrial–scientific utopia. Thus, the persistent marking in cultural discourses of the normative citizen-subject as at once Indian and universal.

Universalizing narratives of liberal humanism have always coexisted with Orientalist discourses in the intellectual constitution of the Indian elite, giving them a double-semiotics to define their relationship to the state

(Dhareshwar 1993). This has also given them considerable space to margin-alize the demands of subaltern groups. Just as the language of rights, democracy or secularism begins to be appropriated by hitherto marginalized groups, upper castes deny the existence of casteism by designating it as 'backward'. Similarly, as minority communities claim their status as citizens, secularism becomes a Western concept. In effect, such a constitution of normative Indianness, while setting up 'class' as 'modern', has also made 'caste' unavailable for critical social analysis. 'Caste' is turned into a problem of macro-structural policy, or is pushed into the domain of the 'private' or the 'anthropological'—shoved into 'traditional India' (ibid.: 115–26). This explains the primitivism marking the modernist literatures of the 1950–60s and elite art forms like the new folk theatre of, say, Girish Karnad (see Cherian 1995; Tharu and Lalita 1995: 91–7). Within mainstream Bombay, the rural-belle motif provides a neat example to encapsulate this theoretical complicity between liberal and leftist models of social analysis. While *Achhut Kanya* meticulously constructed its 'Indian types' for a European market, *Barsaat* was made by the Raj Kapoor–Kirdar Sharma team for an *Indian* national market.

Structurally, the paradigmatic 1950s' 'feudal romance' revolved round the pedigreed, England-educated or Westernized *male* protagonist who returned to the village/countryside to rediscover his Indianness. Under the binaries of tradition/modernity, Indianness/Westernization, countryside/the city were played out narratives in which the Westernized male protagonist was educated into adulthood and love by the emblematic rural belle. The rural belle—associated with a specifically 'tribal' (*non*-middle-class) culture—was set up as 'beyond the grasp of capitalist appropriation'.[22] Framed within an overarching country/city divide,[23] this non-middle-class space occupied by the rural belle was also tangential to that occupied by the female protagonists of the Oedipal narratives analysed by Ravi Vasudevan.[24] However, by collaps-ing questions of caste and gender into the image of the exotic, the rural-belle motif recast the lower-caste woman as legitimate object of desire, containing the threat of disruptive sexuality with which her figure has historically haunted the nationalist imaginary.[25] But, as is obvious, the non-upper-caste woman could be constructed as legitimate sexual partner only through the complete erasure of her caste identity.[26] The crucial 'tribal' woman's caste was transformed here into a signifier of the decorative, rather than functioning as an indicator of a position in the social field of power. Indeed, this was even necessary, given the apolitical all-India idiom that Bombay pioneered. The overarching logic of the feudal melodrama could then work to normalize the excesses represented by both unbridled Westernization as well as folk/tribal primitivism into narratives of an indigenist feudal patriarchy.

The decisive shift that marked the new romance films of the 1980s was that *the rural belle could no longer be sustained as a viable narrative possibility*. She was replaced by her cosmopolitan, upper-middle-class counterpart—the New Indian Woman who lives in Levis jeans but could don her ethnicity on demand. Emblematic of this shift were a whole range of figures from Pinky (Vijeta Pandit) in *Love Story* to Rashmi (Juhi Chawla) in *Qayamat Se Qayamat Tak*. Underlying the changing configuration of the rural belle, I will argue, were the fundamental shifts that were precipitated in the Bombay industry by the newly undertaken project of globalization.

THE 1980s' LOVE STORY: THE 'NEW INDIAN WOMAN'

I have analysed in earlier sections of this chapter the structural changes underlying the emergence of the new 'ordinary' Star in 1980s' Bombay. The 1970s' middle cinema also drew on notions of the 'everyday', used 'ordinary' de-glamourized Stars not only as markers of cultural distinction but also as strategies of product-differentiation. As a new commercial cinema emerges in the 1980s—one that deploys the resources of 1970s' middle cinema to capture a commercial market—the rural belle is transformed into her upper-middle-class ethnic–chic counterpart. Following the line of enquiry opened by Prasad, I contend that this transformation of the rural belle symptomatizes the transition from the 'formal' to the 'real' subsumption of the Indian economy by capital.

Prasad has argued that Bombay mediates the emerging dominance of capital in India through its epic narratives of 'transpatriarchal migration' (from the feudal family to the capitalist state) by mobilizing a Euro-American discourse of romance (1994: 210–16). In the feudal melodrama of 1950s' Bombay, the centrifugal tendencies of romantic love were contained within the authority of the feudal joint family through last-minute revelations which showed that the romance of the couple was already sanctioned by their respective families. However, the symbolic referent of the English-language expression 'I love you'—one that proliferated in the commercial cinemas of 1980s' Bombay—represents an aspiration to the space of the private as represented by the couple of the *nuclear* family:

> Being in English, this expression ('I love you') and the symbolic network into which it transports the couple, are also marked as a social privilege, a mark of social distinction. What is this Other whose recognition is invoked and guaranteed by this expression? This Other, the witness to a coupling that is beyond the formal coupling sanctioned by traditional authority, is as yet unformed, unidentifiable, its only trace being the obsessively recurring English expression that something is being called into existence. Would it be too far-fetched to speculate that this Other is precisely the modern state in which the romance of the nuclear family and the state would dissolve or sublate all other mediating categories? (Ibid.: 210.)

Similarly, Srilata Krishnan, in her re-reading of popular women's literature, has examined the social construction of the New Indian Woman through popular magazines such as *Femina* and *Savvy*. As a member of the global middle class, the New Indian Woman of the 1980s was constructed as being even farther removed from any caste–region–religion markers than her 1950s' counterpart. She was defined primarily by her 'innocent' upper-middle-class status and was, above all, an individual with an *agency* to be publicly visible and to 'fall in love' (see Krishnan 1996a). In the 1980s, it was no longer the male protagonist alone who travelled back to the countryside to rediscover his roots. This symbolic (usually, also literal) journey was now being undertaken by the Westernized heroine too. This changed configuration precipitated several changes in the narrative form of the feudal romance (see Prasad 1996: 27–43). The concept of Westernization emerged as being in seamless continuity with—rather than being opposed to—'Indian tradition'. Further, the city—through its training in consumerism that was now coded as Indian/traditional—was no longer opposed to the country. The earlier opposition between Westernization and Indianness was now reinflected onto a *generational conflict*—a conflict between the generation of the 1950s (India's socialist era) and that of the 1980s (the moment of globalization). A range of 1980s' romance films show lovers as consummating unfulfilled desires of the past. Where generational conflict is not literal, it takes the form of an opposition between the 1950s' parental generation (coded as backward) and the 1980s' young generation (set up as modern). Thus, while *Ek Duje Ke Liye* (Made for Each Other, 1981) portrays the parental generation as clinging on to backward regional chauvinism, *Prem Rog* (The Mania of Love, 1982) sets up the parental generation as clinging onto outmoded and conservative codes of Hindu widowhood.

In the new tradition/modernity opposition around which the 1980s' love stories were constructed, the ordinariness of Star images had important implications—Stars specializing in romantic roles helped produce idealized images of Indian yuppies as the new bearers of Indian modernity, a modernity had retained its links with ancient tradition. The notion of the ordinary invoked by new Stars without screen histories translated, thematically, into a notion of 'innocence of politics', especially of socialism. The young lovers in the 1980s' films do not understand the scheming, politicking 1950s' generation wreaking destruction and violence in their world. The idealization of the 1980s' youth is contingent on the coding of the 1950s' generation as the repository of clannishness and conservatism. Such a setting up of the 1980s' generation—as helpless victims of 'wrong' choices of the 1950s—provided the ideological justification for a reinscription of the new consumerism by the city on the countryside.

In the new tradition/modernity binary of the 1980s, the love marriage and the nuclear family were set up as radical alternatives to the 1950s' worldview. Romantic love—coded as 'bad modernity' for the normative Indian woman of the nineteenth century—was recoded as 'good modernity' for the upper-middle-class woman of the 1980s. The love marriage was pitted against the arranged marriage, which was re-designated as conservative or lacking in choice (Krishnan 1996a). The new tradition/modernity opposition was structured around dystopic manifestations of community living (represented by the feudal joint family) and the nuclear family couple (represented by freedom of individual heterosexual choice). Freedom was set up as being opposed to community living. It is also set up as opposed to politics. In this de-politicization of freedom, the agency of the New Indian Woman played a crucial role. Tharu and Niranjana have analysed in a different context the problematic visibility that women seem to have acquired within the nation in the 1980–90s. Describing the mass participation of women in the anti-Mandal riots, Tharu and Niranjana argue:

> The fact of women 'taking to the streets' became in the hegemonic culture iconic of an idealism that recalled the days of the freedom struggle. The marking of 'women' as middle-class and upper-caste has a long genealogy which, historically and conceptually, goes back into nationalism as well as social reform. Marked thus, 'women' are seen as pure and uncorrupted: hence the significance of their struggle which becomes a disinterested one, since they have no place in the organised political process. However, as a powerful strand of nationalism asserted, it was women, who were entrusted with the task of saving the nation (1996: 240).

Such a coding of the upper-caste and middle-class woman's agency as idealism was worked by Bombay's new love stories into an equation between freedom and couple-formation. Thus, the logic of this new love story meshed neatly with a host of other chauvinistic social initiatives that gained legitimacy within the national imaginary through their foregrounding of the agency and participation of upper-caste women. However, not only was the modernity of the New Indian Woman different from that available to the lower-middle-class woman, it was also the flip side of a process of 'othering' through which the lower-*caste* woman or the Muslim woman, for example, was locked into her caste and/or religious identity (Dhareshwar 1993). As we shall see in the next chapter, not only does Rashmi in *Qayamat Se Qayamat Tak* appropriate tribal culture as ethnic fashion, but her upper-classness is also actively constituted by the new consumerism of the city—a lifestyle and a social privilege restricted almost exclusively to the Hindu upper caste in contemporary India.

A film like *Ram Teri Ganga Maili* (Ram, Your Ganges Has Been Soiled, 1985, henceforth referred to as *RTGM*) foregrounds this transformation vividly. Ganga (Mandakini), the eponymous rural belle, was overdetermined by notions of moral 'purity' not only through the setting of the film in an imaginary Himalayan (North Indian) village at the originary point of the river Ganges, but also through Raj Kapoor's much-hyped search for the face that would encapsulate the mythic resonances that the Ganges has generated in the cultural history of India. Into the countryside comes the suave but sensitive Naren (Rajiv Kapoor) in search, literally, of the 'purity' lost in the city. Marking a significant departure from the feudal romance, however, *RTGM* shows Ganga publicly choosing Ram as her husband. The travails that Ganga subsequently faces follow from this one act of self-conscious choice. Though she is ultimately united with Ram, Ganga is even reduced to prostitution in the intervening space, with her 'client' turning out to be none other than her father-in-law! While the film, in obvious ways, is a neo-nationalistic lament on the degeneration of the mythical Ganga (symbolic of Indian culture) in the new age, I propose that *RTGM* can also be metaphorically read as Bombay's nostalgia for a bygone feudal idyll. The new discourse of romantic love is categorically an urban upper-caste/class discourse, one which, by definition, excludes the rural belle and the tribal woman from their notion of agency and, eventually, their conception of womanhood. The significance of this exclusion, I argue, is that it sympto-matized the entire transformation of Nehruvian nationalism that has been underway for the past two decades. The point to bear in mind is that this exclusion was done in the name of 'individualism' and 'free choice', a rhetoric that not only re-appropriates female agency within the institutions of family and marriage, but also categorically sets up these institutions as 'others' of politics.

But while women as a group were left out of the fictive social contract on which the classical nation-state was based, so also were the lower classes ('the folk'), a category equally crucial to the ideological construction of nationhood. The ideological creation of 'the folk' was based on a systematic disciplining and transformation of the peasantry into citizen-subjects by the institutional apparatuses of the new regime of power. The ideological function of this social category was to set up the nation-state as a community based on deep *horizontal* solidarities, despite the existing hierarchies. Thus the persistent coding in all nationalist discourses of the folk as bearers of primordial 'national traditions' (see, among others, Anderson 1983; Burke 1981).

Consequently, Bombay cinema, as a representative popular cultural form in India, has seen another genre in which the protagonist is placed outside the institutions and practices of citizenship—the genre of the 'anti-hero' or, in other words, 'action cinema'. My attempt in the following section will be to read Bombay's anti-hero genre as elite documentation of subaltern politics, as negotiations between the normative Indian self and subaltern castes and classes. Moreover, while the love story has revolved primarily around questions of couple formation, the anti-hero film revolves around questions of a more political nature. There is, of course, a fundamental relationship between the two—changes in the private are integrally related to changes in the political and vice versa.

Initiated in Ranajit Guha's path-breaking *Elementary Aspects of Peasant Insurgency in India* (1983a) and followed through in the work of the Subaltern Studies collective, there has emerged documentation of a whole realm of popular mobilization whose modes of organization, notions of community, ordering of time, etc., were quite independent of the political idiom of liberal democracy. Read in the light of this new writing of history, my analysis of Bombay's anti-hero genre will attempt to map through it the ways in which the Indian elite have negotiated the socio-political idioms of these 'other' worlds—the world of the thief, the 'rowdy', the 'outlaw'—worlds that were framed in counterpoint to the law of the new state. The new legal system itself (as evident in the detective novel, for example), with its grounding in the figure of the individual, signals the transition to a capitalist state. Further, as Foucault has documented, the new techniques of discipline and the new discourses on sex were preconditionally linked in the very *nature* of power on which the new art of governmentality was premised. This new form of state power was based on continuous and systematic modes of surveillance geared to maximize efficiency (Foucault 1991).[27] But while, in Europe, the institutional and conceptual transformations—that provided the conditions of for the historical ascendancy of the bourgeoisie—performed the function of controlling the despotic powers of the aristocracy and therefore seemed liberating, in India they seemed exactly the reverse.

'FAMILY NAME': INSIDE AND OUTSIDE THE LAW

The question of 'law' in India has a very complex genealogy. At an obvious level, the legal apparatus here, as opposed to that in Western Europe, emerged as one of the most visible signifiers of the colonial state's absolute power. Consequently, nationalism as a mass movement gained crucial momentum from popular mobilization directed against the law. Yet, as we have discussed at several points, despite its ostensible anti-imperialist stance, nationalist discourse shared fundamentally in the worldview of colonial modernity. This included not only the economic and political institutions of the colonial state but also the discursive universe on which these institutions were grounded.

The problem was that, given the nature of pre-existing social structures in India with their own modes of asymmetries, it was impossible for an arrogant and numerically insignificant bourgeoisie to reconstitute the common sense of the lower orders in any effective manner. As Kaviraj suggests:

> 'Illiteracy' implies not just 'lack' or 'absence' of a high discourse, but the presence of a very different one whose rules, codes, emphases and ironies are entirely different [. . .] The culture of the lower orders, therefore, has potent means of not learning, insulating out the cultural instructions coming from the top [. . .] This resulted in [. . .] the most significant cultural fact of modern Indian political life. There were two ways of dividing society—in terms of discourses and in terms of political ideology—and the two divisions would be asymmetric (1991: 81–2).

The approaching climate of political power in the 1930–40s marked this decisive realignment between elite nationalist and subaltern politics (Tharu and Lalita 1995: 1–40). In telling continuity with the colonial rulers, forms of popular mobilization operating outside the institutional procedures of liberal democracy, which had earlier found Congress support, were now re-designated by the *nationalist* leadership as 'law and order' problems (ibid.: 80–90). The meeting of the elite nationalist and subaltern political domains in India has historically been marked by contradiction. In the trajectory of Bombay's anti-hero cinema that follows, I will focus on the most distinctive characteristic of this genre—its fundamental ambivalence to law.

The class-based contradictions around questions of law-making and law-breaking were, further, overlaid by the internal contradictions within the ruling coalition that assumed power at Independence. Given that the Nehruvian ruling bloc was a coalition of feudal, capitalist and professional groups, the legal system of bourgeois democracy too could only be invoked here so long as it paid homage to feudal notions of justice and honour. It is these multiple contradictions in the Indian social formation that provided the structuring trope of Bombay's anti-hero cinema—the motif of the 'family name'. The exclusion of Bombay's anti-hero from codes of citizenship is enacted through his exclusion from the feudal notion of status represented by family name.

Vasudevan's analysis of the crime film of the 1940–50s' Bombay presents an examination of Bombay's anti-hero genre (1991a: 63–91, 1991b: 171–85, 1993: 51–77). Placed within the comprehensive Oedipal triangle of the castrating father, the nurturing mother and the traumatized son, Vasudevan reads the criminality of the 'thief-hero' of the 1940–50s as the symbolic enactment of the Oedipal fantasy of patricide. The crime film of 1950s' Bombay, Vasudevan points out, was split into three clearly differentiated ideological spaces—the space of 'legitimacy' occupied by the father (who has, moreover, banished his wife), the space of 'virtue' occupied by the mother (in the now-dispossessed hero's home) and the space of 'illegitimacy' occupied by the villain who is also the father's double. The conflict between father and son erupts in these films through a contest over the heroine, the father's 'daughter', who is also a symbolic substitute for his absent wife. Since the hero cannot gain his objectives through legitimate means, he is forced into criminal ways. However, through the possibility of moral redemption opened by the heroine and with the aid of the law, he regains his virtue. But this is now a redefined space because authority has passed from father to son. In the process, the heroine has also taken the place of the mother. In this challenge to the father's authority, Vasudevan reads hints of nucleation and the transition to a capitalist culture being enacted in the breakdown of the early studios and the emergence of the Star system in Bombay.

In what is both a related as well as different reading, Prasad has traced an ideological doubling not only at the level of content but also as it 'determined' the form of the Bombay social:

> [I]n the 'classical' Hindi cinema, two resolutions to the narrative crisis would follow in quick succession: one enforced by the traditionally given authority of the exemplary[/feudal] subject(s) of the narrative; the other, following immediately after, and comically redundant in appearance, enforced by the agents of the modern law. The laughter evoked by this redundancy should not distract

from the ideological necessity of this doubling [. . .] Here the law has the 'last word' but this is as yet only a formality, an observance of form (1996: 30–1).

Tracing the shifts in narrative structure between the feudal melodrama of the 1950s and the reformed 'social' of the 1970s, Prasad says:

> This relationship of complicitous supplementarity (between the Law and a feudal code of values) was seriously disrupted in the early 1970s when, in the midst of a national crisis, the cultural economy of cinema underwent something of a transformation. After much groping and fumbling, a new dominant form emerged, in which the law was no longer a supplement but the most important stake of narrative conflict and resolution [. . .] Disinherited, marginalized, and thrown into a world of law and criminality, their stories (the 70s anti-heroes') brought the state to the centre of the narrative and while not eliminating the feudal family romance, relegated it to a somewhat subordinate status, [. . .] a lost object of desire whose repossession is the driving force behind the action (ibid.).

This shift, Prasad moreover suggests, was symptomatic of the emerging dominance of capital in the Indian economy with the bourgeoisie becoming the dominant partner in the ruling coalition. Working within this broad transition from feudalism to democracy (i.e. capitalism) that Prasad has outlined, I will plot the changing configurations of Bombay's anti-hero genre as it has mobilized the concept of family name to negotiate the anti-hero's problematic relationship with the law.[28]

THE TRAMP, THE CITY AND THE CRITIQUE OF THE NATION

Ideologically, the Swadeshi movement charged categories such as the folk and the countryside both as repositories of Indian tradition as well as sites opposed to Westernization. Consequently, when set in an agrarian background, conscious disidentification with the law could only be located in 'outlaw' figures such as Birju (*Mother India*, 1957) or Ganga (*Ganga Jamuna*, 1961)—figures who ran *parallel* legal systems and were literally outside the domain of the state within which the emblematic Indian village was encased. A film like *Jis Desh Mein Ganga Behti Hain* (The Land Through Which the Ganges Flows, 1960) provides an interesting departure in its depiction of 'communists' as outlaw figures. Alternatively, disidentification with the law could be located within the *urban* experience of modernity. It is this urban gangster or outlaw—drawing heavily on the Hollywood genre—who develops into Bombay's vigilante in the 1970–80s. Consequently, in the trajectory that I propose to map, it is the 'tramp', the 'thief', the 'rowdy'—loners in an urban landscape—who emerge as 'others' to the normative middle-class householder.

In their analyses of popular mobilizations, one of the characteristic features of insurgent subaltern consciousness identified by the Subaltern Studies collective has been its 'community membership'. However, as Rosalind O'Hanlon suggests, in the movement from moments of spectacular mobilization to resistance in its less dramatic forms, it might be necessary to reconceptualize resistance itself:

> [T]he very dichotomy between domination and resistance, as we currently conceive it, bears all the marks of dominant discourse in its insistence that it should necessarily take the virile form of deliberate onslaught. Rejecting this, we should look for resistances of a different kind: dispersed in fields we do not conventionally associate with the political; residing sometimes in the evasion of norms, or failure to respect ruling standards of conscience and responsibility; sometimes in the furious effort to resolve in metaphysical terms the contradictions of the subaltern's existence [. . .] sometimes in what only looks like cultural difference (1988 : 224).

In the work of the Subaltern Studies collective, the definition of subaltern consciousness through community membership worked to locate it as the 'other' of the individualized bourgeois consciousness. Yet, as we move from spectacular mobilization to resistance in its more personalized forms, it is important to note that while highlighting the reification generated by capitalism, the feudal notion of family name in Bombay's anti-hero cinema functioned to evoke notions of community in the alienating urban locale of modernity. But, of course, this nostalgia was framed in a manner that completely erased questions of caste. In an important essay cited earlier, Rajadhyaksha (1993a: 55–70) has argued that the way in which the many contending definitions of Indianness were resolved at Independence certain objectified symbols came to function as stand-ins for the desires and promises betrayed by this new imagined community. The motif of family name, I propose, was similarly one such symbolic referent of social justice promised by the nation at its birth. As Rajadhyaksha notes of Raj Kapoor's films, they invert the utopianism of the Nehruvian era to foreground instead a fundamental unattainability of desire.

Now, let us briefly go back to *Awara* (The Tramp), as I propose an alternative perspective to Vasudevan's reading of 1940–50s' crime films. While it is true that the law (with the aid of romantic love) helps Raj regain his social legitimacy, we must remember that at the end of the film it is nevertheless Raj who has to serve a prison sentence. His father, the judge, stands at least 'formally' exonerated by the law. Even as the law is invoked as a guarantor of social justice it still punishes the victim rather than the aggressor.

In 1970s' anti-hero films we see that the father figure has lost this status of legitimacy in the eyes of both society as well as his son. In *Deewar*, for instance, till the end it is only the spectator who knows the 'truth' about Ajay-babu's 'compromise'. Disillusioned with the father figure, the son then tries to reinstate the mother in his place (see Prasad 1994: 278–82). At this point the law however steps in reluctantly to punish the erring son. In the action films of 1980s, however, the father is reinstated in the space of social legitimacy. There is no conflict between father and son. Moreover, the father figure is also ideologically aligned to the law. In the changed cultural space of the nation the motif of family name was now reinflected as the son's desire to regain the organic upper-caste community of his father.

1980s' ANTI-HERO CINEMA: THE 'INHUMAN' VERSUS THE 'ORDINARY'

It will be interesting to introduce here some stimulating work by the cultural theorists Vivek Dhareshwar and R. Srivatsan on the 'rowdy-sheeter' (1993). The rowdy, the authors argue, is the 'other' of the yuppie in the new post-liberalization social landscape of the Indian nation. While in the 1950s, the loss of family name is on account of failed father figures, in the 1980s it is due to the failure of sons to live up to the father's name instead. We have noted earlier Prasad's thesis on the structural similarities between the 1950s' Bombay melodrama and the feudal stage melodramas of nineteenth-century USA. In both, while the class structure remained feudal and populated with the aristocracy, variations were possible and sometimes slaves or peasants were given elevated roles. Usually, however, in such cases, a last-minute 'discovery' would establish the peasant's noble birth. Such tropes in the narrative were not so much a mark of incipient egalitarianism as a mechanism of aristocratic self-legitimatization—a way of figuring the prince or noble's organic relation with his subjects (Prasad 1994: 131–7). Working within the structure of the feudal melodrama, the paradigmatic feudal anti-heroes of the 1950s include, among others, the 'thief-hero' of *Kismet* (Fate) and the 'tramp' of *Awara*. Both Shekhar (*Kismet*) and Raj (*Awara*) are discovered in the end to be of noble birth. They are 'declassified' because their father figures fail in their parental roles. In Shekhar's case, this 'failure' is represented through greed and the 'excess' (symbolized by the second marriage) of his father, Inderjit. In Raj's case, it is Judge Raghunath's paranoia about 'purity of lineage' which leads him to cast his pregnant wife out on the street. Further, in both *Kismet* and *Awara*, the heroines are the 'moral' guardians enabling the successful transfer of 'family name' across the generations. In both films the law, with the aid of the heroine, enables members of a family to 'recognize' each other.

The emerging dominance of capital in the 1970s and 1980s has however meant that the authority of this earlier feudal code is now displaced by the law of the capitalist state. Beginning with *Zanjeer* (Chains, 1973), *Deewar* (The Wall, 1975) and *Trishul* (The Trident, 1978), the 1980s' anti-hero films present the legal system as the primary site of narrative contest, *Shakti* (Strength, 1982), *Meri Jung* (My Battle, 1982), *Ardha Satya* (Half-Truth, 1983), *Ankush* (Restrain, 1985), *Karma* (Duty, 1986), *Tezaab* (Acid, 1988), *Parinda* (The Bird, 1989), *Ghayal* (The Wounded, 1990) and *Prahaar* (The Assault, 1991).

There has, however, been a subtle transformation between the iconic 1970s' anti-hero played by Amitabh Bachchan and the vigilantes of the 1980s. As Prasad has observed, the Bachchan persona, while placed in a relationship of conscious disidentification with the state, was 'nominated' as 'representative' by various subaltern communities in his films—the Muslim in *Zanjeer*, the folk in *Sholay*, the underworld in *Deewar*. The mother figure, in his films, worked as a stand-in for all these 'other' social formations that had to give way to the nation and/or the law. According to Prasad, the tragic denouement of the Bachchan persona was then preordained insofar as he tried to reinstate the mother in the position of the father. Without denying Prasad's argument, the motif of the family name gives another perspective from which to read the trajectory of the Bachchan persona.

The marginalization of the Bachchan vigilante was usually the result of absent or failed father figures. But the crucial point was that the Bachchan narratives went to considerable length to justify the father's failure. The films showed that the fathers had abdicated their paternal functions not out of choice as Judge Raghunath had done in *Awara*. Rather they had failed because of circumstances beyond their control. Inspector Vijay's father in *Zanjeer* is killed. In *Deewar*, Ajay-babu deserts his family to 'save' his family from the dishonour he has brought by being blackmailed into complicity with his evil boss. The fathers of the 1970s were *victims* of a corrupt system. Unaware of the father's 'true' nature, the Bachchan vigilante retained a violently antagonistic stance to the absent father/the law, trying to reinstate the mother in his place.

The shift in the 1980s' anti-hero films is that the father has now become the embodiment of 'idealism' for the son. The son's exclusion from respectable society occurs as he tries to emulate the father's high social ideals. But in order to do so, the 1980s' anti-hero finds he has to 'cleanse the system' first. Mapping the changing configuration of the anti-hero genre through the motif of family name, it appears, as if retrospectively, the anti-hero films of the 1980s are justifying the 1970s' vigilantes' adversarial stance to the law or the father, suggesting that the latter rejected his father because he did not know what his father was 'truly' like.[29]

A film such as *Shakti* provides a powerful 'transition point'. Narrated in flashback, the film opens with the DIG's grandson trying to make up his mind about which 'career'. The DIG then recalls for him his father's life. As a young boy, Vijay (Bachchan) is kidnapped by the local mafia. They hope to use Vijay to blackmail the Inspector into releasing one of their friends. At enormous emotional cost, the Inspector refuses the deal. Though he rescues Vijay soon after, Vijay is convinced from then on that his father does not really love him. This deep-seated sense of betrayal/loss, via a series of events, then precipitates Vijay into a career in crime. At the climactic shoot-out, the Inspector is bound 'by duty' to kill his son. As the dying Vijay breathes his last on his father's lap, the Inspector weeps inconsolably. The final question of a son to his father is: 'Why did you not tell me you loved me before?' (This scene makes for striking comparison with the climactic last scene of *Deewar* where Vijay breathes his last on his mother's lap, shot by his brother as he comes to meet her.)

The vigilantes of 1980s' anti-hero films consciously idealize their father figures. Given the genealogy of the 1980s' vigilante films in the 'mass' cinema of the 1970s, these films are set in urban, lower-middle-class milieus, invoking everyday problems such as lack of housing, education and employment. The father figure here typically comes from a lower-middle-class 'ordinary' background and holds a clerical position or is a lower-rung police official. In the 1980s' anti-hero films, the hero is either directly associated with the repressive apparatuses of the state or, indirectly, through his guardian figure whom he aspires to emulate. The repressive state apparatuses are set up as institutional manifestations of the 'idealism' of the nationalist movement. *Karma* (Duty, 1986) perhaps represents the high point of this process where a benevolent jail warder (Dilip Kumar) transforms three convicts facing death penalties (Anil Kapoor, Jackie Shroff and Shah Rukh Khan) into an anti-terrorist squad.

The Others of the nation are either 'corrupt' representatives of state apparatuses or as inhuman megalomaniacs running parallel dystopic empires. The villain in these films is often not given any tangible motive at all. While monetary greed/political ambition are sometimes presented as ostensible reasons for villainy, in several instances he is shorn of all 'human' moorings. A range of villains from Maharani (*Sadak*, The Street, 1991) to Anna (*Parinda*) can be cited as examples. As Rajiv Velicheti observes of the 'new' 1980s' films in Telugu, 'evil' appears as all-pervasive and senseless, creating an overwhelming atmosphere of danger which can randomly strike *any* person at *any* time (1993). Failing to comprehend the villain's sub-human nature, representatives of the 1950s' generation (the idealized fathers) in 1980s' Bombay, fall prey to this auto-generating violence as they uphold civic, social and human values in a hostile world. Velicheti draws the underlying connections between such representations of 'villainy' and the implicit logic of a police-state this feeds into:

> Such a villain [one without any ostensible 'motives'] helps to propagate a view that evil is all pervading and there is no escape [. . .]

The earlier ethical conception of the universe where good ethics protected people from all kinds of evil no more holds good. [. . .]

The conception of the world as depicted in these films has a number of ideological implications. Firstly, the villain becomes a metaphor for all social disturbances and tensions. Secondly, such a depiction calls, not for social solutions but for a total suppression of them. Thirdly, it fosters the view [that] opposition to violence would be inviting great personal trouble which an ordinary citizen cannot face [. . .] Lastly, such a depiction of the problems and their resolution prepares the ideological ground for the rule of an authoritarian state [. . .] There is a homology between authoritarian notions of state and the hero as depicted in these films. Both are idealizations of authority in terms of a moral duty of protection and both claim absolute power on this basis (1993: 4–5).

Failing to comprehend the villain's sub-human nature the naive father figures, who represent the generation of the 1950s in these films, fall prey to the auto-generating violence even as they struggle to uphold basic human decencies in a hostile world.

Such an idealization of the 1950s' generation is, firstly, the direct opposite of their portrayal in the 1980s' love stories. These narratives also propose counter-violence as the solution to all social problems. Apart from reinforcing the logic of a police-state such an ethic also has disturbing implications for women. As Velicheti has noted, *women* have emerged as the primary targets of violence in the 'new' commercial cinemas of Telugu also. This reconstructed patriarchy, I would argue, is even more rigidly masculinist than the 1950s. Drawing on Gandhism, women in the 1950s were to be inducted into the task of nation-building as guarantors of the new nation's morality. As Rani in *Kismet* or Rita in *Awara*, they functioned as agents for the successful transfer of patriarchal authority ('family name') across generations. The political upheavals of the 1960–70s saw the mother move centre stage. The tragic destiny of the disinherited son in the 1970s resulted from his efforts to reinstal the mother as the agent who could bestow on him the patriarchal inheritance of 'family name'. The idolization by the 1980s' vigilante of his father has not only reduced the mother to relative insignificance, it has also seen the heroine become the 'other' of the chaste, (potential) middle-class housewife—the night-club singer in *Shakti*, the widow in *Prahaar*, the pop star in *Tezaab*. Forced into the public space of the market/the profane world of labour, these middle-class women are now 'deprived' of the 'protection' of 'family'. It is to reinstate *her* within the privacy of the bourgeois home as well as to live up to the name of the father that the 1980s' vigilante has to transgress the law.

Tracing the emergence of vigilante chronicles in 'feudal' America, David Grimstead (1994) argues that they emerged as the paranoiac response of a bourgeoisie trying to re-assert its control in the face of the threatening new world order signalled, for example, in the writings of Marx. Inverting the dichotomy between class-position and morality represented by the 'theatrical melodramas', the vigilante chronicles drew on the absolutist vocabulary of American life to portray the lower classes as vile and vicious:

> [T]he appeal of the vigilante tradition, to both its members and its historians, was that it allowed a comforting connection between class and moral position that democratic society and scholarship eschewed in more sober moments and on less picturesque subjects. The strong strand of class-consciousness, of deep sympathy for society's poor and disadvantaged. [. . .] disappears completely in the complacent equation of social position with moral worth in vigilante chronicle and subsequent history [. . .] Vigilantism was the local version of the United Sates' and the world's frequent politics of simple-minded self-righteousness, the attempt or the pretence of inaugurating the ideal by hanging the real (ibid.: 209–10).

Grimstead's analysis generates obvious resonances with Bombay's anti-hero cinema of the 1980s. As the 1970s' mother figure (with her associations with the society's dispossessed) is marginalized, the law in its 1980s' incarnation targets marginalized groups as the genesis of 'social disturbance' instead; the 'Muslim' and the 'South Indian' in *Parinda*, the 'Muslim' in *Tezaab*, the 'outsiders' in *Ankush*. Moreover, given the emergent aesthetic of the 'ordinary' discussed in the earlier section, this opposition between idealism/innocence and sub-human villainy is greatly refurbished through the attention to the texture of violence that the new thrust on representationalism generated. It is through this representationalism that the ideological ground was prepared for the 1980s' anti-hero to 'break the law to uphold justice'.

The 1970s launched the iconic anti-hero Amitabh Bachchan. In the 1980s, Bachchan—under pressures for novelty generated by the erosion of the industry's economic base—gave way to a string of new Stars. Reinflecting the 1970s' angst, these new anti-heroes drew on the cultural memory of Bachchan while using a discourse of 'endeavour' to rework, in the 1980s' context, the Swadeshi-generated ideological opposition between inherited and acquired wealth. These new Star images played up the idea that these men had made it to the top through determination and hard work rather than through easy money and decadent upper-class privilege.[30] However, as I will show in Chapter 5, the politics of the New Right gave this structure of feeling a de facto upper-caste Hindu coding.

The growing dominance of music also meant that the 1980s' anti-heroes had to be 'musical' stars too. Thus, the 'Jumma Chumma' song-and-dance sequence in *Hum* (Us, 1990) by Bachchan himself. In fact, the emerging prominence of music in Bombay became dramatically evident in the 1990s with Bachchan, for example, starting his own music company, Big B. The album *Aby Baby* (1996) began with Bachchan's recitation of verses from the title song of *Kabhi Kabhi* (Sometimes, 1976), as he tried to reclaim an earlier 'musical' and sensitive persona. But the point at which, in hindsight, all the different strands elucidated here came together most forcefully was the renaissance of the very upper-class suave Bachchan persona through the mega-hit television serial, *Kaun Banega Crorepati* (Who Wants to be a Millionaire?). [This has now also been followed by several romantic roles played by Bachchan in films such as *Nishabd* (No Words, 2007) and *Cheeni Kum* (Less Sugar, 2007).]

The 1980s, to sum up, was the decade that provided the decisive crossover point from a socialist idiom to a new free-market vocabulary of nation-building. Metonymic of the changed equation between English and Hindi, the changed ideological framework within which the nation was conceptualized provided the conditions for the possibility of a 'new' commercial cinema to emerge in Bombay. In the altered cultural space, the technologies or institutional apparatuses mediating the process of structural adjustment made music the dominant segment of the Bombay film industry.

They also fed into a cinematic aesthetic with a heightened sense of representationalism—the new televisual realism. These twin phenomena not only coalesced in the new image of the ordinary Star but also precipitated formal changes in both its major genres. While the love story reworked the new ordinariness into idealized representations of the Indian yuppie, the anti-hero genre renotated ordinariness into a distinctly lower-middle-class non-consumerist lifestyle and ethics. The love story deflected democratizing caste- and gender-based initiatives into problems of bourgeois conjugality. The anti-hero genre, on the other hand, redefined repressive Sate apparatuses as guarantors of social justice.

To go back to the objective bilingualism of postcolonial nations with which this discussion began, Chatterjee has shown us that the most spectacular evidence of this was located in the terrain of culture as the modernity of the West was translated into indigenous idioms. The vocabulary of Bombay cinema was located at this interstice—as the modernity of the colonizer was both contested and re-appropriated by indigenous elite groups. Further, beginning with the 1980s, as the nation became almost 'a pure image', the terrain of culture also gained lethal impact. In this context, a critical analysis of the Bombay industry is hopefully a gesture that follows Marx's dictum of producing 'accurate knowledge'. In that spirit, the next two chapters will now present close readings of representative texts from each of the two genres highlighted here.

Notes

1 Cinematically, conflicts over the 'national–modern' were reworked most dramatically by the classic M. G. Ramachandran melodramas. For analysis of the crucial role of cinema to the politics of the DMK, see Pandian (1992). Work on regional appropriations of the national–modern, as we have remarked in the last chapter, is only just emerging. For a theorization vis-à-vis Bengal, see, among others, Ashish Rajadhyaksha (1993b: 7–16) and Moinak Biswas (1995). For the use of realism to invoke a 'region', especially in the context of the Indian avant-garde, see Rajadhyaksha (2009: 353–94).

2 I refer here, of course, to the theory of the three 'looks' of classical Hollywood cinema. For a critique of the classical model, one which has in many ways proved foundational, see Laura Mulvey (1975).

3   For the most recent development of this thesis, see Prasad (2009).

4   Politically, the chauvinism of the 1980s' regionalisms can be marked, say, by a new phase of the Akali Dal movement in Punjab or the launching of the Telugu Desam Party by N. T. Rama Rao in the Andhra Pradesh. But, even more than specific political markers, the distance between the regional movements of the 1950s and those of the 1980s becomes evident when we consider the case of Tamil popular cinema, for instance. Emerging as a critique of North Indian Brahman domination, the new films of Tamil cinema (such as *Geetanjali* or *Roja*) could be translated into an all-India idiom in which regional markers had been redefined into a new pan-indigenism to suit the demands of transnational capital. A similar phenomenon is also evident in Telugu popular cinema of the 1980s, with directors like Ram Gopal Varma who also makes Telugu films translatable into a similar all-India vocabulary. In fact, with directors like Varma and Mani Ratnam, the changed nature of regionalism since the 1980s becomes dramatic as these *southern* directors move into a national space, claiming an auteurial status inconceivable for earlier directors from South India.

5   For useful documentations, see Geeta Kapur (1987), Ratnabali Chatterjee (1990) and Tapati Guha-Thakurta (1992).

6   I owe this phrase to Rajadhyaksha (1993a).

7   The pioneering work here is undoubtedly that of Chatterjee (1986).

8   Prasad (1994) has analysed the ways in which conflicting notions of the 'modern' were inscribed, for instance, into the specific form of scopophilia mobilized by the Bombay film, the nature of its representations of 'the private', the logic of its 'double-ending', etc.

9   Prasad suggests that the 'heterogeneous mode of manufacture' adopted by the Bombay industry is contingent on the nature of capitalism in the country. Here, the source of finance directs the structure of the narrative (1994: 41–108). While Prasad's is undoubtedly the most comprehensive analysis, introductory references include Eric Barnouw and S. Krishnaswamy (1963: 116–211), Ravi Vasudevan (1991a) and the introductory chapters of Sumita S. Chakravarty (1993).

10 While Behroze Gandhy and Rosie Thomas (1991) locate the images of three female Stars within the changing political climate, from the 1950s to the 1980s, caste, as an analytical category, does not inform their interpretative framework. This is not a minor omission. Placed in the context of my argument so far, it represents the inability of much of the leftist models of social analysis to conceptualize 'politics' in India in categories other than those derived from the classical democracies of Western Europe.

11 The year 2009, in fact, marked the 50th anniversary of Indian television. Recent studies on the Indian television industry include those by *Journal of Arts and Ideas* 32–33 (1999), Nilanjana Gupta (1998) and Melissa Butcher (2003). These new works have provided many indispensable insights into the growth of television in India. I am trying to theorize the ways in which the new electronic/digital technologies, while augmenting the representational aesthetic of 1970s' middle cinema, fed into an intensely new 'realism effect' in the Bombay commercial of the 1980s. I am further suggesting that this new realism was indicative of a whole set of structural transformations that occurred within the mainstream industry with the onset of liberalization.

12 For useful statistics, see Peter Manuel (1993), Anupama Chandra and Kavita Shetty (1993), and Anupama Chandra (1994b).

13 See, among many others, the cover feature by Brian Tellis and Milton Frank (1996).

14 These connections were given dramatic turn when Sanjay Dutt, the real-life son of 'Mother India', was arrested by the police in connection with the 1993 Bombay blasts, a supposed retaliation by the Muslim community to the destruction of the Babri Masjid, in December 1992. For a sense of the outrage in the national media on the nature of money funding the new Bombay cinema, see M. Rahman and Anup Katiyar (1993). In what forms a striking contrast, Subhash Chandra, the 'owner' of Zee TV was given a very different profile by the media. Thus, the *India Today* feature 'Rice to Riches' (Agarwal 1994: 90–1) proudly recounts Chandra's success story. Beginning as a humble rice merchant, the article recounts how Chandra had grown into one of India's major industrial barons, owner also of the massive new Disney-style amusement park in Bombay. The article narrates (with a jingoism that might put nationalist historians to shame) how Chandra had refused to sell more than 49.9 per cent of his shares in Star TV to Rupert Murdoch even though he had been offered a huge sum of money. Chandra's response to Murdoch had apparently been, 'India is not for sale, Mr Murdoch.' This ideological distinction between the 'good' capital of TV and the 'bad' capital of mainstream Bombay has, of course, reached hysterical pitch with the recent murder of cassette industry baron Gulshan Kumar, the alleged implication of music director Nadeem in the killing and all sorts of rumours of extortion charges faced by many of the current superstars such as Shah Rukh Khan. See, for example, Smruti Koppikar (1997).

15 For a discussion on this, see, among others, Rajadhyaksha (2006).

16 For a discussion of the narrative strategies used by television news to construct its truth-effect, see, among others, Margaret Morse (1986).

17 For useful introductions to recent debates on 'melodrama', see Christine Gledhill (1985), Pam Cook (1985: 121–33), and Jacqueline Britton, Jim Cook and Christine Gledhill (1994).

18 In fact, Rajadhyaksha, in his analysis of the 'epic melodramas' of the 1950s, argues that it is the dependent nature of the Indian bourgeoisie on pre-capitalist social structures/institutions that accounts for the sanitized 'Indian village' of the All India Film with its rural belle in her ankle-length *sari* (1993a: 55–70). The rural belle of the 'commercial' industry in Bombay needs, firstly, to be differentiated from the 'other' rural-belle motif that emerged in the so-called political cinema of the 1970s, what Prasad calls the 'developmentalist aesthetic' of directors such as Shyam Benegal and Govind Nihalani (1994: 340–52). See also Tharu and Lalita (1995: 109–17). The interweaving of discourses on 'women' and 'tradition' in India, of course, has a very long history. See, among others, Lata Mani (1987). The Swadeshi, however, generated a new form of nationalist self-assertion; one where the reclaiming of 'Indianness' became explicitly linked to a critique of colonial rule and Westernization in all its aspects. My argument is that the East–West divide signified by the 'rural belle' draws on the cultural memory of this critique, infusing Orientalist constructions of Indian feudalism with a specifically nationalist hue.

19 Beginning with Bombay Talkies productions which included hits such as *Jhoola* (The Swing, 1941) and *Kangan* (The Bangle, 1939), the trajectory of the 'rural belle' that I hope to trace is one which is decisively located within the all-India Bombay commercial. The significant *change*, then, lies in the way in which the 'new' love story of the 1980s draws on a certain *middle-cinema lineage*, to address a 'commercial market'.

20 I am grateful to Srilata Krishnan for showing me her paper (1996a), where she argues: 'The terms tradition and modernity are always value loaded; one has to contend with not two but four umbrella categories—Good Tradition and Bad Tradition, Good Modernity and Bad Modernity. Formations such as family, feminism, marriage, romance and caste [. . .] are constantly travelling from one category to another.' This paper is part of Krishnan's doctoral research from the University of Hyderabad, and helped to give many of my half-formed thoughts concrete shape.

21 For discussions on the social construction of 'secularism' in India, see among others, Tharu and Niranjana (1996: 232–60), Dhareshwar (1993), Tharu and Lalita (1995: 43–116), Tharu (1996) and Krishnan (1996a).

22 Rajadhyaksha and Willemen (1994: 330) define Madhumati, the epony-mous heroine of the film, thus.

23 The classic analysis of the ideological descriptions of landscape in terms of the city/country divide is, of course, that given by Raymond Williams (1973).

24 Vasudevan's thesis has explained the formal structures that 1950s' melo-dramas employ to position women in spaces of 'legitimate' and 'illegiti-mate' desire vis-à-vis the male protagonist (1991a). Especially interesting is his notion of the 'transgressive heroine' who is unable to find self-realization within patriarchal narratives. Given that the lower-caste woman has historically been coded as the ultimate embodiment of uncontrolled female sexuality, it is significant that in the rural-belle trope of 1950–60s' Bombay, she is recast as *legitimate* object of middle-class male desire, as her caste is erased or subsumed as marker of the primitive or the exotic.

25 For an excellent collection of essays on the exclusions built into the na-tional modern, see, among others, Sangari and Vaid (1989). The inevitable exclusions built into the homogenizing project of the nation-state are further developed in Chatterjee (1994a).

26 Dhareshwar (1993: 115) calls this the 'solipsism of caste from the narrative of the "secular" self in India'. Regarding the construction of a normative femininity as it de-legitimizes lower-caste as well as non-Hindu identities from notions of Indianness, see Tharu and Lalita (1995: 77–8).

27 See also the chapter, 'Docile Bodies', in Foucault (1979: 135–70) for a brilliant analysis of the new techniques of 'discipline' and the form of state power.

28 In the recent body of research on Indian cinemas, the action-film genre has received a surprising amount of critical attention. See, for instance, Lalitha Gopalan (2003) and Valentina Vitali (2009). From my perspective, Ranjani Mazumdar (2007) represents the most sustained example of this. I will engage with Mazumdar's arguments in greater detail in Chapter 5. While offering valuable insights into the revenge/action-drama genre, her founding proposition is to bring Bombay's 'angry young man', represented quintessentially by the Bachchan persona of the 1970s, in dialogue with the psychotic anti-hero of the 1990s. She claims that the angry-young-man phenomenon faded away during the 1980s (ibid.: 1), although this is quite at variance with the evidence at hand. Her analysis glosses over significant transformations in the anti-hero genre of 1980s' Bombay. See also Prasad (2007) and Vasudevan (2007), as recent essays that reflect on the narrative structure of Bombay's action-film genre through organizing binaries,

although the binaries invoked by them (as well as their readings) are different from mine. Importantly, both Prasad and Vasudevan also overlook the anti-hero of 1980s' Bombay.

29 For the moment, I have left out of my analysis the configurations of the anti-hero genre as it took shape in the 1990s, where—through films like *Prahaar* (The Assault, 1991), *Krantiveer* (Hero of the Revolution, 1994) and *Khalnayak* (The Villain, 1993)—this interconnection vigilantism and co-option into a military state seemed to have reached a climax.

30 Being Star sons, the media images of Sunny Deol and Sanjay Dutt had obviously had to use different points of entry. But as Rosie Thomas' analysis of Sanjay Dutt's Star image points out, there was a similar reworking of masculinity in Dutt's media image; one which highlighted a masculinity that was wrecking avenge on a corrupt world.

CHAPTER FOUR

LOVE IN THE TIME OF LIBERALIZATION:
QAYAMAT SE QAYAMAT TAK

Narratives, as Fredric Jameson (1981) evocatively puts it, are socially symbolic acts. The overarching narrative framing this book has been the translation of the socio-political idiom of nineteenth-century Western Europe into the postcolonial context. From this perspective, in this chapter, I have attempted a close reading of Mansoor Khan's *Qayamat Se Qayamat Tak* (From Disaster to Disaster, 1988, henceforth referred to as *QSQT*),[1] a representative 1980s' love story, as the conflict-ridden negotiations by a postcolonial bourgeoisie of the philosophico-epistemic structures of the Enlightenment. Chatterjee's work has shown us that—given the trajectory of nation-formation in the postcolonial world—it was in the terrain of 'culture' that the nation, as an imagined community, was most powerfully articulated into existence. In this context, I have argued that the significance of Bombay's cinematic idiom lies in the fact that it represents the hegemonic vocabulary of the cultural terrain in India.

Yet, as the political project of Enlightenment 'modernity' is overtaken by an economic logic which disdainfully overrides the sovereignty of the classical nation-state, some of our most deep-seated assumptions of

Indianness, too, have come to be fundamentally questioned. Thus, as the second decade of the new millennium dawns, *everyone* is agreed that India is marked by decisive changes. What these changes signify, however, continues to be the subject of intense debate. I will argue in this chapter that this sense of urgency, this anxiety to construct coherent narratives from profoundly dislocating historical processes, makes evident the attempts of the dominant ideology in post-Emergency India to suture the gaps in the Symbolic that have been precipitated, as the new mode of commodification of labour power generated by the global dominance of transnational capital interacts with the internal contradictions of the nation.

Prasad has contextualized changing conceptions of intimacy in Bombay cinema within changing forms of the state in India. He has argued that the emerging dominance of capital in the 1980–90s also provided the conditions of possibility for a restructuring of the social terrain. Manifested in the desire for a space of 'the private' as constituted by 'the couple' of the nuclear family, Prasad has read the shift in Bombay's trajectory—what he calls its 'epic narrative of transpatriarchal migration' from the feudal (joint) family to its nuclear counterpart grounded in the capitalist state—as metonymic of the transition from the 'formal' to the 'real' subsumption of the Indian economy by capital. Signified by the English-language expression 'I love you', this aspiration to the private, Prasad suggests, is mediated in Bombay through a new concept of romance: a concept of intimacy based on the idea of two *individuals* being totally and transparently accessible to each other (1993: 71–86).

I have already attempted an analysis of Bombay's love-story genre to explore the possibilities opened up by such an examination of plotting a history of desire in Bombay, insofar as such a history maps onto transitions in India's state formation. My contention is that *within* Bombay's love-story genre the earlier opposition between 'Indianness' and 'Westernization' was now reconfigured as a generational conflict—an opposition between the generation of the 1950s and that of the 1980s, respectively. Crucial to this reworking was the changing configuration of the Indian woman, as the iconic rural belle of the 1950s was now replaced by her ethnic–chic, cosmopolitan, upper-class/caste counterpart—the New Indian Woman defined above all by the agency she displays by falling in love.

In this context, I will now read *QSQT*, attempting to locate the concept of intimacy mobilized by the film within the whole reformation of the citizen-subject that marked the cultural politics of the Mandal–Masjid era. As just mentioned, in the changed cultural space, the New Indian Woman of the 1980s and 1990s emerged as a decisive actor. The thrust of my analysis of *QSQT* will consequently be to identify the pressures generated by this new identity of the upper-class/caste Indian woman on the institution of the joint family and its corollary, the 'arranged marriage'.[2]

ROMANCE AND THE NEW INDIAN WOMAN

As a series of recent studies have noted, the 1980s saw the 1970s' middle cinema expand to capture the 'commercial' market both in Bombay as well as in India's regional centres. The explanation provided by the industry for this move at the time was that the new romance films were providing 'clean entertainment', clearing a space in the cultural terrain from the sensationalist violence spawned by the action cinema of the 1970s. *India Today*[3] carried the feature 'Return to Romance' in 1989. Suggesting a range of reasons for the 'deluge of romance' in 1980s' Bombay—from the jading of the Bachchan persona to the common economic logic of hiring inexpensive newcomers—the article concluded that though it provided the much-needed respite from the violent anti-hero cinema of the 1970s, romance in the new love stories had *lost* its sublimity:

> But there's no going back [to the 1950s]. Love in the 80s is for the most part synthesizer love: it magnetizes the audience with hi-tech and hi-gloss, but not with soul and sensuality [. . .] Love has lost its poignancy: it's become too accessible, too easy [. . .] That yearning which comes from separation, that old romantic concept of unheard melodies being sweeter, and the bitter-sweet agony of unrequited love, has evaporated with time. Accessibility killed it [. . .] Now the boy and the girl are available to each other (Jain 1989: 139).

Overriding all other markers of the new age that had caused love to 'lose its mystery', the article suggested that it was the new visibility—the presence that women had acquired in the changed urban landscape—that was making romance in the 1980s so 'prosaic'. It then went on to explain that films that had retained their Indianness despite pressures of the new

times were the commercial successes of the new age. Analysing the phenomenal box-office success of *Maine Pyar Kiya* (I Have Fallen in Love, 1989) it
argued:

> What seems to have really got to people is the film's advocacy of a
> particularly Indian virtue moth-balled for a long time: *sharam* (coy-
> ness) [. . .] In the end, the family is sacrosanct. And the girl, covered
> from head to toe, is prone to sacrifice. 'Sacrifice conveys love more
> than passion does,' says Sooraj [Barjatiya, the director] (ibid.: 133).

We are now back on familiar ground. It is the lamentable assertiveness
of the New Indian Woman—a reconfiguring of femininity challenging the
earlier sacrificial complex constructed around her—that is being held
responsible for 'debasing' love in the 1980s.

Contesting Anderson's thesis regarding the global export of nationalisms developed in Western Europe, Chatterjee has argued that the most
powerful as well as creative results of nationalist imaginations in Asia and
Africa were posited not on identity but on their difference from the 'modular' forms developed in the West (1994a). The anticolonial nationalisms
of Asia and Africa, Chatterjee has argued, ideologically divided the social
terrain into analogous realms of the material and the spiritual, the outside
and the inside, the world and the home. Moreover, in the terrain of culture,
nations were ideologically conceptualized as being sovereign well before
the battle for political independence had been initiated. Consequently, it
is in the cultural realm, Chatterjee has proposed, that the most spectacular
evidence of these anticolonial nationalisms are located, as they sought
to fashion their own distinctly nationalist modernities, i.e. modernities
different from those of post-Enlightenment Western Europe.

Seen as a territory over which the colonial state had no authority, the
growth of a nationalist consciousness in India meant that the realm of the
home/the family/the social space of women, too, was not on the agenda of
negotiations with the colonial state. Thus, Chatterjee has argued that
despite the cataclysmic changes that have marked the lives of Indian women
over the last century and a half, their histories are curiously absent from
the agenda of nationalist politics. It was only after the nation became
independent that it became legitimate for the state to intervene in women's
issues (1989: 233–53, 1994a, b).

Contemporary feminist historiographers have argued that even the mass participation of women in the nationalist struggle did not signify their emancipation in any real sense.[4] Familial ideologies of the middle class became the constricting force, mediating their entry into the labour market and economic sphere. Further, given that the nationalist movement endorsed the Hindu Brahmanical bias of colonialist scholarship, the normative femininity constructed in the late nineteenth and early twentieth centuries worked to actively marginalize large sections of lower-caste as well as non-Hindu women in various ways. It is only in the 1970s that we can locate the next phase of the women's movement in India. Emerging as part of a wider critique of the Nehruvian state, a radical new generation of feminist scholars and activists have questioned the entire grid of assumptions built into nationalist constructions of womanhood—the very structure of the family and the nature of its oppression of women, the common-sense assumption which invariably places on women the onus of maintaining the rubric of the family, of their right to choose *between* political and family life and so on.

From this perspective, if we read the popular media of the period against the grain and go back to *India Today*'s nostalgia for the lost 'poignance' of romance in 1980s' Bombay, then the women's movement—and the explosive demands for social change of which it is metonymic—emerge clearly as the illegitimate demands repressed by the nation. It is against these radical critiques of Indianness, which emerged from a range of social positions in the 1960s and 1970s, that the dominant ideology of the day is anxiously re-asserting faith in old certitudes.

However, as popular media was forced to register, a crucial actor rewriting the script in the modern cultural space was the New Indian Woman of the 1980s. In 1992, *India Today* carried a cover story, 'The Changing Indian Woman'. Though largely in the mode of an inspirational biography—the article focused on only a few highly successful upper-class urban women—it registered 'trends' such as late marriages (the average childbearing age of the Indian woman now having risen to 26), single women, higher rates of divorce and so on. A later issue of the same magazine carried a special feature on the exciting lifestyles of the new supermodels (Jahagirdar and Chandra 1994). Similarly the upmarket Indian women's magazine *Femina,* which typically carries articles on 'controversial' subjects such as live-in relationships and divorce, devoted many issues to the New Indian Woman after Sushmita Sen and Aishwarya Rai not only won the Femina Miss India pageant in 1994 but were also crowned Miss Universe and Miss World, respectively. These two women continue to passionately capture upper-middle-class imagination in India even today. And while it would obviously be difficult to empirically match the authenticity of the claims of popular magazines, it is clear that simultaneous with the euphoria over the 'opening' of India's markets was the recognition that some of the nation's most solidly grounded social institutions were coming under intense pressure—an unmistakable new equation between the sexes that was throwing overboard the passively sacrificial Hindu/Indian woman of nationalist discourse.

Interestingly then, paralleling the 'celebrations' of the identity of the New Indian Woman there appeared in the media a whole spate of features asserting the *continuity* of traditional institutions even in the new age. The *India Today* feature, 'Arranged Marriages: Cool Calculations', for instance, eulogized the 'flexibility' of the arranged marriage thus:

> Shyamolie [the representative New Indian Woman] sums up the mood of the young people in the 90s: self-seeking and pragmatic. Unabashedly so [. . .] Choice and compatibility are the new buzz words. And the decision to opt for a quasi-traditional marriage stems from a rational assessment of material and emotional needs [. . .] While education, women's emancipation and exposure to the West through the media have contributed to altered attitudes, the joint family system and a rigid hierarchical social structure—both cited as historical reasons for arranged marriages—have become more flexible (Chandra 1994a: 135).

Supporting what it termed as the trend towards 'pragmatism', the article noted that while in a survey conducted in 1973, 39 per cent of respondents had felt that love was an essential ingredient for marital happiness, two decades later only 11 per cent mentioned love in the same breath as financial security and material comfort. And one of the fundamental reasons for this new 'openness', the article argued, was the confidence or assertiveness that women in India have now acquired.

A similar logic underwrites a subsequent feature in the same magazine, 'Stress and Marriage' (Jain 1994b). Noting the growing tribes of marriage counsellors and family therapists, the article lists a range of factors contributing to the stress in marriages in contemporary India. Overshadowing the new consumerism bolstered by television, the increasingly competitive job market and so on, here too the responsibility of the new stress in marriages is placed on the 'career woman' and the repercussions of her new identity. While ostensibly professing sympathy with the New Indian Woman, this article ends with the hoary voice of 'Indian tradition' warning us of the dangers of being seduced by the 'superficial glamour' of the West. To avert the inevitable historical destiny of AIDS and traumatized children from broken homes, it goes on to say that the new kinds of 'freedom' opened up by consumer capitalism need to be modulated, above all, into the configuration of sexual politics as has existed in India *traditionally*.

Consequently, as opposed to the new stressed-out marriages, a subsequent feature, 'The Joint Family: Change Amidst Continuity', re-affirmed the continuing relevance of traditional institutions such as the joint family even in the new age (Jain 1994a). While noting that the new joint family is a 'joint family with a difference', i.e., one based on a maximizing of self-interests of each of the constituent nuclear units, the article rationalized this change as the 'adaptability' of an old institution to 'changing times'. Therefore, as the New Indian Woman goes out to work, the article happily noted, the mother-in-law now becomes a convenient baby-sitter. Or, the mother-in-law becomes a handy substitute for household help for the woman who cannot be bothered with the hassles of housekeeping anyway. Or, the new joint-family arrangement becomes convenient as prices of real estate soar. Obviously, in what the article reads as 'flexibility' of an older social institution we can see the ways in which earlier forms of community living are now being inflected by the ruthless logic of capitalism with its singular emphasis on 'productivity'. Completely deflecting initiatives of the women's movement, which has actively tried to strengthen solidarity among women (for example across the much feared mother-in-law/daughter-in-law divide), the new joint family is not a place where women become sensitive to each other's needs. Rather, it is an arrangement where the new upper-class woman now further marginalizes her older, 'feudal' counterpart. Similarly, as opposed to an older type of the joint family—which, by according social privileges in proportion to age did, at some level, provided the elderly with real authority—the new joint family has practically marginalized the aged. As the article noted, privileges in the new joint family are proportionate to one's income. However, even as the younger generation demands its privacy, as new pressures on productivity are exerted, the article argued that these modifications are entirely natural as a centuries-old social institution adapts to the new times. Its conclusion, already suggested by its title, was that the joint family has survived. It is vibrant even in the new age.

Working at the intersection of philosophy and psychoanalysis, Žižek elaborates the double scansion that inevitably marks the dialectical process; the necessary delay between changes in 'content' and changes in 'form' in the terrain of the Symbolic:

> The crucial feature of [the] dialectical 'retroactive unmaking' is the interval separating the process of the change of 'contents' from the formal closing act—the structural necessity of the *delay* of the latter over the former.
>
> [. . .] First, we have the 'silent weaving of the Spirit', the unconscious transformation of the entire symbolic network, the entire field of meaning. Then, when the work is already done [. . .] it is time for a purely formal act by means of which the previous shape of the Spirit breaks up also 'for itself'. The crucial point is that *consciousness necessarily comes too late*; it can take cognizance of the fact that the ground is cut from under its feet only when the infectious illness already dominates the field (1991: 63–5).
>
> [. . .]
>
> The double scansion of this process enables us to grasp in a concrete way the worn-out formula of the 'negation of negation': the first 'negation' consists in the slow, underground, invisible change of substantial content which, paradoxically, takes place *in the name of its own form*; then once that form has lost its substantial right, it falls to pieces by itself—the very form of negation is negated, or, to use the classic Hegelian couple, the change which took place 'in itself' becomes 'for itself' (ibid.: 186).

According to Žižek, then, changes in the symbolic network first erupt as changes in 'content' which appear under the guise of 'strengthening the old form'. Then, once the 'silent weaving of the spirit' has finished its work, the old form can fall off. With respect to calls to return to traditional values in contemporary Western Europe, Žižek remarks that the falsity of this position lies precisely in the fact that these so-called traditional values have to be re-established. But they are not the same. Their meaning has changed *precisely to the extent that their form has remained the same*. Applying Žižek's analysis to the renewed assertions by the popular media in India of the adaptability of traditional forms of family/marriage, we can see the ways in which an emerging capitalist logic here is changing the *contents* of pre-capitalist social institutions till such time as their old forms wear off, for themselves.

A subsequent *India Today* article brought out these contradictions clearly, coding the new thrust on 'choice', 'privacy' and 'pragmatism' into an earlier vocabulary of community living. This was a survey of college students conducted in Delhi, Calcutta, Chennai and Bombay (Pathak 1994). The survey noted that the euphoria over India's 'catching up' with the world was but the flipside of a general relief that an antediluvian 'socialist ideal-ism' had at last been left behind. The new generation of Indian students, the survey proudly proclaimed, were completely unapologetic about their competitive attitude to life, their unabashed self-interest. Such attitudes, the survey suggested, were markers of the 'maturity' of the new generation as opposed to their 'honest but immature' predecessors swearing by Che Guevara and looking for 'causes' to uphold. Of course, it was forced to somewhat reluctantly admit that a price had to be paid—the new genera-tion was probably the most lonely, calculating, overstressed generation of young people that India had ever seen. However, it optimistically concluded that this singular emphasis on individualism might well lead to collective good; the new generation might well be the harbinger of 'social revolution'. It is through such a structure of feeling—overdetermined by notions such as 'dynamism of the market' and 'efficiency of private enterprise'—that liberalization has justified the demise of the Nehru–Mahalanobis model of development.[5] Thus, the disquiet underlying the popular media lies in its attempts to translate an earlier language of socialism into the language of a free-market economy.

I have just discussed Žižek's thesis on the structurally necessary delay between changes in 'content' and changes in 'form' that marks the dialectical process. Žižek further argues that this idea—of consciousness always coming too late, of things becoming what they always-already were (parallel to Lacan's notion of 'in between the two deaths' [1992] and Hegel's notion of repetition in history)—does not represent a model of ontological evolutionism. It demonstrates, rather, the absolute impossibility of accordance between being and knowledge and object and notion. Moreover, this discord does not represent a failure or inadequacy to reach the Ideal. It is instead the positive condition for the consistency of the object. The radical moment of the dialectical process is to recognize in the condition of impossibility, *the conditions of possibility*. Re-reading the Hegelian notion of the 'negation of the negation', Žižek describes as the *point de capiton* or the 'quilting point' this turnaround, this point of reversal, at which an entity turns into its opposite. The significance of the ideological quilt is that it gives consistency to the Symbolic, totalizes an ideology by bringing to a halt the play of signifiers, while in itself being nothing but 'pure difference', a signifier without a signified. At this point an external relation between an entity and its opposite or negative turns into an *internal* self-negation. The 'invisible' agent that makes this process happen—enabling a transformation that however destroys its own grounds of existence—Žižek calls the 'vanishing mediator' (1989: 71–6, 87–9, 201–7; 1991: 16–21, 182–97).

As several contemporary social philosophers have argued, there seems to be a structural link between the principle of enumeration on which the post-despotic state of Western Europe was based, and repeated trends of ethnic cleansing that have swept through 'modern' civil societies.[6] Fascism, it is being increasingly speculated, represents such a Žižekian internal self-negation of liberalism. In the transition from its liberal 'socialist' moment in the Nehruvian era to the proto-fascist guise that post-Independence India has assumed now, one can cite several 'vanishing mediators'—struggles by landless peasants, the women's movement, movements by lower-caste groups, religious minorities and so on—that erupted in the 1960s and 1970s. Loosely paralleling Žižek's analysis of 'Jacobinism', the radical illusion of democratic projects in India also seems to lie in their failure to recognize the ways in which their utopias were *already* realized. It is precisely in the way that the BJP now designates itself as only truly 'secular' party, as the media uses the discourse of 'women's choice' to endlessly display and sexualize them, as upper castes disclaim 'casteism' in the interests of 'national progress', that we can see the ways in which earlier radical projects, in their 'notional content', have been realized. As Žižek says, 'The illusion proper to the "vanishing mediators" is that they refuse to acknowledge, in the corrupted reality over which they lament, the ultimate consequence of their own act—as Lacan would put it, their own message in its true inverted form' (1991: 185).

As I have argued, the New Indian Woman of the popular media too represents such an 'inverted image' of the women's movement: the woman who now translates the discourse of 'women's empowerment' *into* the language of consumer capital. To relate this discussion of the rewriting of gender roles and the accompanying changes in forms of marriage and family to *QSQT*, my analysis of the film s that its most significant aspect was the way in which, while tapping into the resurgent Hindu neo-nationalism,[7] the film refocused the anxiety of this new Hinduism onto the construction of the new couple.

THE ARRIVAL OF HISTORY AND THE 'NEW INDIAN MAN': THE MEDIA IMAGE OF *QAYAMAT SE QAYAMAT TAK*

While retaining its form, capitalism in its present stage has changed its 'contents' so as to incorporate a small class of women into its structure. In doing so, however, there has also been a complementary refiguring of masculinity, the much-hyped 'New Indian Man' who has emerged as a sort of Derridean supplement[8] to the New Indian Woman of the 1980s. The new thinking or sensitive man is a man who is 'liberated' and 'modern', a man who truly understands his successful and intelligent female partner.[9] The ideological function of the new couple, I will contend, is to modulate the explosive social critiques of the women's movement into the institutions of (the nuclear) family and marriage.[10] My reading of *QSQT* will, consequently, now focus on the new masculinity promised by the film.

In this, *QSQT* was clearly reworking an earlier cinematic image of the sensitive hero popularized by Rajesh Khanna in the late 1960s. As is well known, the Rajesh Khanna persona was constructed by Gulshan Nanda, a

Hindi novelist emerging out of the social romance tradition of Hindi literature (Orsini 1995). After an unsuccessful literary career, Nanda went on to establish a reputation for himself as a scriptwriter in Bombay. In hugely successful films like *Kati Patang* (Torn Kite, 1970) and *Amar Prem* (Eternal Love, 1971), Rajesh Khanna's screen persona[11] popularized a social-reform-oriented middle-class narrative that perhaps has its earliest manifestations in Indian cinema with the New Theatre productions of the 1920s and 1930s. The significance of this literary–cinematic tradition for my reading is that, like in Hollywood, the 'sensitive hero' in Bombay too emerged out of narrative traditions crucially negotiating female desire. American cultural theorist Tania Modleski has, in fact, made an interesting observation regarding the women's films of 1940s and 1950s Hollywood which also had a 'feminized' rather than a 'macho' hero. Modleski suggests this was because the feminized hero allows the heroine to 'postpone the powers of patriarchy' (1987: 327). Drawing on Modleski, I analyse *QSQT* to show the ways in which the New Indian Man of 1980s Bombay re-inflected the 'sensitive hero' image of the 1960s and 1970s into a specifically post-liberalization idiom.

As mentioned earlier, the new love story of 1980s' Bombay draws significantly on 1970s' middle cinema. Given this trajectory, *QSQT* was a small-budget film. Its pre-release publicity was relatively low key. Further, as with the new commercial films of the 1980s, the media image of *QSQT* also focused on playing up its 'difference' from the typical song-and-dance entertainer. In this attempt to construct difference, the most important marketing strategy used by *QSQT* was that of foregrounding the intellectual credentials of its young director, Mansoor Khan, son of the producer Nasir Hussain. It was publicized that Mansoor Khan was a computer scientist with degrees from both Cornell *and* the Massachusetts Institute of Technology. As opposed to the average 'commercial' director who made only second-rate films, therefore, it was anticipated that *QSQT* would be 'different' from the mainstream Bombay 'commercial'. A representative interview in *Filmfare* profiled Mansoor Khan thus:

> His office at Nasir Husain Films Pvt. Ltd. is small but tidy. On one side of the wall is a shelf of books. A pretty girl is glued to an IBM computer, which rests prominently alongside the shelf. The

remaining space is taken up by the official-looking mahogany desk. Behind it sits 29-year-old Mansoor Husain Khan, clad in jeans and a checked shirt. He reminds you of one of those yuppies who spend their time zooming up and down Bombay's suburban lanes in fast cars, or lounging around with beautiful girls [. . .] 'I hate bullshitters, fast cars and dumb women,' he says forcefully, squashing my first impressions of him (Shanmugam 1988: 55).

The article went on to list Mansoor Khan's 'trendy' hobbies—astronomy, amateur telegraphy and sailing. As opposed to being just a 'rich kid', Mansoor Khan was constructed as the cosmopolitan, intelligent, modern man. Therefore, the article argued that *QSQT*, Khan's debut venture, too was a film in which the idealistic young lovers had been given a 'slice of realism culled from everyday life'.

I have argued in the last chapter that the changes precipitated by the liberalization process in Bombay's production base saw the emergence of televisually mediated aesthetics premised on the everyday as well as the entry of a whole new crop of actors and actresses. In this tradition, *QSQT* also introduced a 'fresh' lead pair. Moreover, unlike Star images of the 1950s, which played up certain feudal notions of glamour, the media images of Aamir Khan and Juhi Chawla insisted on their 'ordinariness', reinforcing the idea that they were just like the middle-class spectators in the audience.

However, given that *QSQT* was produced by Khan's uncle and directed by his cousin, its pre-release publicity focused almost exclusively on Khan. There were huge hoardings put up all over Bombay asking, 'Who's Aamir Khan?' Though pre-release interviews with Khan are not many, once the box-office collections of *QSQT* started picking up, there emerged a whole spate of interviews with him in all the prominent film magazines. Moreover, the media constructed Khan as the iconic 'Mills and Boon hero'. Further, given the timing of these interviews, they reinforced dramatically a public identification between *QSQT*'s promise of a new masculinity and the 'real Aamir'. A representative *Stardust* interview constructed Khan's persona in these terms:

There is something very ugly about this beautiful place people poetically call tinsel town [. . . But instinct] told me that Aamir

Khan was different [. . .] Alone with Aamir and that smile that can crack crystal. Facing me is a boy who is quiet, [. . .] intelligent [. . .] Behind those eyes and that face that has set the country ablaze is somebody else. Somebody who is honest, not afraid to say what he wants, express what he feels. A frank somebody called Aamir [. . .] (Merchant 1988a: 39).

Article after article reiterated this idea—of a sensitive young man trying to place his success in perspective, of a sincerity or idealism that made Aamir Khan decisively different from the crassly materialistic Star. In fact, there was an interesting paradox here. To sell the idea of a teenage heart-throb, the fact that Khan was already married was kept a closely guarded secret before the release of *QSQT*. Curiously, when this became public knowledge, it did not damage the image of boyish honesty that Khan had cultivated, but came to be seen instead as a reinforcement of the idealism he was constructed as representing. In a subsequent *Stardust* article, 'Love Triumphs', Khan announced that he had been married three years earlier. As Khan now recollected his 'real life' drama, his secret marriage with his 18-year-old Hindu girlfriend in the face of stiff parental opposition, he described how painful it had been for him to hide the woman he so dearly loved: 'I hated to lie [. . .] but I couldn't just think of myself [. . .] Nasir Uncle and my family had put in a lot of money, it was my cousin Mansoor's first film [. . .]' (Merchant 1988b).[12] Coded thus, Khan's 'professionalism' became another marker of his loyalty to his family; a further proof of the sincerity of his feelings. Moreover, contributing to the New Indian Man image, Khan's wife, Reena, was said to be involved in his every decision. To reinforce the idea of the young man's sensitivity were thrown in odd comments like: 'I respect her [Reena] a lot. She still goes by her old sur-name. I don't see why after 20 years of living with it, she should suddenly change it for me' (ibid.).

The article concludes triumphantly:

Two and a half years ago an unknown young man and an unknown young woman pledged a promise to spend the rest of their lives together. Ignoring all obstacles, fighting all odds, they had a secret marriage. Then something happened. The young man didn't remain unknown [. . .] Just last month I had written how this young man could look back in anger. Something very commendable in a world of humans who hate what they've left behind. Now he has proved himself beyond even that. He has the courage to look back in honesty too (ibid.).[13]

It was the odd article indeed that questioned this media image of Khan as embodiment of all the youthful idealism that 'romance' popularly suggests. However, the *Showtime* article, 'Games Aamir Plays', revealed that though *QSQT* was Khan's first film to be released, he had stalled the release of an earlier film, *Raakh* (Ash, 1989), made by his friend, Aditya Bhattacharya, in order to not destroy his 'lover boy' image. Like any other 'professional' in the industry, the article indicted, Khan too had ditched his friend to further his own career:

Earlier Aditya had problems releasing his film because his hero Aamir then was an unknown young actor trying to achieve stardom [. . .] So what went wrong? Nothing except that Aamir Khan became a star. And his face his fortune, he is the lover boy and nothing would induce him to voluntarily change that image [. . .] (Nivedita and Sandhya 1988: 45–6)

Though, in comparison, *QSQT*'s heroine, Juhi Chawla, received insignificant publicity, she was publicly recognized as a former Miss India. Moreover, after a disastrous debut with *Sultanat* (Sultanate, 1986), Chawla had taken to acting in B-grade Tamil and Kannada films and even changed her screen-name for both! Pre-release interviews with Chawla are almost non-existent. After the commercial success of *QSQT*, too, it was Khan on whom most of the media's attention was focused. In one of the few interviews with Chawla that appeared after the release of *QSQT*, she acknowledged that the pre-release publicity had been one-sided. But she 'explained' this as simple nepotism (Sadarangani, 1988). In the following sections, my attempt will be to indicate that there was a *structural* logic to the fact that it was Khan, rather than Chawla, who emerged as the quintessential lover in *QSQT* or, in fact, the national imaginary.

THE DHANAKPUR CONNECTION, OR WHY DOES MADHUMATI COMMIT SUICIDE?

In Proppian terms, the *QSQT* narrative can be plotted thus:

Initial Situation	Liminal Space	Final Situation
[Dhanakpur/countryside]	[Delhi/city]	[Countryside]

The Dhanakpur segment, i.e. the pre-credit segment of *QSQT*, can also be read as the narrative's prehistory, 'explaining' the displacement of the rural gentry from their 'organic' location in the countryside to the impersonal milieu of the city of Delhi. The opening shots of the film invoke arcadian images of Dhanakpur. Mid-shots from a straight-on angle, the camera pans over lush fields to frame landlord Jaswant Singh resting on a *khatia* (a camp bed) with his *munshi* (accountant), while his younger brother Dhanraj supervises the farmhands. While an obvious point of comment is the idealization of the feudal aristocracy, the establishing shots also reinforce the feudal code of respecting elders. Into this picture enters *munim* (village priest/mediator of marital alliances) Totaram, with an invitation to their neighbour's son, Ratan Singh's, wedding.

The primary concern of the narrative is therefore articulated. In the brief exchange of pleasantries that follows we come to know that Jaswant Singh has been a parent-figure to all his siblings. The *munim* ends by telling Jaswant that it is now time for Jaswant, too, to 'settle down'. Jaswant replies that he will do so once his youngest sister Madhumati has been married. This, then, remains the unfulfilled dream of *QSQT*. Jaswant, the ideal brother/parent-figure, is not able to set up his own familial space because of the 'disaster' that Madhumati brings upon the family through her relationship with Ratan.

Yet, underlying the initial impressions of leisure, Dhanakpur is actually bristling with change. The intrusions of the off-screen space of modernity/the city into Dhanakpur's idyllic world are marked not only by the jeep standing in Jaswant's fields that the camera casually pans over. But through Totaram we come to know that Dhanraj was also educated in the city and that their other sister, Parvati, too lives in Delhi after her marriage. However, the changes wrought by modernity/the city into Dhanakpur's social fabric are much more fundamental. We soon come to know that Madhumati has lost her virginity and honour. She is pregnant, but Ratan now disowns his responsibility in the affair. Raghubir Singh, Ratan's father, being aware of his son's responsibility, refuses to entertain the possibility of a marital alliance on the ground that a woman who has lost her 'purity' before marriage is not good enough to be the family bride. Having failed to obtain justice from Raghubir, Jaswant decides that his entire family will move to Delhi to avoid the collective shame that is certain to befall them. At this point Madhumati commits suicide, setting the stage for the ensuing family feud.

As the editors of the *Encyclopaedia of Indian Cinema* have also noted, *QSQT* presents a re-staging of the Romeo–Juliet myth (Rajadhyaksha and Willemen 1994: 448–9). From this perspective, the immediate point of comment is *QSQT*'s mobilization of a specific North Indian feudal/upper-caste identity, the notion of the 'Rajput'. This definition of caste identity is, of course, crucially predicated on the control of female sexuality. Invoked in endless popular myths about queens who 'voluntarily' committed sati to defend their honour against 'lustful' Muslim invaders, such fundamentalist re-tellings of Indian history enjoy wide currency within the nation today. Represented by the notion of a woman's honour, such definitions of 'Rajputness' legitimize only those expressions of female sexuality that are within the confines of a monogamous, patriarchal marriage.

However, as recent feminist historiography has shown, such a definition of caste identity emerged in India only in the nineteenth century, concomitant with the consolidation of the colonial state in India and the accompanying changes that it introduced in property laws that worked to the disadvantage of women across the social hierarchy.[14] In the process, the many (and conflicting) pre-colonial discourses on sexuality and gender relations were marginalized, and the monogamous, patriarchal marriage set up as the norm.[15] The emergent neo-nationalism of Hindutva, which has also castigated feminism as 'Western', however, naturalizes such patriarchal gender constructions in its aggressively masculine world. While women are the custodians of honour, men are their valiant protectors. An entire cult of blood and firearms is then exalted as the essence of a virile and purifying Hindu/Indian culture that is going to be reborn.[16]

Given this cultural context, it is significant that Madhumati does *not* face any active condemnation from her family. In fact, as Jaswant tells Ratan, it is 'human' to err. And although Madhumati is unaware of it, in a remarkable gesture, Ratan's mother actually tries to intervene on her behalf. By doing so, she also ideologically distances herself from her own family and the ground is prepared for Rashmi's (Chawla's) subsequent identification with her grandmother. Though premarital pregnancy is coded as a 'mistake', the narrative unequivocally blames *Ratan*, rather than Madhumati, for the whole affair. The discourse drawn upon is one where a man's word is, literally, his identity. Thus, Ratan, the 'emasculated' Rajput, lacking the courage to stand by his word, represents the most indicting lack in Dhanakpur's social world. The function of collective villainy consequently falls squarely on the 'bad' Rajput family of Ratan, his elder brother Randhir and their father Raghubir, who have gone back on their promise and violated what, in popular consciousness, constitutes the defining characteristic of the true Rajput.

But while Madhumati is obviously humiliated by Ratan reneging on his promise, the troubling question still remains: why does she kill herself? This is significant because, unlike in the conventional Bombay film, Madhumati's family stands by her. Although this plays up Ratan's 'cowardice', abortion *is* mentioned as a possibility. Further, despite Dhanraj's dramatic outburst (given that Parvati's husband Bhagwan Das has a prosperous business in Delhi, which Bhagwan has already invited Jaswant to join), the family also has the option to move elsewhere.

In Žižekian–Lacanian terms the unconscious is not some transcendent, unattainable thing. It is, rather, an overlooking, with the overlooking itself being its condition of possibility. Apropos Hegel's theory of repetition in history, Žižek suggests that when an event erupts for the first time it is experienced as an arbitrary, traumatic event—something which could have also *not* happened. It is only through repetition that it finds its place in the symbolic network and is granted the status of symbolic necessity (1989: 55–84). I have discussed earlier the anxiety in the national imaginary caused by the New Indian Woman and have argued that the dominant ideology coded the related social changes as merely notional changes of 'content' within *older* forms of family/marriage. From this perspective, Madhumati has to die because otherwise the narrative would have to be 'written differently'.[17] It is necessary that Jaswant, Raghubir's wife and Madhumati *all* use the vocabulary of 'shame', 'honour' and 'betrayal'—remaining conceptually bound to a feudal code of values—so that they are trapped in the contradiction that Raghubir later makes explicit. In a feudal system of representation, a woman's worth is guaranteed by her 'virtue', which is represented within this symbolic network by absence, especially the absence of sexual desire and sexual knowledge. This is thus a framework that is structurally incompatible with the discourse of a woman's 'right to (sexual) pleasure'.[18] By coding premarital sex as 'error', the narrative of *QSQT* plays up Ratan's guilt—and implicitly Madhumati's victimhood—*repressing* the discourse of women's rights. This is the act of 'overlooking' that we witness in the Dhanakpur section of the film. It is necessary for Madhumati to remain symbolically bound to a feudal code of honour in order for the narrative to 'overlook' the Real of Dhanakpur's world—the anxiety of the phallic woman, the trauma caused by the woman asserting her 'right to choose'. The most deep-seated change in Dhanakpur's social fabric caused by the offscreen space of modernity/the city is, therefore, this free-market discourse of 'choice' that has filtered in, unawares. To decisively transfer the guilt on to Ratan, Madhumati has to die (honourably, by committing suicide,) instead of starting a new life in the city. Dhanraj Singh can then appropriate Madhumati's assertion of her 'right to sexual pleasure' into the symbolic universe of shame/betrayal and shoot Ratan in an act of 'Rajput valour'.

The 'right to die', as manifested through suicide, Foucault suggests, causes such conceptual confusion within us because it attests to an individual's determination to die, whereas the post-despotic state that emerged with the Enlightenment in Europe legitimizes itself primarily through the idea of fostering the 'right to live' (1990: 131–60). With specific reference to India, Gayatri Chakravorty Spivak (1985, 1988), Lata Mani (1987, 1993) and Rajeswari Sunder Rajan (1993) have debated in different contexts the conceptual problems in reading acts such as sati either in terms of 'intentionality' or existential choice (see also Loomba 1993). Focusing instead on the phenomenology of pain, Rajan makes the important point that it is an inherent *resistance* to pain that impels either the individual or collective suffering subject towards action: '*It is therefore as one who acts/reacts rather than as one who invites assistance that one must regard the subject in pain*' (1993: 302; emphasis added).

Madhumati's suicide can, now, be read in the context of an earlier scene. On hearing of Ratan's wedding plans, Madhumati's immediate response is not to turn to her brothers for help. Instead, she goes to Ratan's home and asks *him* to refuse the alliance. It is only after Ratan backs out that she tells her family of their affair. All efforts having failed, she overhears her brothers agonizing over their next move. The camera zooms in to reveal her horrified expression as she realizes the 'disaster' she has brought upon them. Her suicide is a gesture that, she hopes, will save her family from shame. In effect she commits a double transgression. Not only does she make a sexual choice but, in a society based on the power of fostering life, she chooses to die. By focusing exclusively on Ratan's guilt, however, the narrative 'overlooks' this assertion of female agency. It is only when the discourse of a 'woman's right to choose' erupts for the second time, with Ratan's niece Rashmi, that it achieves the status of symbolic necessity. However, since it is Ratan who is coded as the 'failed' partner in the first generation, the symbolic debt opened up by Madhumati's suicide will now be repaid by her nephew Raj, the New Indian Man. Thus, Raj sees Rashmi for the first time at Dhanakpur while Rashmi remains oblivious of his gaze. So, even though the move from Dhanakpur to Delhi of both the families makes it inevitable that Raj and Rashmi both learn the language of consumerism, the market discourse of free choice is mobilized in such a manner that female agency is effectively controlled in the second generation too.

The move of Jaswant's family from Dhanakpur to Delhi is, moreover, framed by two highly charged images. The first is that of Dhanraj behind bars, imprisoned by the new law that translates the heroism of Rajput honour into the prosaic language of crime. The second is that of the train carrying the rest of Jaswant's family to the city. Given the historically loaded allegories of modernity that the train as an image in Bombay cinema has carried, this shot marks the decisive conceptual re-grounding that the move from the countryside to the city signifies in the film. I will return to these images later. My aim will be to show that the narrative returns to a reformed countryside at the end. Before it can do so, however, the protagonists have to traverse the liminal space of the city. So, we will now analyse the semantic re-grounding signified by Delhi.

THE DELHI GENERATION

The city in *QSQT* functions as the liminal space that Jaswant's family have to traverse in order to repay the dead Madhumati's symbolic debt. In Delhi, Jaswant's family soon become prosperous textile merchants. This trajectory is extremely significant given that it is from a similar section of the regional bourgeoisie, one that has only recently become urbanized as a consequence of its displacement from ownership of agricultural land, that political parties such as the BJP draw their maximum support. While within the narrative world of *QSQT* the reasons for this forced emigration are located in a premarital pregnancy, in the master-text that a section of the bourgeoisie is currently mobilizing, it is primarily the 'Muslims' (said to be 'spooning off the state') who are imaginatively held responsible for this dislocation. As noted earlier, *QSQT* significantly refocuses the anxiety of the Hindutva ideology on to the women's movement. Here, the upper-caste woman asserting her choice is now held responsible for the traumas currently besieging her social class. It is ultimately on account of Madhumati that Jaswant cannot ever marry.[19]

Even in Delhi's urban milieu, both families retain their caste identities. The process of capitalist urbanization is thus presented in seamless continuity with feudal practices of self-description. Thus Raj, the New Indian Man, goes to 'Rajput College'. In spite of being city-bred, he retains 'aristocratic'/feudal hobbies like game-hunting. And for a family friend's wedding, all the men in Jaswant's family wear the traditional Rajput *pagdi* (the ceremonial turban which denotes caste-status). As Niranjana has observed in a different context, the conjuncture of multinational capital and Hindu neo-nationalism in the 1980–90s has meant that the 'Hindu' coding in recent films is indistinguishable from secular/cosmopolitan coding (1994: 79–82). Thus, Raj is normally shown only wearing jeans and T-shirts. Only Raj's Muslim friends wear pathan suits. The farewell party at the Rajput College is peopled with teenagers dressed in Western clothes, dancing to rock-n-roll. Raj himself sings the catchy pop number '*Papa Kehte Hain Bada Naam Karega*' ('My Father says his Son will be Famous Someday'). In everyday life Raj addresses his father as 'pitaji'—a Sanskritized usage of Hindi, befitting the feudal aristocracy. For the purposes of the college social, however, this becomes transformed into the Anglicized 'papa'. Their plush upper-class home too has all the signs of the new consumerism that has been the hallmark of the penetration of multinational capital.

There has, however, been a significant 'lack' in Raj's upbringing. Being in prison, Dhanraj has not been able to school his son into the feudal values that Dhanakpur represents. This lack has been filled by Raj's uncle, Jaswant Singh. Within the diegesis, it is Jaswant, the 'true' father, who accounts for the definite feminization of the hero. Thus, though a Rajput, Raj is sensitive and romantic. He has no 'material' ambitions such as being an engineer or succeeding in business. He wishes only to leave his mark in the ethereal world of love. As he sings:

Banda yeh khoobsurat kaam karega
Dil ki duniya mein apna naam karega.
Meri nazar se, dekho to yaaron, ke meri manzil hai yahaan.

(This man will accomplish the beautiful task of leaving his mark
in the world of romance. That is his destiny.)

As Rajadhyaksha and Willemen have also noted, it is through this very emphasis on 'matters of the heart'—and the connotations of passivity/ femininity this evokes—that Raj is repeatedly placed in confrontations with his father Dhanraj. One of Dhanraj's first requests to his family after his release from prison is that there be no mention of the traumas that the family has gone through. In a startling instance of the 'return of the repressed', however, immediately following shots of Dhanraj taking his place as head of the family at the dinner table and occupying the proprietor's chair at work, is the arrival of the court summons from Raghubir. This necessitates that Raj go to Dhanakpur, initiating the whole subsequent chain of events culminating in his and Rashmi's death.

Father and son also have completely different notions of achievement. The two opposing definitions of masculinity come to a climactic confrontation on the evening of Rashmi's forced engagement to Roop Singh. Raj and Rashmi's attempt to elope has been thwarted. Beaten up by Rashmi's father's thugs, Raj has to then face the wrath of Dhanraj Singh. Dhanraj, on his part, has decided to whip Raj to death for disregarding the suffering caused to their family by that of Rashmi's. Therefore, when Jaswant tries to intervene, Dhanraj even rebuffs Jaswant in a shocking transgression of the feudal code of respecting elders. However, overwhelmed by regret at his own behaviour, when Raj does finally return home, Dhanraj lovingly embraces his son. This scene is important because Raj—throwing overboard notions of the macho Rajput—openly bursts into tears on his father's shoulders. This is also the last meeting between Dhanraj and Raj and implicitly enacts the entire family's acceptance of Rashmi. It also shows that it is the philosophy of the true father, Jaswant, that has been passed on to the new generation. Dhanraj's code of living by the gun (*'khoon bahana to Rajputon ki shaan hain'*/'shedding blood in battle is the glory of the Rajput race') has been tempered into the language of love and understanding.

The redefinition of masculinity that *QSQT* undertakes is thus centrally predicated on a critique of arbitrary, despotic and feudal codes of male behaviour. Represented by Jaswant Singh, male identity in *QSQT* is premised on the ability to perform nurturing, rather than protective, functions. Witness this moment of extreme confusion in the text. Dhanraj has been released from prison before his term. Raj is jubilantly calling the rest of the family down to the living room. Over the image of *Jaswant*, Raj's voice excitedly says, 'Maa!'

From the initial shots of the film itself, Jaswant's 'feminization'—his nearness to the world of nature and feeling—is played up.[20] At a later point Jaswant himself reminds Dhanraj how he had nursed Raj as a child. In fact, we can now read back and ask—unlike Rashmi, why does Raj *not* have grand-parents? The answer, I would contend, is that both Raj's grandparents have to be dead so that Jaswant can take on the role of provider as well as nurturer to his siblings. Raj's closeness with Jaswant parallels Rashmi's attachment to her grandmother. By taking on nurturing functions, Jaswant ideologically distances himself from his own (the 1950s' generation) and allies himself with Rashmi's grandmother instead, as bearer of 'good tradition'.

Moreover, such a feminization of the hero in *QSQT* is also the obverse of the discourse of the 'woman's right to choose'. As Rajadhyaksha (1990), Velicheti (1993) and Niranjana (1991) have all analysed in different con-texts, the new femininity of 1980s' and 1990s' popular cinema is enabled by the new consumerism. The re-appropriation of tradition—on which the new consumerism is based—has meant that, as opposed to being the bearer of regional specificity, the new woman is now simply marked as 'Indian'. Further, the ideological burden placed on the new woman is to modulate 'good tradition' into 'good modernity'. It is at this intersection of American English (or the new consumerism) and emergent notions of 'ethnic traditionalism' that *QSQT*'s heroine, Rashmi, is located. Rashmi's defining behavioural characteristics include her highly formal usage of Hindi as well as what is coded as her desirably deferential attitude to her 'elders'. For the major part of the film she is dressed in virginal white. She usually also wears only *ghagra cholis*, a dress that appropriates the identity of the iconic rural belle as ethnic fashion[21] and is significant to the extent that Rashmi wears this apparel in Delhi's urban milieu.

Moreover, as with Raj, her traditionalism cohabits effortlessly with a certain cosmopolitanism. She is completely familiar with the language of a consumer culture. She speaks fluent English, wields a camera, plays Frisbee with her boyfriend, goes camping and is at ease in settings of plush hotels. Like the other New Indian Women of the 1980s' and 1990s' commercial films, Rashmi also displays a certain sexual abandon. It is she who initiates the relationship. She is taking photographs of the setting sun as Raj enters her frame, a romantic silhouette at sunset. She then gives Raj her photograph and asks him to meet her the next evening. Later, as the two try to find their way out of the jungle, she not only gives Raj all 'relevant' details such as her age, educational background and marital status but, as scored beautifully through the '*Ghazab Ka Hai Din*' ('It's a Miraculous Day') number, tells him openly that she has fallen in love without, of course, placing Raj under any obligation to reciprocate. Finally, it is Rashmi who runs away from her home on the night of her engagement to Roop Singh.

In a perceptively argued essay, Teresa De Lauretis suggests that the ideological function of conventional/Oedipal narratives, is 'to seduce women into femininity'. Rereading Freud, she observes:

> The end of the girl's journey, if successful, will bring her to the place where the boy will find her, like Sleeping Beauty, awaiting him, Prince Charming. For the boy has been promised, by the social contract he has entered into at his Oedipal phase, that he will find [the] woman at the end of *his* journey. Thus the itinerary of the female's journey, mapped from the very start on the territory of her own body [. . .] is guided by a compass pointing not to reproduction as the fulfilment of her biological destiny, but more

exactly to the fulfilment of the promise made to the 'little man' of his social contract, his biological and affective destiny—and to the fulfilment of his desire (1984: 133).

With regard to the new women of Telugu cinema, Niranjana (1991) and Velicheti (1993) have both observed that the sexual aggressiveness of the new heroines is sanctioned only insofar as it either cannot be consummated or is coded as 'childishness'. With reference to *QSQT*, Rashmi's modernity—her assertion of choice—is problematic to the extent that it posits the institutions of marriage and family as the only legitimate conduits into which this desire can be channelled.

Rashmi's 'feminism', then, needs to be qualified. Thus, we can recall that even though Rashmi takes the initiative in the relationship, it is a little more than innocent prattle since she does not know Raj's true identity. It works instead to highlight Raj's emotional conflicts as he defers his desire out of loyalty to his family. Of course, once Rashmi actively seeks his 'guardianship', he stands by his word and takes on a protective role.

This is not to deny that Rashmi's decision to question her father's overbearing attitudes and its corollary—a system of marriage in which women lack *any* element of choice—is laudable. The difficulty arises because within *QSQT* too, the 'problem' of women is presented as merely a problem arising out of 'incompatibility'. The solution, consequently, is to portray a sensitive husband such as Raj, as opposed to the father's choice, i.e. Roop Singh. Deflecting critiques of women's enforced restriction within the de-politicized realms of domesticity and childbearing, *QSQT* sets up the active desire for these very roles as a woman's 'free choice', fitting in with De Lauretis' analysis of the 'destination' of female desire in Oedipal narratives.

BACKLASH: THE 'NEW' FAMILY

Questioning the inherent formal subversiveness attributed to melodrama by critics such as Thomas Elsaesser, Mulvey has suggested that the 'excess' generated by Hollywood melodrama works instead as a 'safety valve' to contain the sexual contradictions of bourgeois patriarchy.[22] Mulvey has proposed instead a distinction between melodramas structured by a female point of view and those which play out male Oedipal dramas to foreground the pressure exerted by feminine desire on melodrama's conventional form

(1994: 121–34). I have argued earlier that though Jaswant's family has to move to Delhi to repress the trauma of the dead Madhumati's transgressive desire, by coding her as 'victim', the narrative transfers the agency of repaying the symbolic debt opened by her suicide onto Raj. Bracketed within two versions of the 'Papa Kehte Hain' number, it is Raj's desire to leave his mark in the world of romance that the post-credit segment of QSQT consequently articulates.

The 'family' that Raj and Rashmi set up is, moreover, presented as utopian. This is a family ostensibly based on complete equality between partners, unlike that of the relationship between spouses of the 1950s' generation, where women are shown to lack any decisive authority. In fact, if we go back further, we can recall the scene from the pre-credit sequence of the film where Raghubir threatens to kill his wife if she dares to intervene on Madhumati's behalf. Similarly, Randhir also reminds his daughter, Rashmi, at a later point that it is 'tradition' that a wife does only as her husband wants her to. The point being made here is that it is up to Roop Singh to decide whether Rashmi should continue her education.

However, given that Raj is acting out the philosophy of his 'true' father, Jaswant, his and Rashmi's marriage is predicated on nurturance or support. The formation of the couple through Raj and Rashmi thus symbolically enacts the unfulfilled desire of the narrative to establish a familial space for Jaswant himself. Importantly, Raj and Rashmi set up home in a ruined temple, i.e. a physical space that already has divine sanction. Also, they have what is defined by Hindu rites as a Gandharva wedding, giving their cohabitation social respectability. This is then a marriage that enacts the ultimate market fantasy of 'free choice'. Thus, when Rashmi confesses her complete lack of culinary skills, Raj, the New Indian Man, blames himself. 'I should have asked you first if you could cook,' he says. One of the most popular dialogues of the film was, in fact, Raj asking Rashmi, 'I too have several shortcomings. Would you stop loving me because of them?' Dialogues such as these were played up as hallmarks of the realism that Mansoor Khan was meant to have infused into the film. Within the diegesis, they play up the innocence of the lovers, making parental opposition all the more unjustified.[23] As the young lovers sing—'Akele Hain To Kya Gham Hai' ('What Does it Matter that We are All Alone').

However, while the enmity between the families provides the immediate reason for Raj and Rashmi setting up home 'somewhere far away from civilization', I would argue that another function is also served by locating the couple in the countryside. This is not to deny Bombay's convention of picturizing 'love' in backgrounds that seem straight out of the *National Geographic*. But such a convention in *QSQT* gains its significance from its purported naturalism—the idea that, like the middle cinema of the 1970s, *QSQT* was a commercial film presenting pictures of the everyday. My contention is that by setting up home in the wilderness, Rashmi can give up her education by choice. Consequently, the narrative is able to side-step the entire range of problems currently besieging the institutions of family and marriage and attributed to the New Indian Woman who is defined primarily through her successful career. It can instead reassert traditional gender roles as natural. Thus, we have Raj going into the jungle to gather firewood while Rashmi cooks his favourite food (vegetarianism serving here as a marker of an upper-caste status).

Raj's ambition is not merely to 'fall in love'. He also wishes to 'leave his mark' in the world of romance and desires a kind of 'intense living'. Thus, once couple-formation has been achieved, the narrative logic makes it imperative that both Raj and Rashmi die before mundane questions of the everyday intrude on their idyll. This, in turn, takes us to representations of villainy in *QSQT*. Given the film's thrust on a redefinition of masculinity, it is among the male rather than female characters that role-conflicts in *QSQT* erupt. While the thugs who try to molest Rashmi in the jungle represent 'bad modernity', Ratan/Randhir/Raghubir Singh represent 'bad tradition'. While Jaswant was ahead of his time, Raj is obviously the New Indian Man, retaining his Rajput valour even as he endorses the philosophy of free choice. Thus, he tells Rashmi that their parents do not own them and that they have the right to make their own choices.

The burden of the narrative, therefore, is not so much the construction of an Other as the creation of a space for the new consumerism within the older feudal view of the countryside—a reformed Dhanakpur, a cohabitation of patriarchal ideologies that Raj and Rashmi's nuclear family in the wilderness visually enacts. If we go back for a moment to Žižek's 'vanishing mediators', Raj and Rashmi's family then is the true/inverted image of the popular struggles of the 1960–70s, especially the women's movement, a chauvinistic definition of intimacy now set up as the ultimate female fantasy.

THINGS CHANGE PRECISELY INSOFAR AS THEY REMAIN THE SAME

Let us return to the shot of Dhanraj handcuffed before the new law, marking the transition from Dhanakpur to Delhi. In his analysis of narrative form, Jameson identifies three different 'levels' of interpretation, suggesting that in the third, the historical level, form itself becomes the bearer of ideological content (1981: 74–102). Following Jameson, Prasad has analysed the ways in which the form of the 1950–60s' Bombay melodrama was overdetermined by the ideological contradictions of the Nehruvian era. He has also drawn attention to the pressure that the emerging dominance of capital in the 1980–90s seems to be exerting on the feudal form of the Bombay film (1996: 27–43).

The problem with the textual form of *QSQT* then is that, while changing in notional content, its form seems to fit an earlier feudal mould. The denouement of the film is the (implied) incorporation of the nuclear unit constituted by Raj and Rashmi into Jaswant's extended family, containing the centrifugal possibilities generated by their romance. My contention, however, is that it is the shot marking the transition to the new law which presents the key moment in the analysis of narrative form here. If we recall Žižek's thesis of the necessary delay between changes in content and changes in form that marks the dialectical process, then changes in the Symbolic first erupt as changes in content, which are, moreover, coded as strengthening the *old* form of a social institution.

From this perspective, the 'double ending' of the feudal melodrama as analysed by Prasad formally enacted the endorsement of the exemplary feudal subject by the law of the capitalist state. Thus the melodrama of 1950s' Bombay always saw the police 'arriving late', after the hero had already vanquished the villain. In *QSQT*, in contrast, there is a violent disjunction between the exemplary Rajput, Dhanraj Singh, and the new law. The code of feudal chivalry here has been decisively replaced by the dull, grey ('formally' equalizing) law of the capitalist state. Consequently, it is the reclaiming of a *feudal* 'distinction' that is now the aim of the post-credit segment of the narrative.

Considering Raj's ambition to leave his mark in the world of romance, the death of the couple has to be spectacular. However, the post-credit sequence is also set in the changed semantic context signified by the city, i.e. Delhi. Thus, in contrast to Dhanraj Singh who shoots Ratan in broad daylight in the feudal world of Dhanakpur, Randhir Singh has to hire a mercenary to kill Raj. But for Raj, to be killed by a mercenary would take away from the 'Rajputness' he retains despite his sensitivity. The only possible denouement, then, is the one we actually have. First, Raj kills the mercenary who has, in the meantime, shot Rashmi. Then, as the ultimate act of Rajput valour, Raj kills himself with the knife (clearly a phallic symbol) that Rashmi has presented him. By doing so, not only does Raj repay his symbolic debt to Madhumati, but he also evokes the splendour of feudal chivalry in death even as he mobilizes the market fantasy of free choice in life. This, then, is how things have changed, precisely to the extent that they have remained the same. While *QSQT* works within the mould of the feudal melodrama, its ending suggests a change of equations—it is no longer the law that endorses the feudal subject. It is rather the citizen-subject who is now trying to reclaim the 'distinction' or 'exemplariness' of an earlier feudal era. Thus, the absence of the police at the climactic confrontation. Instead, we again have Dhanraj carrying his rifle.

Drawing homologies between the structure of the detective story, the process of archaeological excavation and psychoanalysis, Mulvey (1989: 177–201) has pointed out that in all three, it is through the act of re-telling that events of the past are brought to consciousness. The transformative power of narrative analysis, Mulvey argues, is that it is only through such an act of re-telling that unassimilated traumas may first be recognized, and then worked through. An analysis of popular culture from this perspective, she goes on to suggest, can enable us to work through the repressed collective traumas of a society. Using Mulvey, I have attempted to read a representative love story of 1980s' Bombay to excavate the contradictions of caste/class–gender that mark the present-day nation. As the New Right aggressively occupies the terrain of culture, re-narrating our pasts to ourselves seems a task of great historical urgency.

Notes

1   See Appendix I for plot summary.

2   The significance of *QSQT* to the 'new' love stories of 1980–90s' Bombay is
    evident from the fact that it has also been the object of analysis of two other
    recent studies of 1980s' Bombay cinema, Sanjukta Tultul Ghosh (1992)
    and Lalitha Gopalan (1993). My reading of the film, however, differs
    substantially from both. Ghosh analyses *QSQT* in terms of a completely
    ahistorical set of Proppian 'narrative functions'. Further, my reading of
    the film differs from Gopalan's analysis in two major ways. Analysing Bom-
    bay's love stories from the perspective of the cinematic technique of *coitus
    interruptus*, Gopalan argues that this technique operates in *QSQT* through
    the way in which the second-generation romance in the film is sanitized
    of the 'excesses' of the first. Endorsing her broad argument about *coitus
    interruptus* as a technique that reinforces state-attitudes to the 'population
    question', my reading proposes that it is the *lower* middle class, the referent
    of the anti-hero genre, that is the target of the state-drive on the 'small
    family norm'. The upper middle class represented by *QSQT*, on the con-
    trary, is haunted by the cultural memory of a feudal past; the whole re-
    launching of 'tradition' that marks the Hindutva project. The Raj–Rashmi
    romance needs to be seen, instead, in terms of the way in which the joint
    family is being reconfigured in the new conjuncture of Hindu neo-nation-
    alism and multinational capital. This leads to my related, and second,
    disagreement with Gopalan's analysis. Reading *coitus interruputus* as a tech-
    nique that tries to salvage the unpenetrated female body as a displaced
    stand-in for a unified Indian nation, Gopalan notes that internal critiques
    of nationhood emerging in the 1970s and 1980s have seen a related re-
    placement of the *coitus interruptus* technique by sanitized representations
    of sexuality. She goes on to suggest that the idea of woman-as-nation has
    therefore now been replaced by an anxiety over retaining women within
    the domestic space, an anxiety she attributes to the new fundamentalist
    common sense popularized by the Hindu Right and its paranoia of the
    need to 'protect' the nation from the enemy within. From this perspective,
    Gopalan argues that the tragic denouement of *QSQT* is preordained inso-
    far as both Raj and Rashmi transgress 'normative' gender roles constructed
    by the Hindutva ideology. While obviously tapping into the resurgent
    Hindu neo-nationalism, I argue, however, that it is precisely this rewriting
    of 'traditional' gender roles in *QSQT* that represents the film's mediation
    of *upper*-middle-class anxieties caused, among others, by democratizing
    initiatives such as the women's movement.

3 While I have drawn the majority of my examples in this chapter from *India Today*, this is not because of any unique feature of this magazine. My argument, on the contrary, is that the conclusions drawn in this book must stand or fall at the general level. *India Today*, too, from this perspective, has been used only as a representative instance of popular journalism aimed at the urban upper class/caste, the symbolic referent of films like *QSQT*.

4 For documentations, see, among others, Sangari and Vaid (1989), Sen (1990) and Tharu and Lalita (1991, 1995).

5 This was a model of industrial development that emphasized the growth of heavy industry under the public sector. It aimed at transforming India from an agricultural economy into an industrial one by channelling investment into the production of capital goods. Created by Indian Statistician Prasanta Chandra Mahalanobis in 1953, the model provided the theoretical framework for India's Second Five Year Plan in 1955, by appointment of the then Prime Minister Jawaharlal Nehru.

6 The most remarkable insights in this regard have undoubtedly come from the works of Foucault. With specific reference to the postcolonial context, Chakrabarty (1995) and Chatterjee (1997) have speculated on the implications of the logic of counting to the new constructions of identity that have emerged in the [post-]/colonial state.

7 It will be appropriate to keep in mind that *QSQT* was released barely a year after Roop Kanwar's sati in September 1987. For an insightful discussion of the media debates surrounding this event, see Rajan (1993). The Roop Kanwar sati, of course, was itself part of a gradual process of communalization of civil society in the 1980s. The crucial role of women in the construction of communalism perhaps coalesced most intensely in the debates surrounding the Uniform Civil Code and the infamous Muslim Women's Bill (1985). Again, for excellent analysis of the Shah Bano case, see Pathak and Rajan (1992). Sangari (1995) also provides a comprehensive critique of the relationship between notions of 'community' and 'women' as conceptualized by *both* leftist and liberal models of social analysis.

8 Jacques Derrida defines 'supplement' as a combination of something that is missing and something that is extra: 'The overabundance of the signifier, its *supplementary* character, is [. . .] the result of a finitude, that is to say, the result of a lack which must be supplemented' (1978: 290).

9 In fact, there emerged a series of New Indian Man images across the Indian media in the 1980s, with the glossy back-and-white 'Complete Man'

series of television advertisements for Raymonds fabrics being perhaps the most striking example. Others would include the Nivea advertisement with its punch line declaring it is 'For men who dare to show they care' or the Digjam series of advertisements with its campaigns focusing on the 'modern' relationship between the New Man and his 'feminist' partner. In fact, one of the Digjam ads shows the New Indian Man saying, 'I have nothing against feminists as long as they don't lose their femininity' as he looks at his feminine feminist partner, while she stands pouting at a distance.

10 While obviously formed by a different history, the pressure exerted by feminist movements globally has also seen a re-figuring of masculinity in Hollywood. See Susan Jeffords (1993).

11 For a profile of Rajesh Khanna, see Rajadhyaksha and Willemen (1994: 117). For an excellent analysis of 1970s' middle cinema, see Prasad (1994: 295–339).

12 This article appeared in *Stardust* as the 'Scoop of the Month'. Celebrity film-journalist Cyrus Merchant rates this as among his best interviews.

13 Over the decades since *QSQT*'s release, developments in the 'Aamir Khan story', as it were, have quite neatly carried forward this thinking-man image. Following a few initial flops after *QSQT*, Khan has today come to represent *the* intelligent/thinking face (actor/director/producer) of the Bombay industry. His 'perfectionism'—he appears in only one film a year—is almost the subject of folklore. He does not accept Indian film awards because he says they lack credibility. Virtually all his recent films have been major box-office hits and have received critical acclaim, with *Lagaan* (The Tax, 2001) getting the Oscar nomination for 'Best Foreign Language Film' clearly being the high point. Changes in Khan's personal life have continued to be cast in the same thinking/'sensitive man' mould as well. So, although he divorced Reena in 2002 and has been married to Kiran Rao, who he met on the sets of *Lagaan*, since 2005, the media still carefully projects him as a very caring father to his teenage son, Junaid. Not much information is available about daughter Ira though. Kiran Rao is herself constructed as an 'intellectual woman'. Allegations of an affair with journalist Jessica Heines were quietly buried. Similarly, his invitation to ex-wife Reena to the engagement ceremony of his nephew, Imran Khan, in 2010 was well publicized. Moreover, not only did he 'launch' Imran, son of Nasir Hussain, in *Jaane Tu Ya Jaane Na* (Do You Know or Don't You, 2008), but he also organized major promotional events, very similar to the pre-release publicity of *QSQT*, prior to the launch of Imran's debut film.

14 For a stimulating analysis of these interconnections, see Sangari and Vaid (1989: 1–28).

15 For discussions on alternative sexual ethics existing in pre-colonial India, see, among others, Sangari (1990) and Tharu and Lalita (1993: 199–219).

16 For analyses of the sexual politics of Hindutva, see Suddhabrata Sengupta (1991), Pradip K. Datta (1991) and Tanika Sarkar (1991).

17 I use this phrase in a manner similar to Teresa De Lauretis (1984: 105–57).

18 As a useful marker of the ideological distance between Bombay and Hollywood, see Hilary Radner (1993), where the New Woman of 1980s' and 1990s' Hollywood is valued, instead, by her sexual *expertise*.

19 Perhaps we also need to keep in mind that *QSQT* was a film made by a *Muslim* production house.

20 We can recall here the opening shots of the film. As opposed to the literal and symbolic distance that the feudal landlord in Bombay maintains, from his land as well as the labour it signifies, Jaswant is shown as causally resting in his fields, on a camp-bed, with his accountant. Jaswant can be effectively contrasted with Thakur Raghubir Singh, for example. The establishing shots here first frame the magisterial 'Thakur Haveli' (feudal mansion). This is cut to a top-angle shot which slowly cranes down, displaying the opulence of the mansion, to show the Thakur resting on his divan supervising the purchase of wedding jewellery, while the rest of the family *sits on the floor*.

21 I have argued in this book a new translatability between films from South India and those of Bombay—a feature contingent on the new nature of regionalism in the country. In this context, it might be useful to draw parallel between the 'ethnic' costume of Rashmi and that of the epony-mous heroine in *Geetanjali* (1998), for instance, which came to be known, literally, as the 'Geetanjali dress' among fashionable young women in the urban cities of South India. *Geetanjali*, initially made in Telugu, was also released in Tamil and Malayalam and is considered to be an unofficial 'remake' of the Hindi film *Yaad Rakhegi Duniya*, (The World Will Remember, 1992).

22 Among many others, see also Cook (1985: 73–81) for a useful summary of the debates.

23 The most dramatic of these instances first shows Rashmi's father and uncle going to a mercenary's house in the dead of night. With a subhuman laughter, the mercenary promises to kill Raj, looking at his knife. The scene dissolves to *Raj* sharpening his axe because he wants to gather

firewood from the forest so that Rashmi and he can make their evening tea. This is *after* parent-figures on both sides are also shown as having (unknowingly) very much liked/approved of the young man and young woman respectively from the 'enemy' camp. So Rashmi's uncle mistakes Raj for Roop Singh, Rashmi's husband-to-be, in the initial (comic) sequence. Similarly, before they know her family background, Raj's parents explicitly state on several occasions that they would like just such a pretty bride as Rashmi for their son.

CHAPTER FIVE

IN THE NAME OF THE FATHER: *TEZAAB*

> Ladies and Gentlemen,—It was discovered one day that the patho-
> logical symptoms of certain neurotic patients have a sense. On this
> discovery the psychoanalytic method of treatment was founded. It
> happened in the course of this treatment that patients, instead of
> bringing forward their symptoms, brought forward dreams. A sus-
> picion thus arose that dreams too had a sense (Freud 1982: 109).

Dreams, as Freud evocatively reminds us, have always held a special place
in human existence, even in ancient civilizations where they were endowed
with magic and the powers of prophecy. The genius of psychoanalysis, then,
was to provide a conceptual apparatus by which one could translate the
language of the unconscious, of which dreams are but one manifestation,
into the language of 'rational' discourse.

The important point for our purposes is that, as a semiotic strategy,
psychoanalysis insists on 'symptomatic' readings, i.e. readings which, by
definition, assume that there cannot be any one-to-one referencing between

the 'original' unconscious traumas and their manifestations within the domain of consciousness. The manifest content of a dream is always only a displacement and/or condensation of repressed desires. Drawing on Freud, psychoanalytic cultural theory argues that the texts of mass culture can similarly be read 'symptomatically', i.e. as the manifest content of repressed desires/traumas of a *social* psyche. And the work of cultural analysis, from this perspective, is one of reading back from texts of popular culture to confront the latent repressions that shape the social unconscious.

In the manner of the analyst, this chapter will read N. Chandra's *Tezaab* (Acid, 1988),[1] a representative action film from 1980s' Bombay, as a popular manifestation of the repressed traumas that shape the social unconscious of post-Nehruvian India. It might be appropriate, then, to begin by laying out the formative cultural discourses within which the anti-hero cinema of 1980s' Bombay took shape.

'SEX', 'VIOLENCE' AND THE LIBERALIZED NATION-SPACE

The distinctive marker of the cultural discourses within which the 1980s' version of Bombay's anti-hero cinema emerged was that they were deeply imprinted with two related sets of anxieties: the growing incidence of 'violence in society' and the 'criminalization of politics'. Moreover, while some sections of the popular media interpreted the increasing social unrest in the country as resulting from representations of violence on screen, others argued that cinema was instead mirroring the increasing unrest within civil society itself. Recent political theory has shown us that the 'objective' contradictions that shape present-day India derive from the ways in which the programme of the 'structural adjustment' of the economy undertaken since the 1980s is interacting with internal contradictions (of caste/class, region and gender) of the post-Nehruvian nation.[2] And given the wide-ranging critiques that the Nehruvian state has come under over the last three decades or so, I will argue that the media's concern over violence in society was a manifestation—within the imagination of the upper middle classes—of the growing unease at what was now clearly seen as erosions of traditional class privileges.

Thus, the flip side of the state-led euphoria over the opening of the economy was the evident discomfort in acknowledging the massive social upheavals that were simultaneously accompanying India's new modernization agenda:

> According to sociologists, policemen and psychologists, even a mere eight or ten years ago, instances of destructive anger manifesting themselves between couples, families and anonymous citizens were comparatively rare because there were institutional restraints to inhibit such short-fuse explosions [. . .] Today, it is as though a vigorous shake had altered the kaleidoscope that is Indian society, loosening all rules of behaviour [. . .] While expectations, fuelled by the new god of consumerism, are rising relentlessly, so are the prices which make a mockery of all such expectations. Then, there's corruption at every turn, unemployment, a new assertiveness among women which is confusing men [. . .] (Jain 1994c: 132–3).

In such a milieu, the article went on to observe, anger erupted in bizarre psychopathic forms. Within the sphere of popular film criticism, too, emerged a similar concern over the loss of traditional values: a 'decline' in the nation's morals. A subsequent feature wistfully recalled:

> Those [the 1950s] were the days when it seemed that only good films were made. [. . .] Today, every film has to have violence [. . .] It is perhaps a reflection of our times: light romance made way for the confident strides of an angry young man called Amitabh Bachchan [. . .] The age of innocence was over (Tripathi 1988: 88–9).

Referring to the new quirky range of villains of 1980s' Bombay, another article argued:

> The Good then has taken a back seat in Indian cinema. Unfortunately, this trading of places reflects more fundamental and disturbing changes [. . .] Why the change of heart? Once upon an unevil time one looked for villains on screen. Today, they crowd the newspapers and the neighbourhood [. . .] Good and evil are mixed up: the boundaries between the two have become blurred. As they have between the hero and villain [. . .] Real life villains are now coveted; they become the celebrities at parties, they are

the men behind all the big projects. In a society-on-the-make it matters not how you make it but that you make it (Jain 1988: 152).

Given the 'inverted' morality of the 1980s, the article went on to observe that it was now the 'screen rapists', the 'national disintegrators' and the 'underground dons' who had emerged as Bombay's major filmic attractions, while the heroes themselves had become 'dull and lustreless'. It ended by making the following case for the villains' new popularity:

> Most of all, villains personify power. The plot unfolds according to their dictates until that fateful last reel [. . .] Not only does the villain get the money, he also gets the girl—at least until judgement day [. . .] Nor is the bad guy—often a comic-book character—frightening anymore. The emotion he invokes is envy—for those mirrored walls, star ships, disco dens, his mile-long desk, strobe-lit floor and outlandish outfits (ibid.: 153).

Underlying the optimism over globalization was therefore also an extreme nervousness that in the new 'structure of feeling' naturalized by the market, traditional ethics would no longer hold. Greed, competitiveness, and a new thrust on 'commercial success' seemed to be already blurring earlier distinctions between 'good' and 'bad'.

Further coded as infiltrations of a corrupting Western modernity, the concern over the increasing violence in cinema also spilled over into denunciations of the new (consumerist) sexuality that was simultaneously exploding on Bombay's screen. As hero and villain traded places, so did heroine and vamp. The feature cited above went on to ruefully note:

> Inevitably, between the anti-hero and the heroic villain, vamps have died an unnatural death [. . .] It is the new breed of heroines who struck the fatal blow—they do all that the vamps did and still get to marry the hero [. . .] In today's love stories, it is almost natural to show the boy and the girl living together (ibid.: 159–61).

Chatterjee (1995a) has shown us that a fundamental ambivalence marks the nationalist modernities of the postcolonial world vis-à-vis the modernity promised by the Enlightenment in Europe. This ambivalence, Chatterjee has argued, is the result of the historical interconnection between the Enlightenment's promise of universal self-determination on one hand and the whole project of the colonization of the non-West on the other. Further given the 'objective' presence of colonial power in the domain of the state, Chatterjee (ibid.) has also suggested that the nation, as an imagined community in the East, found its most powerful articulation in the cultural rather than the political terrain. The fact of British colonialism meant that the nation in India, too, was most forcefully imagined into existence in the realm of culture.

In this context, the anxiety that we have just noted in the popular media, over the loss of 'traditional values' in 1980s' Bombay cinema, derives its urgency from the fact that the contemporary stage of capitalism could erase entire 'national cultures' with ease. And the unease with the changing ethical universe of 1980s' Bombay gained its historical resonance from this volatile juncture, as the nation collectively tried to dream of new notions of community and new modes of being together.

BEYOND THE BOUNDARY:
THE 1980s' ANTI-HERO AND THE MEDIA IMAGE OF *TEZAAB*

In this backdrop, let us begin our reading of *Tezaab* with an analysis of the 'rowdy-sheeter' by Dhareshwar and Srivatsan (1993). In the new cultural landscape of India, the 'rowdy', they propose, is the Other against whom the 'yuppie' defines himself. His non-assimilation into the political idiom of the elite is indicated by the fact that even leftist models of social analysis locate the rowdy outside of any class-membership:

> The term lumpenproletariat (lumpen: shabby; paltry; rabble or riff-raff), used as a category in Marxian social theory, also situates them outside any social semiosis of class; a lumpen is precisely one whose relationship to money is unmediated by any value; any bonds of class solidarity or ties of community. The 'lumpen', then, is sub-human, the 'other' (thus subaltern?) from whom the 'yuppie' (the unavoidable representative figure of the global middle-class) differentiates him and his social space.
>
> [. . .]
>
> If we take the term 'subalternity' as a shorthand for the critique of various 'norming' and exclusionary narratives, such as the nation,

secularism, citizenship, etc. can one use that critique to interrogate the everyday practice of 'citizenship' (or 'democracy') that sustain and define our conception of the public sphere? (Ibid.: 202–03.)

I have argued in Chapter 3 that the feudal notion of status signified by family name can be used as a structuring trope to trace Bombay's anti-hero's ambivalence to law/citizenship. I have also argued that there was a paradigmatic shift in Bombay's anti-hero genre from the 1950s to the 1980s. While in the 1950s, Bombay's anti-hero was excluded from 're-spectable society' on account of a 'failed' father-figure, in the 1980s, the anti-hero transgressed the law trying to emulate an idolized father-figure.

Emerging as a critique of colonial modernity by the 1980s, Bombay's anti-hero had transformed into a vigilante instead, championing the modernizing drive of the nation-state and inverting, in the process, melodrama's traditional critique of class and hierarchy by locating social problems within the marginalized and the dispossessed. To recall the analysis of the rowdy with which we began this section, let us now place beside it a close analysis of *Tezaab*'s media image. As we shall see, a repeated emphasis on lower-middle-classness, i.e. ideas of hard work, sincerity and family values, not only formed the ethical core of the film's media image but would also be the focus of its narrative. Let us then begin with an analysis of the media image of the film's director, N. Chandra.

It was well known that before his (fascistic) portrayal of the problems of urban unemployment in *Ankush*, Chandra hailed from the lower middle class, even living in the Bombay *chawls* (tenements) in his youth. Working with a small budget and a virtually unknown cast, the success of *Ankush* however brought Chandra instantly into the limelight. His next film, *Pratighaat* (Revenge, 1987), another small-budget film without any major Stars, similarly turned out to be among the major grossers of the year. Consistent with the narrative logic of *Ankush*, *Pratighaat* also portrayed a middle-class woman as an avenging angel. Even before *Tezaab*, therefore, Chandra had already established his image as one of the most promising directors of the new breed of 'violent' films emerging in 1980s' Bombay (see, for example, Chandra 1989).

In terms of budget, however, *Tezaab* was Chandra's first major film. Dinesh Gandhi, one of India's wealthiest diamond merchants, financed the film. This also explains the massive media publicity *Tezaab* received. In terms of cast, however, as with Chandra's earlier films, Madhuri Dixit and Anil Kapoor were both at the time minor figures in the industry. I will now underline the ways in which this notion of lower-middle-classness was reiterated through both Dixit's as well as Kapoor's Star images: a combination of class status and violence that it would be the burden of *Tezaab*'s narrative to justify.

I have argued in the third chapter that the changes in Bombay's production base precipitated by liberalization led to a realignment of dominance from the Star to the music segment of the industry in the 1980s. In this context, Madhuri Dixit's rise to stardom perhaps best represents the new dominance of music in 1980s' Bombay. Although *Tezaab* was Dixit's first hit, she had entered the industry four years earlier. A string of flops had, however, reduced her to playing minor roles in B-grade films. At this point in her career she suddenly began to be promoted by one the most prominent directors in the industry, Subhash Ghai. He inserted a major five-page advertisement in all the trade papers reintroducing Dixit as the Star to be born. The advertisement read: 'This is the girl who has flopped in 1986. She is reborn in 1987. In 1988 she will be a Star.' Despite Ghai's flamboyance, however, the flops continued. But Dixit continued to get roles in several big-banner films. It was also at this point that rumours began of affairs with several men that mattered—Ghai himself, N. Chandra, even Anil Kapoor. On her part, these were rumours Dixit never overtly denied. What she did instead was to play up an 'ordinariness' that would implicitly counter such allegations. As she described herself:

> I feel very bad when people say I am being promoted by Subhash*ji* or Anil or some other hero. But at the same time I feel people's suspicion is understandable. Frankly, what have I done in the last three years to deserve the kinds of films and banners I am getting today? [. . .] Sometimes my success surprises me. I am not the glamorous, gutsy, flashy, outgoing, go-getting kind [. . .] I am a casual, introverted, solitude-loving, girl. That's why I used to shun parties [. . .] (*Filmfare* 1988: 22).

The Other of Dixit's media image was the Westernized starlet who, it was suggested, would stoop to any level to get ahead in her profession. As opposed to Dixit's supposedly 'well-bred demeanour' and her 'classical' beauty, the 'typical' aspiring starlet was described by *India Today* in such pejorative terms:

> Stars and starlings now gyrate, strip, smoulder, pout, bump-and-grind, clinch, rape and deliver dialogues loaded with double meanings [. . .] It was, one could say, inevitable. Cinema is the moving mirror of the times. And they have changed [. . .] Helping boost the trend are the New Young Things—NYTs—swarming tinsel town. Trapped in a never-stopping revolving door, the dare-bare-guys-and-dolls pumping the temperature of Bollywood drop their clothes and inhibitions at the whirr of a camera (Jain 1991: 50–1).

The NYTs—symptoms of the new age of fast cars, Coca Cola and MTV—were the Others against whom Dixit represented 'traditional' values. In such a context, Dixit's acceptance of her role in *Tezaab*, which required her to go very much against the grain of the media image she had cultivated, was cause for major controversy. The article titled, 'Changing . . . Madhuri Dixit's Shocking New Lifestyle!', remarks:

> Madhuri has changed and there is no doubt about it. When I first saw her almost a year ago I was most pleasantly surprised. She was pretty, very pretty in an old-fashioned demure sort of way. She spoke softly. What was a decent girl like her doing in a place like films, I had wondered [. . .] Ever since, there has been a constant process of erosion [. . .] I would not ever have expected what I saw a few weeks ago on the sets of N. Chandra's *Tezaab*. She was wearing a very revealing costume, very unlike her usual top-to-toe attire. But what actually surprised me was the ease with which she did all the suggestive and provocative gesticulations . . . I couldn't believe that this confident coquette dancing in front of my eyes was the same bashful girl I had met a year ago (*Stardust* 1988: 45).

Such a change of image was accompanied by allegations that she had ditched her mentor (Ghai), had walked out on her co-Stars, held up the releases of several films—in short, that Dixit had learnt the tricks of the trade. It was only *after* the phenomenal success of the '*Ek Do Teen*' ('One, Two, Three') number in *Tezaab* that she came to be described as a dancing sensation, a label Dixit held till she left the industry after her marriage.

Chatterjee (1989) has argued that nationalist discourse in India elaborated itself premised on an ideological division of the social realm into analogous sets of dichotomies such as the material/the spiritual, the world/the home, the masculine/the feminine. In the new urban space saturated by all kinds of liberalized objects—global televisual junk, fast food joints, malls—fashion, and its bearer, the body, have emerged as key sites encrypting the changed politico-cultural climate of India. Social definitions of Indianness have consequently had to find new strategies to yoke together the visibility of women with earlier notions of traditionalism. Within the 1980s' anti-hero genre, as represented by Dixit's media image, the strategy for doing so was to play up a non-consumerist lifestyle.

Thus, as opposed to the NYT who partied through the night, Dixit was apparently never to be seen at discotheques. Her family was constructed as very 'traditional'. (It was, of course, upper caste.) All her career decisions (including 'payments') were said to be jointly taken with her parents. She would always be accompanied to shoots with one of her parents and was reported to have had very few friends in the industry. She would supposedly never wear make-up at home, and would always be dressed in *salwar-kameez* as opposed to Western clothes, etc. (Moreover this image has subsequently received a perfect closure with Dixit's 'arranged marriage' to a highly 'respectable' medical practitioner in the US.)

Thus, while the explosion of lewd sexuality was attributed by the popular media of the 1980s to a range of factors—the frontbenchers who now invaded the theatres, the new fly-by-night producers, a thriving porn video industry, and even 'films from South India'(!)—Madhuri Dixit was ideologically constructed as maintaining a distance from the 'bad modernity' of the NYTs even while doing 'bold' dance numbers as her sexuality was sanctioned by the mediating authority of her traditional upper-caste family. As we shall see, this family image was crucial in distancing the lower-middle-class woman from the discourse of free choice, the definitive marker of the feminist, in *Tezaab*. Moreover, while Dixit's media image re-notated her sexuality as being in consonance with traditional 'Indian values' by playing up a middle-class lifestyle, Anil Kapoor's media image performed a similar ideological function by playing up reified motifs of working-class culture such as hard work and dignity of labour.

Like Dixit, Kapoor's entry into the industry had also been a non-event. He had, however, built himself an image as a 'character actor' by the time of *Tezaab*'s release. However, in striking parallel to Dixit, charges of manipulativeness had started being levelled at Kapoor also, as he began to be promoted by scriptwriter Javed Akhtar. This is a significant detail because this was the same Javed Akhtar of the Salim-Javed team which had scripted Bombay's iconic 'angry young man' persona in the 1970s through Amitabh Bachchan super-hits such as *Zanjeer* and *Deewar*. It was a similar 'angry young man' image that Javed Akhtar attempted to script for Anil Kapoor in films like *Meri Jung* (My Battle, 1982) and *Mashaal* (The Torch, 1984)—films that proved to be turning points in Kapoor's career. Moreover, with films such as *Woh Saat Din* (Those Seven Days, 1983), *Andar Baahar* (Inside/ Outside, 1984), *Karma* (Duty, 1986) and *Mr India* (1987) behind him, Kapoor's track record was much better than Dixit's at the time of *Tezaab*'s release.

Again, similar to Dixit, Kapoor also attributed his not getting better roles earlier to the fact that he had had no mentors in the industry and that he was just an 'ordinary' guy from Chembur (a lower-middle-class locality in Bombay) trying to make it on his own. Thus, he consistently played up his hard work, his sincerity and dedication—ethics implicitly opposed to the degenerate lifestyle signified by inherited wealth and traditional upper-class privilege. As Kapoor recalled in a post-*Tezaab* interview:

> I started from scratch. And I've inched my way up [. . .] They're
> [i.e. his screen rivals] either sons of big people or they are backed
> by big names. I'm an ordinary guy from Chembur trying to make
> it big [. . .] so it's tough competition. But I know I'm good (Komal
> 1989).

The article sympathetically recalls how, in his pre-stardom days, Kapoor had apparently followed Sanjay Dutt[3] all the way to a five-star hotel one day, only for a 'bit' role in *Rocky* (1981), and how that had been Kapoor's first sight of a squash court where he was now a regular. These claims of hardship and deprivation need, however, to be taken with a generous helping of salt given that Anil Kapoor's brother, Boney Kapoor, is a film producer. In fact, *Woh Saat Din* and *Mr India* had both been home productions. However, in contrast to his upper-class screen rivals, the media insistently played up the ordinariness of Kapoor's lifestyle. There-fore, as opposed to the crassly materialistic Star who would sign on any role just to make a fast buck (the equivalent of the NYTs against whom Dixit's media image had been constructed), Kapoor emphasized that he cared for the quality of roles he selected:

> I'm happy with what money I have. Money is not more important than the role. Money doesn't give me more security than doing good films [. . .] Some people are lucky when they lay maximum stress on the monetary aspect of things, but not me [. . .] My work is my high (ibid.).

Given this sustained emphasis on middle-classness, let us now analyse the enormous implications of this class position for the actual narrative of the film.

GOVERNMENTALITY: LAW, FAMILY AND THE NEO-LIBERAL NATION

We have noted earlier that the preoccupation with family name can be used as a structuring trope of Bombay's anti-hero genre. In *Tezaab* this preoccu-pation is manifested through the changing significations that gather around the different names that Anil Kapoor himself takes on in the narrative— from Mahesh Deshmukh, the patriotic adolescent of small-town Nasik, to Munna, the rowdy or social outcast of Bombay, back to Mahesh Deshmukh, the future citizen of modern India. As Mahesh encapsulates in a climactic confrontation with Guldasta, the reformed informer of main villain Lotia Khan (Kiran Kumar) and Mahesh's arch enemy: 'The city of Bombay gave me the name Munna. It also gave me another name, "rowdy" or outcast. Having got rid of them both, I am going to a new city, with a new name, to start a new life.'[4]

Given this background, let us approach *Tezaab* through Foucault's notion of 'governmentality' (1991). Foucault argues that the fundamental change in the nature of power that occurred in the transition from the despotic to the post-despotic state in Western Europe was that while the theory of sovereignty was based on a fundamental distinction between the power of the prince and all other forms of power, the art of governmentality involved establishing continuous and multiple networks, in both an upwards and a downwards direction. He outlines:

Upwards continuity means that a person who wishes to govern the state must first learn how to govern himself, his goods and his patrimony, after which he will be successful in governing the state [. . .] On the other hand, we also have a downwards continuity in the sense that, when a state is well run, the head of the family will know how to look after his goods and his patrimony, which means that individuals will, in turn, behave as they should [. . .] (ibid.: 90–1).

Let us now analyse the narrative structure of *Tezaab* in the light of Foucault's thesis. The function of the pre-credit segment of the film—which stretches to almost 40 minutes—is to sketch in the dystopic nature of the 'base time'/present of the narrative. This is crucial because, in the manner of the 'whodunit' plot, Inspector Gaggan Singh will take on the role of the detective in the *post*-credit segment and attempt to unravel the mystery behind the degenerate nature of *Tezaab*'s present.

We will return to this point. Here, let us merely underline that *Tezaab*'s plot follows the generic structure of the detective story and unfolds primarily through flashback sequences. Importantly, both flashback sequences are located in the post-credit segment of the film. The first flashback (which I shall refer to as f1), located in the inspector's memory, sketches in an ideal 'past' to offset the degraded 'present' with which the film begins. The second flashback (f2), located in Mahesh's memory, performs the function of providing reasons for this process of degeneration.

We can map the structure of the plot of *Tezaab* thus:

Pre-credit segment	Credits	Post-credit segment	
		f1	f2
Base-time		'Past'	Intervening events between 'past' and base-time)

Drawing on Tzvetan Todorov's *narratologie*/'narrative structure', Mulvey proposes that the detective story is based on a double-time structure (1989: 177–201). There are two stories to be told. The first precedes the narrative and is the story of the crime. This story is gradually unfolded in the course of the second, which is the story of the investigation. So also with *Tezaab*.

At the beginning of the film, a crime has already been committed. Bombay has become a city where fathers live off their daughters while rowdies, rather than the police, protect people. In the second story, the story of investigation, Inspector Gaggan Singh reconstructs, through Anil Kapoor's biography, a second narrative explaining the reasons for Bombay having become the city that it is. The point to remember is that Mahesh (Kapoor's character) is explicitly coded as paradigmatic of his generation.

To return to Foucault, the pre-credit segment of *Tezaab* is further subdivided into two distinct sequences. The first sequence comprising Mohini (Madhuri Dixit) and Shyamlal (Anupam Kher) depicts the 'aberrant family' while the second depicts the law and order problem in Bombay. The film opens in the middle of the night. In expressionist *mise en scène*, the establishing shots frame a Gothic mansion. To the sound of eerily tolling bells, silhouettes of swarthy men flicker across its walls. As they walk up to the door one of them pours a brown liquid on a potted plant. The plant goes up in a puff of fumes leaving behind a black mess. This is inter-cut with '*Tezaab*, a Violent Love Story' in bold red letters. Inside, a top shot frames a drunken man sprawled on a bed. The goons haul him up. They are main villain Lotia Khan's men. Shyamlal, the debtor, has not repaid his loan though his daughter Mohini has already given 25 shows. The scene then changes to an aerobics session with Shyamlal trying to threaten the studio-owner, Saxena, by saying that Mohini will not give her performance that evening unless he is given the additional money. Thus, within the first 10 minutes, we already have a 'character sketch'—Shyamlal is an alcoholic, a debtor and, above all, a father who appropriates his daughter's labour.

The disastrous Shyamlal–Saxena rendezvous is followed by the spectacular '*Ek Do Teen*' dance number that catapulted Dixit to stardom. As Shyamlal has still not repaid his debt, Lotia Khan and his men have come to the show to retrieve their money. Spotting them from the backstage, Shyamlal runs away. To substitute for his loss, Lotia abducts Mohini. In the audience at Mohini's show is also a lone woman. In terms of narrative function she links the two sequences of the pre-credit segment together. She is Munna's (Anil Kapoor's) sister, and as she watches Lotia Khan kidnap Mohini she rushes to a nearby post office and telegrams her brother asking him to return to Bombay immediately.

The telegram dissolves into the second sequence of the pre-credit segment. It is again a dark night in a slum somewhere in the vicinity of Bombay. Munna the rowdy or *tadipaar* (outcast by law) is coming to collect his *hafta* (the weekly protection money extorted by street gangs). A top shot reveals people running helter-skelter. One of them quickly puts out a chair and a table. In the soundtrack, continually, are the slow, confident strides of a man. The camera cuts to focus on a glistening knife, heavy leather boots. Two men quickly pay their *hafta*. A third gives an excuse. In a flash his hand is pinned to the table and a knife jabbed between his fingers. He screams but finds his fingers unscathed. Perspiring profusely, he looks up. A point-of-view shot tracks his eyes to reveal a scornful, rugged face. Munna warns him never to lie again. Insolently, Munna then collects money from the others, asking them to hurry up because he has to go to the police station to give his 'attendance'.[5]

There are, however, in the slum also a group of urchins to whom Munna plays big brother. As the sequence ends, one of them complains to Munna about a new rowdy in town, Mukut Bihari. To protect the children, Munna hatches a clever plot and single-handedly takes on the new rowdy. As Munna walks back, one of the boys runs up to him again, this time with the telegram that has just arrived from Bombay. The next shot shows Munna on a train superimposed on which the credits begin to roll.

So Bombay/the nation not only faces the problem of an aberrant family but also one of law and order. In accordance with Foucault's thesis on governmentality, the narrative of *Tezaab* will have to negotiate both these interrelated areas. Significantly, the narrative agent who will undertake this task of cleansing the narrative's 'present' is Inspector Gaggan Singh, both literal representative of law and also, as we come to know immediately after the credits, Munna's surrogate father.

The post-credit segment of *Tezaab* opens at the headquarters of the Bombay police. The Inspector's team has launched a search for the famous pop star, Mohini. At this point one of his men informs the Inspector that a rowdy-sheeter, Munna, has illegally entered the city limits. Looking at the rowdy profiled in the police records, however, the inspector recalls (through the first flashback) having met a very different Mahesh Deshmukh in the past. This makes him determined to also investigate the mystery behind Kapoor's transformation from Mahesh Deshmukh the patriot to Munna the rowdy.

So let us now use f1, the flashback located in the inspector's memory, as a detour into some crucial questions of caste, class and gender raised by *Tezaab*'s narrative.

IN THE 'NAME OF THE FATHER'

We have noted the insistence with which the media images of *Tezaab*'s Stars drew attention to their middle-class lifestyles. As we shall see, the significance of *Tezaab*'s emphasis on middle-class values lies in the way in which this entire 'structure of feeling' in the 1980s came to carry a de facto upper-caste Hindu marking. From this perspective, the most significant point about f1 is that the lost patriotism recalled by the inspector is located within the distinct ambience of a lower-middle-class family of small-town Nasik. It begins with the young Mahesh jubilantly running into a bank with the cup he has just won for being the Best Navy Cadet. Both of Mahesh's parents work there in clerical positions. With the inspector who happens to be accidentally present, Mahesh's parents joke that their son must have been a patriot in his last life, martyred in the nationalist struggle, because ever since his childhood Mahesh has apparently wanted to dedicate his life to India. Seconds later, the bank is raided by Chota Khan, Lotia Khan's younger brother. The flashback shows Mahesh heroically saving a young woman and her baby as well as helping the inspector capture Chota Khan. Ignoring Chota Khan's threats, Mahesh's parents, in the meantime, valiantly try to raise the alarm and are both killed in the process. Thus within minutes, the happiest day of Mahesh's life turns into the saddest. The flashback ends with Mahesh's father breathing his last as he tells his son to fulfil his ambition of becoming an admiral, an ambition in which he is sure to have the support of the whole nation. As representative and witness of the nation to this tremendous sacrifice, the inspector now decides that it is his responsibility to help Munna return to his earlier life.

THE DEATH OF MERIT

Political theorist Sudipta Kaviraj's insightful formulation provides us a vital clue to understand the larger contemporary resonance of *Tezaab*'s insistent highlighting of 'patriotism' and 'merit' as middle-class values. Kaviraj has argued that the nature of politics initiated in the Indira Gandhi era generated a tendency towards an extreme centralization of the political process so that, by the 1980s, a crisis within the Congress party could translate, almost directly, into a crisis of the political structure of the state. The new nature of politics not only saw a replacement of political ideology with empty rhetoric but also the introduction of irresponsible feudal forms of power and patronage within the institutional apparatuses of a bourgeois democracy (see Kaviraj 1988). Given this political climate, the significance of locating idealism within a specifically middle-class ambience in f1 is that the Deshmukh family represents precisely that construct of the national imaginary that would literally set the nation ablaze during the anti-Mandal agitations that engulfed India barely a year and a half after *Tezaab*'s release.

As is by now familiar, largely as a populist gimmick to accommodate the increasingly articulate claims to citizenship of hitherto-marginalized groups such as the lower castes and minority religious communities, the Janata Dal government, in September 1990, announced its decision to implement the recommendations of the Mandal Commission, introducing 27 per cent reservations for 'Other Backward Castes' in government service and the public sector. This was in addition to the 22.5 per cent reservations for Scheduled Castes and Scheduled Tribes that already existed. This lead to a nation-wide outcry, with several upper-caste youth immolating themselves at what was coded as a policy reinforcing casteism. The question continually invoked during the anti-Mandal riots was, 'What about the *poor Brahman*?' The Deshmukh family of small-town Nasik, the representative upper-caste family deprived of its 'rightful' share of social privileges because of minorities 'spooning off' the state, would emerge as the most powerful imagined construct to fuel this paranoia about the 'death of merit' in the nation.

It is significant, therefore, that although Mahesh and his friends go to an English-medium college, none of them becomes a high profile executive. In fact, it is about Mahesh's lower-middle-class status that Shyamlal at one point taunts his daughter. Mohini lashes back:

Yes, it is true that Munna's father was only a clerk. But he still maintained his family with his own income. He did not live off them. Munna has only a dilapidated house to live in. But that is still much better than mansions as ours that have been mortgaged. To meet his expenses, Munna has a job that pays him only Rs. 500. But that is far better than people like you who are neck-deep in debt.

The question of 'employment' (and let us recall the war cry of the anti-Mandalites over the loss of government jobs for 'meritorious' upper-caste men because of reservations) thus assumes utmost importance as *the* marker of eligibility for the subject-position of the 'male' in Bombay's anti-hero genre of the 1980s.

The obverse of this is that eligibility for the subject-position of the 'female' in *Tezaab* becomes restricted to only that section of women who comprehensively occupy the space of 'the private' or the home. As Mohini tells Mahesh at a subsequent point in the narrative, she wishes above all to retreat into quiet domesticity by giving up her career as a pop star into which she has been forced. Thus, an analysis of the trope of family name in *Tezaab* opens out into two interrelated areas—the construction of the private and public spheres by Bombay's anti-hero cinema—the small-town middle-class family that will be reconstituted by Mahesh and Mohini in the end, and the 'others' against whom this normative family is defined.

CASTE AND THE PUBLIC/PRIVATE DIVIDE

In a fascinating study of nineteenth-century Bengal, Sumit Sarkar (1992) has analysed the cultural semiotics of the lower orders of the urban middle classes, the intermediate stratum between the world of elite–nationalist politics and the space of the subalterns. While English education brought success for some, for many more it brought only the humble clerical job (*chakri*) in government or mercantile offices. Plagued with a sense of alienation in the new regimented schedule of the office, helpless in the face of bitter everyday encounters with a racist and impersonal bureaucracy, this city-based literati—as Sarkar analyses—is attracted to an uneducated, rustic 'saint-figure' such as Sri Ramakrishna Paramahamsa (1836–86). Within the discourse of the rustic saint, Sarkar shows that the conception of 'evil' intertwines *kamini* (woman), *kanchan* (gold), *dasatya* (bondage) and *chakri* (clerical job):

[L]ust, as embodied invariably in women, gold, and the bondage of the office job. Wives with their luxurious ways instil into their husbands a thirst for money, and this in turn forces men to office work. The temptations of *kamini* and *kanchan* are age-old themes, but their association with *chakri* is new [. . .] A deeply depressing, claustrophobic world, where failure and poverty only help to consolidate caste and gender—over which Ramakrishna presides, an icon that gives, perhaps, a little comfort, but not hope (ibid.: 1545).

Keeping in mind the historicity of the experiences of the nineteenth-century Calcutta *bhadralok* (gentleman), it is still worth asking: what are the socio-political processes that have transformed the much-despised world of the *chakri* into the seat of idealism a century later? A series of recent studies have documented that the popular base of the current Hindutva project lies in a social stratum very similar to that of the Calcutta *bhadralok* a century earlier—the urban lower middle classes continually teased by the new signs of 'good life' but without viable options for upward social mobility (see, among others, Heuze 1992).

Given the new assertiveness of various subaltern groups, this is also that segment of the upper castes which is most haunted by a persecution complex. The idealism that the inspector in *Tezaab* recalls through the Nasik bank robbery case then forms the necessary ideological obverse of the present upper-caste hysteria—the obsession that 'meritorious' upper-caste young men are now being deprived of their 'rightful' social place in the nation because of the state's policy of 'appeasing minorities'.

Hence, it is significant that, in the film, Mahesh and his parents are the only people who work for a living. Shyamlal, a decadent feudal aristocrat, considers an office job beneath his dignity. His refusal to work and his parasitical dependence, first on his wife and then on his daughter, become the distinctive markers of the aberrant family. Similarly the only other upper-class character in the film, the studio-owner Saxena, is also reprehensible. While Saxena offers to 'buy' Mohini for Rs 50,000, Shyamlal is perfectly happy to sell even his blessings if he is paid enough.

The high point of exploitation is, needless to say, represented by Lotia Khan. Lotia Khan sells women into prostitution, forces little children into bonded labour and takes advantage of all other vulnerable social groups.

To claim the subject-position of the 'male' in this situation, i.e. to be 'man enough to be a man', Mahesh needs to occupy the public sphere in a certain way and be in a certain position of socio-economic power. Given, however, that such socio-economic power has historically been accessible to only a very small section of upper-caste Hindu men in India, it is this very exclusive definition of masculinity that *Tezaab* endorses with a vengeance.

The film's emphasis on middle-class values serves to ideologically distance a segment of the upper castes from the gross disparity of privileges obviously appropriated by a tiny elite in the nation. However, mobilizing a discourse on 'endeavour', the film also legitimizes desire for the new consumerism by coding it as 'nationalist'.

And in order to effect such a redefinition, while Mahesh's declassification into 'rowdy' enacts one facet of upper-caste paranoia, Mohini's career as pop star enacts the obverse. The nineteenth-century discourses on social reform in India constructed the normative Indian woman as the woman who, by acquiring the requisite education and practising the requisite refinements, could become the fit bearer of a glorious and ancient Indian tradition. This normative Indian womanhood was moreover defined vis-à-vis both the 'vulgar' lower-caste woman of the marketplace as well as the 'immoral' woman of the West.

The new internationalization of finance in the 1990s gave rise to a new upper middle class in India that sought to define itself in terms of the internationalism of the free market. Ostensibly de-racinated, the identity of this class derives from its participation in the global consumer market. As a member of this class, the identity of the New Indian Woman (the feminist) is similarly constituted within this discourse of free-market internationalism. Her modernity is defined through her free choice, which she displays not only through her successful career and her public visibility, but also, most significantly, through 'falling in love'.

Placed in relation to the specifically lower-middle-class modernity of *Tezaab,* the point to stress is that the New-Indian-Woman-style modernity is however re-inflected here to underline a certain traditionalism. (Recall the ideological distinction between the NYTs and Madhuri Dixit.) Importantly, all the three major female characters in *Tezaab* are working-women. The first, Mrs Deshmukh, is the happily married working-woman.

Her husband already has a legitimate place in the public sphere. Consequently, her career evokes no oppressive connotations. Instead, it becomes an extension of her marital happiness. This is also the lifestyle that is the symbolic referent of Mohini's deepest desires.

However, the second workingwoman, Mohini's mother, compares herself to a 'prostitute'. In fact, she chooses to leave Shyamlal because she can no longer fathom the extent of his debauchery. Mohini's mother is a classical dancer and she had married Shyamlal out of love. Yet, instead of seeing herself as the privileged bearer of an ancient tradition, Mohini's mother compares her public visibility to the vulgar marketplace woman.

The third, Mohini herself, describes her celebrity status in similar terms. Placed alongside nineteenth-century discourses of social reform, it is therefore with the 'coarse' lower-caste woman that Mohini and her mother compare themselves in order to highlight their oppression. The celebrityhood evoked by the pop-star phenomenon—which, in the New-Indian-Woman-style modernity, would be a marker of her feminism and an assertion of free choice—becomes a marker of a woman's exploitation in the film. As Mohini tells Mahesh, she is convinced that her father will never get her married because *she* is his source of income.

THE ENEMY WITHIN: THE PATRIOT VERSUS THE ROWDY

Mahesh subsequently recalls for the inspector (through the second flashback, f2) that his romance with Mohini has encountered opposition from two interrelated quarters. The first, not surprisingly, is Shyamlal, the representative of the aberrant family. Yet, by himself, Shyamlal is only a minor irritant. It is because of Shyamlal's connection with Lotia Khan, representative of the law and order problem besieging Bombay, that things have gone so completely beyond control.

We may recall that even in the ideal past of Nasik (represented through f1) there was still an indigestible surplus, an inexplicable evil threatening the peace of small-town India in the form of Chota Khan. Unlike Mahesh, who is a victim of circumstances, Mukut Bihari, Lotia Khan and Chota Khan are all 'naturally' criminal. Crime then is the Other against which patriotism in *Tezaab* is defined.

So when the inspector at the beginning of the post-credit segment catches up with Munna—who is in turn on his way to rescue Mohini—and tells him that he must arrest him, the rowdy retorts, 'But what is my crime?' The inspector answers that if the law has thought it fit that Munna should remain an outcast from Bombay it must have its reasons. But as the rowdy is quick to remind the Inspector: 'For its own selfish ends, this very society had also made Lord Ram an outcast for 14 years. What was *his* crime?'

This confrontation between the inspector and the rowdy is crucial because it provides the ideological frame within which the state (as well as the spectator) will now fundamentally have to rethink Munna's social status. And given the comparison with Lord Ram that is invoked, Munna's crimes are transformed into acts of service to the oppressed, while Munna himself emerges as a modern-day Robin Hood. Of course, the ambiguity of Munna's identity as criminal is present in the pre-credit segment itself, where he saves the slum children from 'real' rowdies. In addition, this confrontation with the inspector also provides cues through which Munna's other crimes are now redefined as heroism; as efforts to save vulnerable women such as Mohini. Finally, Munna is 'humanized' through his acquaintance with Babban Shinde. An acquaintance from college days, Babban is a true friend who ultimately dies trying to save Munna from Lotia Khan's wrath.

Therefore by providing Munna with friends, family and love, the narrative ideologically distances him from 'natural' rowdies like Lotia Khan. As opposed to even Shyamlal who has human failings, Lotia is the embodiment of a mysterious, self-generating evil, embodying all social practices against which respectability is defined. Crucially, he is also the only character in the film who is defined explicitly through his religious identity —that of the Pathan. This idea of the Pathan recalls popular myths of warrior tribes of the North West Frontier Provinces of Pakistan and Afghanistan. And, in what is a strange construct, Lotia seems to have no ostensible motive for his debauchery.

In fact, Lotia Khan's enmity with Mahesh is also curious. He is angry with Mahesh not because the latter was instrumental in his younger brother, Chota Khan, being captured in the Nasik case. (He casually tells Shyamlal that going to jail is just a 'professional hazard'.) Lotia's enmity stems, instead, from the fact that during that particular term of imprisonment Chota Khan became a drug addict. Being the first in the Pathan's family to have become so, Chota Khan had disgraced his 'family name', a crime for which Lotia Khan holds Mahesh responsible! The fitting revenge in Lotia's feudal code is an eye for an eye: to disgrace Mahesh's younger sister, Jyothi, to avenge his younger brother. Thus Lotia sends his thugs to abduct and rape Jyothi.

This feudal coding of the villain was crucial to *Tezaab*. But this point will take us back to an observation we had put aside in the introductory sections. Noting the inverted morality of 1980s' Bombay where the villain, rather than the hero, was emerging as the major source of filmic attraction in the popular media, this inversion, I had suggested, was the result of pressures generated by the new consumerism. It was the villain's power and his money, his fancy clothes and high-tech hideouts, I had argued, that were the source of envy for the man in the crowd. With reference to *Tezaab*, then, the ideological slip that occurs is that neither Lotia Khan nor Shyamlal have any structural links with the consumerism signified by the pop-star phenomenon. In fact, as *opposed* to the reference to the contemporary evoked by the pop-star phenomenon, both Lotia Khan (the major villain) and Shyamlal (the minor villain) are remnants of a feudal past. Shyamlal has pretensions to feudal aristocracy while Lotia is a money-lending Pathan. Lotia Khan is not a high-tech villain like Mogambo (*Mr India*), nor even a 'national disintegrator' like Dr Dang (*Karma*). Therefore, the reification of human relationships ostensibly brought about by the new consumerism is deflected in *Tezaab* onto the category of 'history'. And this observation will, in turn, direct us to the comment with which we had begun our analysis of the film, namely, its double-time structure.

TIME, HISTORY AND *TEZAAB*'S NARRATIVE FORM

We had noted that, like the detective story, *Tezaab*'s plot has a double-time structure. In his capacity as detective, Inspector Gaggan Singh journeys into the netherworld of Bombay to unravel the mystery of its degenerate present. There he discovers two kinds of criminals who are, nevertheless, related to each other in a structural sort of way. The first, represented by Mahesh, are those who have become rowdies to uphold justice. The others, represented by Lotia Khan, are those who are criminal by nature.

Mulvey links the structure of the detective story, archaeological excavation and the psychoanalytical process by suggesting that all three involve a process of re-telling—a reconstruction of past events which shifts the plane of narrative action from the axis of space to that of time:

> It is tempting to see the detective story as the myth or legend of the newly constituted industrial cities that had grown up *outside* order. The nether world of the city, seething with bars, prostitutes and criminals [. . .] could provide a mythic terrain for scenarios of adventure [. . .] similar to the no man's land through which the heroes of antiquity travelled. But whereas the ancient folk-tale heroes embarked on a linear journey outside the city space, the journey of the urban detective is a descent into the hidden world of what is repressed by bourgeois morality [. . .] (1989: 186–7).

In *Tezaab,* moreover, there is a dramatic overlap of the detective-story structure with the analytical process. The inspector collapses in himself the role of the detective as well as the analyst, and orders Munna (when the two meet after many years) to remember all those forgotten chapters of his life that have transformed him from a patriot to a rowdy.

The flashbacks also perform crucial ideological functions. By highlighting a disjuncture between the narrative's past and its present, they create the impression that both Inspector Gaggan Singh and Mahesh are travelling back in their memories to the misty beginnings of time when Bombay was a completely different city. Yet, in diegetic time, the interval between the past (recalled) and the present (with which the film begins) is actually only two years. Given the distancing effect created by its double-time structure, further reinforced through flashbacks as primary narrative devices, the narrative form of *Tezaab* works to create the overarching impression that the interval spanned by the diegesis is much longer time than it actually is. And, as explained below, the crucial ideological result of the distancing effect brought about by the use of flashbacks as the primary narrative device is to suggest that Muslims are 'naturally criminal'.

Clearly, Hindu characters in the film have acquired the desirable work ethics of modernity. Shyamlal is merely the deformed remnant of the past that Mahesh has left behind. No such change is, however, visible in Muslim characters. Both in the past as well as in the present, they remain criminals.

The distancing effect created by *Tezaab*'s narrative structure therefore works to suggest that Muslims have always been thus. The only solution, as the inspector discovers, is to kill Lotia Khan. Therefore, in the end he actually orders Mahesh to break the law because the emblematic young man of India today needs such a cathartic purgation of his anger. The 'real' acid disfiguring Bombay's social fabric—in the same way that Shyamlal had disfigured his wife's face—is the Muslim. The reconstitution of the family and the restoration of law and order can only be achieved once this acid has been neutralized.

We began this chapter with a discussion of the methodology that psychoanalysis, with its emphasis on symptomatic readings, provides us in terms of being able to confront the repressed traumas that structure a social psyche. In the spirit of the analyst we then located *Tezaab*, a representative action film of 1980s' Bombay, within the general concern with 'sex and violence' that seemed to haunt contemporary popular media. This anxiety about the changing ethical universe of the nation, we further saw, was a symptom of a growing upper-caste/class paranoia at the loss of their traditional class privileges, privileges they had come to regard as natural. Cinematically, Bombay's new action hero, the paradigmatic upper-caste/ class young man who has become a rowdy on account of being denied his rightful social place, emerges at this juncture as a crucial narrative figure mediating this anxiety.

Placed within the broader media concern about the death of merit in the nation, *Tezaab's* thrust on lower-middle-classness as well as its mobiliza- tion of a discourse of endeavour (the emphasis on hard work, dignity of labour, etc.), function as important narrative tropes here. Through them, a section of the traditional elite is ideologically distanced from the gross disparity of social privileges appropriated by a tiny section of society and deflected onto lower castes (as during the anti-Mandal agitations) or on to minority communities (as asserted by the resurgent Hindu fundamental- ism). These latter social sections are now constructed as spooning off the state and hence are the *real* rowdies. And because it is the writ of the real rowdies that now runs large, the popular media argues, meritorious upper- caste young men such as Mahesh Deshmukh are being pushed beyond the pale of respectable society and upper-caste women—genteel women who should ideally reside in the protected space of the home—are also being forced into the marketplace.

The paradigmatic Lacanian subject is a subject defined by 'lack' or self-loss, a subject alienated both from its organic nature as well as from the phenomenological world. The accession into the Symbolic effects the most extreme form of this self-alienation because henceforth the subject is completely subordinated to an objective system of signification—the discourse of the Other—which will determine its identity. Further within the Lacanian paradigm, the terrain of culture is structured around the paternal signifier, the 'name of the father' or the symbolic father who exceeds all 'actual' fathers and instead finds support through a range of institutions or through associations with other privileged signifiers such as money, power and the law. The symbolic father is therefore an ideal representation—a representation to which no actual father can correspond. It is a representation that also consequently effects a brutalizing sense of inadequacy in any (male) actual subject who comes of age within culture.

The obvious relevance of this Lacanian notion to the social psyche of post-Nehruvian India seems to be borne out given the excruciating sense of inadequacy that Bombay's action hero of the 1980s feels in his attempt to live up to the father's name, an inadequacy for which various dispossessed social groups are now held responsible. To regain his lost sense of wholeness then, the popular imagination of India seems to chillingly suggest, these minorities must be exorcised.

Notes

1   See Appendix II for plot summary.

2   Kaviraj, for instance, has argued that as the result of leadership tussles within the Congress caused by Nehru's death, the nature of politics initiated by Indira Gandhi substituted the Nehruvian model of 'planned development' with empty 'socialist' rhetoric—vacuous slogans not meant to be translated into policies (1988). However, this very coding of the state as 'socialist' proved fundamental to a whole range of oppositional struggles that emerged contemporaneously, struggles to which the Emergency was imposed as response in 1975.

3   This is important because Sanjay Dutt best represents the new generation
    of Star sons who made their debut in the industry in the 1980s, but cru-
    cially through the genre of romance films. Sanjay Dutt's lifestyle however
    greatly fitted that of the proverbial black sheep, the much-indulged son
    of very famous Star parents, the late Nargis and Sunil Dutt.

4   The translations of the dialogues from Hindi are mine.

5   Tracing the trope of homelessness (and the related trope of the 'footpath')
    in Bombay over the decades, Mazumdar (2007) draws on Max Weber to
    propose that one of the defining features of the urban experience in
    India/South Asia is its 'unintendedness'. The 'unintended city' is the
    underside of the original master plan. While the official city caters to the
    urban elite, the 'unintended city' is the space inhabited by poor migrants,
    for example, who flock to the city for work and a better life. It is a space
    marked by uprootedness and resentment, anger and rejection. The dis-
    tinctive feature of homelessness in 1990s' Bombay is that the pathological
    element in the anti-hero is greatly accentuated. The new stranger in the
    city, Mazumdar argues, does not speak a social idiom but remains co-
    cooned within his own warped individual obsessions (ibid.: 1–6). Huge and
    important differences with Mahesh of *Tezaab* immediately open up—not
    only is Mahesh not primarily an economic migrant (in Mazumdar's sense)
    when he moves to Bombay but he is also distinctly coded as being 'typical'
    of his generation. His desire for revenge is shown as being driven by com-
    pletely understandable motives. In fact, it is the whole burden of *Tezaab*'s
    narrative to explain why talented young men from a certain social class in
    India might feel violent resentment towards the existing socio-political
    system. In a reading somewhat related to Mazumdar, Prasad argues that
    in the urban films of 1990s' Bombay, the earlier epic confrontation
    between the countryside (or the memory of a place left behind) and the
    city (the new place) was displaced onto a new set of binaries—the reality
    of the urban hero's life (whose tragic destiny is foretold) and his fantasies
    of romantic love and a 'normal' middle-class lifestyle. In a thought-
    provoking analysis of *Satya*, Prasad points out that the film cannot retain
    even a fragmentary memory of a village or the character Satya's prehistory
    (2007: 90–2). The confrontation between the community and the law in
    1970s' Bombay—where the perspective of the subalterns (slum-dwellers,
    Muslims or the gangster who has been forced into crime) was central—
    had now been replaced with a new logic where the sordid lives of urban
    underdogs seem to have an inbuilt tendency towards despair and all-
    pervading, senseless violence. The city in the 1990s emerged as a self-

sufficient space for staging epic conflicts and allegorical narratives. In the process, the pathological anti-hero moved centre stage. For Prasad, this new portrayal of the city meant that the reformist possibilities of the old leadership could no longer be imagined as viable (ibid.: 93–8). While endorsing Prasad's argument, I propose that *Tezaab* and the decade of the 1980s provide a crucial mid-point in this (seemingly) inexorable trajectory of Bombay's anti-hero cinema. Here, the community of the subalterns is just beginning to be imagined as the genesis of social decay and the desire for a violently authoritarian state making its initial mark on the screen. Consequently, the hero/vigilante, instead of being pathologized, is represented as embodying the idealism of a generation.

AFTERWORD, OR 'ON THE PASSAGE OF A FEW PEOPLE THROUGH A RATHER BRIEF MOMENT IN TIME . . .'

I draw the title of my Afterword from a major exhibition on the *Situationist International* curated by Mark Francis and Peter Wollen with Paul Herve Parsy at the Musee national d'art Pompidou, the Institute of Contemporary Arts in London and the Institute of Contemporary Arts in Boston, Massachusetts, in 1989–90. Doing so is a means of emphatically acknowledging the so-called Western lineages of this book. It is also an act of looking back and taking stock of the terrific pace at which India has moved on in the last couple of decades.

In the period since the ideas presented in this book first took shape, much water has flown down the Krishna and the Godavari. The BJP has been in power in Karnataka, the first South Indian state in which it has formed a government since May 2008. More than Urdu news broadcasts, its current object of hate is Bangalore/Bengaluru's 'Westernized' (pub-) culture, its special target being young urban women. Its electoral fortunes at the Centre have, however, waned considerably since the 1990s and there is much churning in the party as the baton is passed on to a new generation of leaders from those that led the Babri Masjid agitations.

In the sphere of 'formal' state-sponsored education there have been flagship programmes such as *Sarva Shiksha Abhiyan* (Education for All), launched in 2001, by the then BJP-led Central government with the aim of universalizing elementary education. This has been followed by the intense debates on the National Curriculum Framework (2005) of the NCERT and its related programme of rewriting school textbooks (especially after the BJP years), with the aim of putting the child at the centre of the education process and of trying to break stereotypes of gender, rural–urban divide, etc. These have, in turn, been overtaken by the recently passed Right to Education Act (2009), with its controversial proposal to restructure tertiary education. Along with this, new regulations have been introduced to allow foreign universities to set up offshore campuses in India.

Bombay cinema, in the meantime, has become majestically 'Bollywood-ized'. From the publication of *The Encyclopaedia of Indian Cinema* in 1994 (with which we began our discussion) to the world premiere of Mani Ratnam's *Raavan* on 16 June 2010 at the British Film Institute in London, the clock has come full circle. (It is another matter that in an unusual turn of events for a Mani Ratnam film, *Raavan* has dramatically flopped at the box office.)

How, then, do we join the dots, even as the world races on?

For Lacan, narrative is itself a primordial fantasy. Lacan says that we tell ourselves stories—with a neat beginning, middle and end—to give an imaginary sense of coherence to our lives; arrange things in a temporal cause–effect fashion to cover up the traumatic 'lack' (or the *objet petit a*) that, in reality, marks the place of the subject. Emerging from a very different tradition, that of political theory, Kaviraj (1992) makes a related point. For him, too, there is an inevitable element of 'fraudulence' in all historical narratives. Apart from establishing 'truth-value', history (in the sense in which one 'does' it at universities), Kaviraj proposes, also has a colligatory function—that of establishing connections between events (ibid.). Even so, reports of the same event told by different reporters differ as to how connections are made, where the ruptures lie. Derrida thus situates the deconstructive stance, which uses concepts of a logocentric order of representation even as it seeks to avoid being trapped within metaphysics of presence:

> The movements of deconstruction do not destroy structures from the outside. They are not possible and effective nor can they take

accurate aim, except by inhabiting those structures. Inhabiting them *in a certain way*, because one always inhabits, all the more when one does not suspect it (1976: 24).

Let us use Derrida, then, to look back at the way I have situated Bombay cinema. Broadly, I have located Bombay as the Enlightenment's 'other' scene. By approaching Bombay cinema through an analysis of notions of modernity that underwrite the postcolonial world my aim has been, after him, to inhabit the 'discipline' of Film Studies *differently*. In doing so, I have tried to also critique one of the fundamental assumptions of 'modern' knowledge—knowledge that invariably assumes the Western subject as the agentive self and his/her cultural formation as the norm.

Indeed, as Spivak observes, all mainstream disciplinary formations give the impression that they are self-contained entities. But these apparently crystalline disciplinary mainstreams would instantly run muddy with the dredging operations that postcolonial studies can provide. She also notes that it is not accidental that, despite Derrida's repeated invocations of disciplinary matters and the crises of European consciousness, the few attempts at harnessing deconstruction to these ends have generally not been considered germane to deconstructive literary or philosophical critique (1999: 1).

Charting the dramatic changes in the US academy from the old 'Comparative Literature' of the 1920–30s to 'Area Studies' in the 1950–60s to 'Cultural' and 'Postcolonial Studies' in the 1980–90s, Spivak (2003) has traced the changing contours of the broad academic discipline of 'English' as it has attempted to deal with changes in the student body. She shows how the old Comparative Literature, which emerged in the US in the aftermath of the Second World War, has radically changed in profile in the context of a new globalizing world—a world where, there has been a 500 per cent increase in Asian immigration to the US since 1965, for instance.

However, even if the academic front since the 1980–90s has been seized by the postcolonial initiative, Spivak cautions us that Postcolonial Studies itself can become an alibi of neocolonial knowledge if it places colonialism securely in the past and/or suggests a continuous line from the past to the present. In such a context the task for the postcolonial academy, Spivak suggests, 'is to learn to use the Enlightenment from below; strictly speaking, abuse it' (1992: 3). As she makes a passionate plea for a *new* Comparative Literature in the US, one not so overwhelmingly determined by the market, Spivak draws on Freud's notion of the uncanny to imagine the contours of this discipline-to-come.[1] The general sense of Freud's use of the word *unheimlich* is that of turning the homey (familiar?) into the strange or frightening. Through a painstaking reading of Freud's essay 'The Uncanny' (1955a: 217–52), she then wrests Freud's notion of the uncanny from its specific narrative into a more general *imaginative* move that the new Comparative Literature will have to make as it tries to theorize collectivities, border crossings and questions of identity in ways radically different from prevailing ideas of American multiculturalism. In the process, Spivak shifts Freud's signifier of the uncanny—the vagina—onto colonialism, decoloniza-tion and postcoloniality, which also 'involve[d] special kinds of traffic with people deemed 'other'—the familiarity of a presumed common humanity defamiliarized' (2003: 77). I find Spivak's move richly suggestive for my own apparently 'unfamiliar' mode of locating the Bombay film industry. Like Spivak, I too must in the end leave it for the future reader to decide. But my reason for approaching Bombay cinema through an analysis of the language-question is similarly an attempt to make 'unfamiliar' the prevailing contours of Film Studies in the hope of a new Film-Studies-to-come.

I have cited Rajadhyaksha's work on several instances in the book. In direct polemic with the Bordwell, Staiger and Thompson's formulation of the 'Hollywood mode of production', Rajadhyaksha has similarly argued that the 'Hollywood mode' produced ways of talking about films (and comprehending technology) that itself need to be historicized from Indian cinema's point of view (1995, 2009). By locating Bombay cinema within the subtle shifts of dynamics between 'high' and 'popular' culture in India, my aim has likewise been to show that Bombay cinema derives its unique idiom from the multiple contradictions that marked the coming into being of an anticolonial bourgeois democracy.

Following the line of enquiry opened by Chatterjee, I have read Bombay cinema as an instance of the bilingualism of post-colonial modernity—as the conflicting idioms of the terrains of 'politics' and 'culture' in non-Western societies that are the trace of a deep historical scar. Enlightenment Reason, Chatterjee has shown, has functioned for the last 200 years as the carrier through which the universalist urge of capital travelled across the globe. In this journey a certain notion of modernity, emerging out of the marriage between Reason and metropolitan capital, became the most lethal conduit for the West as it sought to conquer new markets. Anticolonial nationalisms, while they challenged overtly racist ideologies, did not however have in their arsenal the theoretical wherewithal to challenge the world-historical contradiction between capital and the nation-people. Instead Chatterjee has argued that the logic of a 'passive revolution' determined that the life of the people was again sought to be absorbed into the body of the state, albeit in a fragile and contradictory fashion.

With regard to the bilingualism of the postcolonial world, the conceptual idiom signified by Hindi—contesting the universalist claims of English —nevertheless endorsed the rationality of the colonial state, blocking a resolution of the historical–political contradictions between metropolitan capital and the vast subaltern sectors in India. Moreover, given the conjuncture of English and Hindi since the 1980s, there has been a new overlap between the terrains of politics and culture as the ideology of Hindutva has appropriated the colonial logic of counting/enumeration to redefine Indianness in virulently exclusionistic idioms.[2]

Additionally, the logic of a passive revolution, Gramsci argues, is that it incorporates into its thesis a part of its antithesis (1971: 106–14). As Chatterjee has shown with reference to India, the Gandhian intervention in the early twentieth century provided the channel through which the ideologies and aspirations of the nation-people were reinscribed within the framework of a bourgeois political order. After Independence, the 1960–70s marked a period of renewed assertion by the nation-people to claim the emancipatory dreams signified by the birth of a 'national' state. The 1980s, from this perspective, mark the critical crossover point when the egalitarian promises of 'Nehruvian socialism' were again comprehensively subsumed by a new free-market logic through the programme of structural adjustment. The rhetoric mobilized to do so was that of efficiency, technological sophistication and an accompanying discourse on 'secular merit'. Furthermore, the new logic of capital found hospitable climate in the changed nature of politics initiated during the Indira Gandhi era. To hark back to Kaviraj (1988) briefly, present-day India represents a case where even a passive revolution has failed as despotic/feudal forms of power were reinserted into the apparatuses of a bourgeois state.

Moreover, it was this unique conjuncture that provided the constitutive ground for the new 1980s' Bombay commercial. The realignment of dominance within the different sectors of the Bombay industry and the rise to prominence of the music sector symptomized this intersection of new electronic/digital technologies (such as television, satellite and computer networks) with the revival of caste-based and religious fundamentalism. Thus the technical sophistication of the new Bombay commercial (what I have called its televisual realism) cohabited skilfully with ideologies that now targeted feminism (e.g. *QSQT*) or secularism (e.g. *Tezaab*) as Others of the nation.

In conclusion then, what should our feelings be as we look back at (fragments of) the century gone by? And then the more mundane question: how does one take leave, in a book? My indebtedness to the genius of Freud informs its every page. It seems fitting, therefore, to turn to Freud once again. On the first page of his crucial paper on 'Mourning and Melancholia' (1917), Freud mentions, almost offhandedly, that mourning can be sparked not only by the loss of a loved one but equally by an abstraction, '[. . .] such as one's country, liberty, an ideal' (1953d: 237). He proposes here the question of how best to consider the relationship of our psychic and political futures to our pasts. Through my readings of the Bombay industry at a particularly fragile moment in the nation's history, I have likewise tried to imagine ways of negotiating brutal alternatives that might still be available to (or possible for) us in India today. In the final analysis, trying to follow Freud, I too have sought to bring psychoanalysis in conversation with film and political theory in the hope of repositioning the reader to the last century's continuing narrative of utopianism and despair.

Notes

1 But this is not to overlook Spivak's unsettling general resistance, here the references are too many, to psychoanalysis as a lexicon for social/political/ cultural analysis.

2 This exclusionistic logic has vitiated the public sphere in alarming ways over the past few years—ranging from Bihari taxi-drivers being targeted as 'outsiders' in Bombay/Mumbai to violent protests to stop the release of a film over a Star's 'conciliatory' remarks on Pakistani cricketers.

PLOT SUMMARY OF *QAYAMAT SE QAYAMAT TAK* (1988)

The two landlord families of Jaswant Singh and Raghubir Singh live in the idyllic village of Dhanakpur. Raghubir's younger son, Ratan, has had an affair with Madhumati, Jaswant Singh's youngest sister, but both families are unaware of this. Now, she is also pregnant. In the meantime, Ratan's marriage has been arranged with someone else. When Madhumati confronts Ratan, he turns out to be a coward. Jaswant Singh approaches Raghubir but that also proves futile. Madhumati commits suicide in despair. As revenge, Dhanraj Singh, Jaswant's younger brother, kills Ratan on his wedding day in full view of the wedding guests. He is consequently sentenced to life imprisonment.

Jaswant Singh meanwhile has decided that the family will move to Delhi. Years pass and, completely by accident, Dhanraj Singh's son, Raj (Aamir Khan), falls in love with Rashmi (Juhi Chawla), who is the only daughter of Randhir Singh, Raghubir Singh's elder son.

While Raj and Rashmi do not initially know each other's family backgrounds, they decide they will not be pawns in a meaningless feud. They elope. But this is not acceptable to either family and the film ends with both Raj and Rashmi being killed.

PLOT SUMMARY OF *TEZAAB* (1988)

Mahesh Deshmukh (Anil Kapoor) is a patriotic young man who wants to become an admiral in the Indian Navy. Both his parents, who work in clerical positions in a small bank in Nasik, are killed in a bank robbery by Chota Khan, younger brother of Lotia Khan (Kiran Kumar). To fulfil his ambition, Mahesh and his sister Jyoti move to Bombay, where Mahesh meets and falls in love with his college-mate Mohini (Madhuri Dixit). Mohini, in the meantime, is being pressurized by her corrupt father Shyamlal (Anupam Kher) to give up education and become a pop star because he has to repay his debts to Lotia.

Shyamlal does not want his daughter to waste her time with a poor man like Mahesh. Mohini defies her father and runs away from home. At this point, Shyamlal and Lotia discover that they have a common enemy in Mahesh. (During his prison term after the Nasik bank robbery, Chota had become a drug-addict, an act for which Lotia holds Mahesh responsible.) Mohini and Mahesh's planned wedding is now interrupted and Jyoti—Mahesh's sister—abducted by Chota. In the violent fight that ensues,

Mahesh kills Chota and is sentenced to a year's rigorous imprisonment. Mohini is forced into a career on the stage by her father. Through various tribulations after his release from prison, Mahesh meets Mohini and the couple is finally reunited.

FILMOGRAPHY

PRIMARY TEXTS

FILM	DIRECTOR	PRODUCER	YEAR
Qayamat Se Qayamat Tak (From Disaster to Disaster)	Mansoor Khan	Nasir Hussain Films	1988
Tezaab (Acid)	N. Chandra	Dinesh Gandhi/N. Chandra Productions	1988

SECONDARY REFERENCES

FILM	DIRECTOR	YEAR
Achhut Kanya (The Untouchable Woman)	Frantz Osten	1936
Ankush (Restrain)	N. Chandra	1985
Ardha Satya (Half-Truth)	Govind Nihalani	1983

FILM	DIRECTOR	YEAR
Awara (The Tramp)	Raj Kapoor	1951
Barsaat (Rain)	Raj Kapoor	1949
Betaab (Restless)	Rahul Rawail	1983
Cheeni Kum (Less Sugar)	R. Balki	2007
Deewar (The Wall)	Yash Chopra	1975
Ek Duuje Ke Liye (Made for Each Other)	K. Balchander	1981
Ek Jaan Hain Hum (We are One)	Rajiv Mehra	1983
Ganga Jamuna (Ganga and Yamuna)	Nitin Bose	1961
Ghayal (The Wounded)	Raj Kumar Santoshi	1990
Geetanjali	Mani Ratnam	1989
Jawani (Youth)	Ramesh Behl	1984
Jhoola (The Swing)	Gyan Mukherjee	1941
Jis Desh Mein Ganga Behti Hai (The Land Through Which the Ganges Flows)	Raj Kapoor	1964
Junglee (The Uncivilized)	Subodh Mukherjee	1961
Kangan (Bangles)	Frantz Osten	1939
Karma (Duty)	Subhash Ghai	1986
Kashmir Ki Kali (The Belle of Kashmir)	Shakti Samanta	1964
Khalnayak (The Villain)	Subhash Ghai	1993
Kismet (Fate)	Gyan Mukherjee	1943
Love Story	Rajendra Kumar /Rahul Rawail	1981

FILM	DIRECTOR	YEAR
Mashaal (The Flame)	Yash Chopra	1984
Meri Jung (My Battle)	Subhash Ghai	1982
Nishabd (No Words)	Ram Gopal Varma	2007
Painter Babu (Mr Painter)	Ashok	1983
Parinda (The Bird)	Vidhu Vinod Chopra	1989
Prahaar (The Assault)	Nana Patekar	1991
Ram Teri Ganga Maili (Ram, Your Ganges Has Been Soiled)	Raj Kapoor	1985
Rocky	Sunil Dutt	1981
Roja	Mani Ratnam	1992
Shakti (Strength)	Ramesh Sippy	1982
Teri Bahon Mein (In Your Arms)	Umesh Mehra	1984
Trishul (The Trident)	Yash Chopra	1975
Zanjeer (Chains)	Prakash Mehra	1973

BIBLIOGRAPHY

ADVANI, Rukun. 1992. 'Master English, Native Publisher: A Publishing Perspective on English Studies in India', in Rajeswari Sunder Rajan (ed.), *The Lie of the Land: English Literary Study in India*. New Delhi: Oxford University Press, pp. 112–29.

ADVANI, Shalini. 1996. 'Educating the National Imagination'. *Economic and Political Weekly* 31(31): 2077–82.

AGARWAL, Amit. 1994. 'From Rice to Riches'. *India Today*, 15 August, pp. 90–1.

AHMAD, Aijaz. 1989a. 'Jameson's Rhetoric of Otherness and the "National Allegory"'. *Social Text* 17 (Fall): 3–25.

——. 1989b. 'Third World Literature and the Nationalist Ideology'. *Journal of Arts and Ideas* 17–18: 117–35.

——. 1991. 'Disciplinary English: Third Worldism and Literature', in Svati Joshi (ed.), *Rethinking English: Essays in Language, Literature, History*. New Delhi: Trianka, pp. 206–63.

——. 1993. *In Theory: Classes, Nations, Literatures*. London: Verso.

ALTHUSSER, Louis. 1971. 'Ideology and Ideological State Apparatuses', in *Lenin and Philosophy, and Other Essays* (Ben Brewster trans.). London: Monthly Review Press, pp. 127–88.

AMBEDKAR, B. R. 1967. *Annihilation of Caste*. Pune: Prakashan Press.

AMIN, Shahid. 1983. 'Gandhi as Mahatma: Gorakhpur District UP, 1921–1922', in Ranajit Guha (ed.), *Subaltern Studies*, VOL. 3. New Delhi: Oxford University Press, pp. 1–61.

ANDERSON, Benedict. 1983. *Imagined Communities: Reflections on the Origin and Spread of Nationalism*. London: Verso.

————. 1998. *The Spectre of Comparisons: Nationalism, Southeast Asia and the World* London: Verso.

BAGCHI, Jasodhara. 1991. 'Shakespeare in Loin Cloths: English Literature and the Early Nationalist Consciousness in Bengal', in Svati Joshi (ed.), *Rethinking English: Essays in Literature, Language, History*. New Delhi: Trianka, pp. 146–59.

BALDICK, Chris. 1983. *The Social Mission of English Criticism 1848–1932*. Oxford: Clarendon Press.

BALIBAR, Etienne. 1991. 'Racism and Nationalism', in Etienne Balibar and Immanuel Wallerstein, *Race, Nation, Class: Ambiguous Identities*. London: Verso, pp. 37–68.

BANERJEE, Sumanta. 1989. *The Parlour and the Street: Elite and Popular Culture in Nineteenth-Century Calcutta*. Calcutta: Seagull Books.

BARNOUW, Eric and S. Krishnaswamy (eds). 1963. *Indian Cinema*. New York: Columbia University Press.

BARTHES, Roland. 1972. *Mythologies* (Annette Lavers trans.). London: Vintage.

BEJNAMIN, Walter. 1968. *Illuminations* (Harry Zohns trans.). London: Collins and Fontana.

BHABHA, Homi K. 1994. *Nation and Narration*. New York and London: Routledge.

BISWAS, Moinak. 1995. 'The Couple and Spaces: *Harano Sur* as Melodrama'. Paper presented at the seminar 'Making Meaning in Indian Cinema'. Indian Institute of Advanced Study, Shimla.

BLACKBURN, Robin (ed.). 1975. *Explosion in a Subcontinent: India, Pakistan, Bangladesh and Ceylon*. London: Penguin/New Left Books.

BOURDIEU, Pierre. 1984. *Distinction: A Social Critique of the Judgement of Taste* (Richard Nice trans.). London: Routledge & Kegan Paul.

BRASS, Paul. 1974. *Language, Religion and Politics in North India*. Cambridge: Cambridge University Press.

BRITTON, Jacqueline, Jim Cook and Christine Gledhill (eds). 1994. *Melodrama: Stage, Picture, Screen*. London: The British Film Institute.

BROOKS, Peter. 1985. *The Melodramatic Imagination: Balzac, Henry James, Melodrama, and the Mode of Excess*. New York: Columbia University Press.

BURKE, Peter. 1969. *The Renaissance Sense of the Past*. London: Edward Arnold.

———. 1978. *Popular Culture in Early Modern Europe*. London: Harper and Row.

———. 1981. 'The Discovery of Popular Culture', in Raphael Samuel (ed.), *People's History and Socialist Theory*. London: Routledge & Kegan Paul, pp. 216–26.

BUTALIA, Urvashi. 1991. 'English Textbook, Indian Publisher', in Svati Joshi (ed.), *Rethinking English: Essays in Language, Literature, History*. New Delhi: Trianka, pp. 321–46.

BUTCHER, Melissa. 2003. *Transnational Television: When Star Came to India*. New Delhi: Sage.

CADAVA, Eduardo, Peter Connor and Jean-Luc Nancy (eds). 1991. *Who Comes After the Subject?* New York and London: Routledge.

CHAKRABARTY, Dipesh. 1992a. 'Death of History: Historical Consciousness and the Culture of Late Capitalism'. *Public Culture* 4(2) (Spring): 48–65.

———. 1992b. 'Who Speaks for Indian Pasts: Postcoloniality and the Artifice of History'. *Representations* (Winter): 1–26.

———. 1993. 'The Difference-Deferral of Colonial Modernity: Public Debates on Domesticity in Nineteenth Century British Bengal'. *History Workshop* 36 (Autumn): 3–64.

———. 1995. 'Modernity and Ethnicity in India: A History for the Present'. *Economic and Political Weekly* 30(52): 3373–80.

———. 2001. *Provincializing Europe: Postcolonial Thought and Historical Difference*. Delhi: Oxford University Press.

CHAKRAVARTY, Sumita S. 1993. *National Identity in Indian Popular Cinema, 1947–1987*. Austin, TX: University of Texas Press.

CHANDRA, Anupama. 1989. 'Mean Street Moghul'. *India Today*, 28 February, pp. 117–19

———. 1993. 'The Madhuri Magic'. *India Today*, 15 September, pp. 124–34.

———. 1994a. 'Arranged Marriages: Cool Calculations'. *India Today*, 31 July, p. 135

———. 1994b. 'Music Mania'. *India Today*, 15 November, pp. 100–07.

——— and Kavita Shetty. 1993. 'Hitting the Right Notes'. *India Today*, 30 November, pp. 149–56.

CHANDRA, Bipan, Amales Tripathi and Barun De. 1979. *Freedom Struggle*. New Delhi: National Book Trust.

CHATTERJEE, Partha. 1986. *Nationalist Thought and the Colonial World: A Derivative Discourse?* New Delhi: Oxford University Press.

——. 1988. 'On Gramsci's Fundamental Mistake'. *Economic and Political Weekly* 23(5): 24–6.

——. 1989. 'The Nationalist Resolution of the Women's Question', in Kumkum Sangari and Sudesh Vaid (eds), *Recasting Women: Essays in Colonial History*. New Delhi: Kali for Women, pp. 233–53.

——. 1994a. *The Nation and Its Fragments: Colonial and Postcolonial Histories*. New Delhi: Oxford University Press.

——. 1994b. 'Secularism and Toleration'. *Economic and Political Weekly* 28(29): 1768–77.

——. 1995a. 'Talking About Our Modernity'. Paper presented at the workshop 'Cultures of Modernity'. Centre for Studies in Social Sciences, Calcutta. [Published as *Our Modernity* (Rotterdam/Dakar: SEPHIS CODESRIA, 1997).]

—— (ed.). 1995b. *The Disciplines in Colonial Bengal*. Calcutta: Samya and Centre for Studies in Social Sciences.

——. 1997. 'Beyond the Nation? Or Within?' *Economic and Political Weekly* 33(1–2): 30–34.

—— (ed.). 1998a. *Wages of Freedom: Fifty Years of the Indian Nation-State*. New Delhi: Oxford University Press.

——. 1998b. 'Community in the East'. *Economic and Political Weekly* 33(6): 277–82.

——. 2004a. 'The Nation in Heterogeneous Time', in *The Politics of the Governed: Reflections on Popular Politics in Most of the World*. New York: Columbia University Press, pp. 3–27.

——. 2004b. 'Populations and Political Society', in *The Politics of the Governed: Reflections on Popular Politics in Most of the World*. New York: Columbia University Press, pp. 28–52.

——. 2008. 'Democracy and Economic Transformation'. *Economic and Political Weekly* 43(16) (19 April): 53–62.

CHATTERJEE, Ratnabali. 1990. *From the Karkhana to the Studio: Roles of Patrons and Artists in Bengal*. New Delhi: Books and Books.

CHERIAN, Anita. 1995. 'Modernism, The Folk and Contemporary Indian Theatre'. Paper presented at the National Research Seminar on 'English Studies in the Nineties'. University of Hyderabad, Hyderabad.

COOK, Pam (ed.). 1985. *The Cinema Book*. London: British Film Institute.

DASGUPTA, Jyotindra. 1970. *Language Conflict and National Development: Group Politics and National Language Policy in India*. Berkeley: University of California Press.

DATTA, Pradip K. 1991. 'VHP's Ram at Ayodhya: Reincarnation through Ideology and Organisation'. *Economic and Political Weekly* 26(44): 2517.

DAVIS, Lennard. 1987. *Resisting Novels*: *Ideology and Fiction*. London: Methuen.

DE LAURETIS, Teresa. 1984. *Alice Doesn't*: *Feminism, Semiotics, Cinema*. London: Macmillan.

DEAN, Mitchell. 1994. *Critical and Effective Histories*: *Foucault's Method and Historical Sociology*. New York and London: Routledge.

DERRIDA, Jacques. 1976. *Of Grammatology* (Gayatri Chakravorty Spivak trans.). Baltimore: Johns Hopkins University Press.

———. 1978. *Writing and Difference* (Alan Bass trans.). Chicago: University of Chicago Press.

DESAI, A. R. 1959. *Social Background of Indian Nationalism*. Bombay: Habeli Press.

DESCOMBE, Vincent. 1991. 'Apropos of the "Critique of the Subject" and the Critique of this Critique', in Eduardo Cadava, Peter Connor and Jean-Luc Nancy (eds), *Who Comes After the Subject?* New York and London: Routledge, pp. 120–35.

DESHPANDE, Satish. 1993. 'Imagined Economies: Styles of Nation-Building in Twentieth Century India'. *Journal of Arts and Ideas* 25–26: 5–36.

———. 1995. 'Communalising the Nation Space: Notes on Spatial Strategies of Hindutva'. *Economic and Political Weekly* 30(50): 3220–7.

DHARESHWAR, Vivek. 1993. 'Caste and the Secular Self'. *Journal of Arts and Ideas* 25–26: 115–26.

———. 1995a. '"Our Time": History, Sovereignty, Politics'. *Economic and Political Weekly* 30(6) (11 February): 317–24.

———. 1995b. 'Postcolonial in the Postmodern or, The Political after Modernity'. *Economic and Political Weekly* 30(30): 1904–12.

———. 2010. 'Politics, Experience and Cognitive Enslavement: Gandhi's *Hind Swaraj*'. *Economic and Political Weekly* 45(12) (20 March): 51–8.

——— and Tejaswini Niranjana. 1996. 'Kaadalan and the Politics of Resignification: Fashion, Violence and the Body'. *Journal of Arts and Ideas* 29: 5–26.

——— and R. Srivatsan. 1993. '"Rowdy-sheeters": An Essay on Subalternity and Politics'. Paper presented at the Sublatern/Anveshi Studies conference, Hyderabad. [Published in 1996 in Shahid Amin and Dipesh Chakrabarty (eds), *Subaltern Studies IX*: *Writings on South Asian History and Society*. New Delhi: Oxford University Press, pp. 201–31.]

DIRKS, Nicholas, B. 1990. 'History as Sign of the Modern'. *Public Culture* 2(2) (Spring): 25–32.

DOANE, Mary Ann. 1985. 'The Woman's Film: Possession and Address', in Christine Gledhill (ed.), *Home is Where the Heart Is*: *Studies in Melodrama and the Woman's Film*. London: British Film Institute, pp. 283–98.

DURING, Simon. 1993. 'Postmodernism or Post-colonialism Today', in Thomas Docherty (ed.), *Postmodernism: A Reader*. Cambridge: Cambridge University Press, pp. 448–62.

DYER, Richard. 1986. *Stars*. London: British Film Institute.

DYSON, T. 1992. *Infant and Child Mortality in India*. London: London School of Economics.

DWIVEDI, S. 1981. *Hindi on Trial*. New Delhi: Vikas Publishing House.

Economic and Political Weekly. 1994. 'Secularism, Modernity and the State'. Special Issue, 29(28).

ENGELS, Friedrich. 1902. *The Origin of the Family, Private Property and the State* (Ernest Untermann trans.). Chicago: C. H. Kerr and Company.

FABIAN, Johannes. 1983. *Time and the Other: How Anthropology Makes its Object*. New York: Columbia University Press.

FANON, Frantz. 1990 [1965]. *The Wretched of the Earth* (Constance Farrington trans.). London: MacGibbon and Kee.

Filmfare. 1988. 'Madhuri Dixit'. 19 October, p. 22.

FISKE, John. 1989. *Reading the Popular*. Boston: Unwin Hyman.

FOUCAULT, Michel. 1972. *The Archaeology of Knowledge and the Discourse on Language* (A. M. Sheridan Smith trans.). New York: Pantheon.

———. 1979. *Discipline and Punish: The Birth of the Prison* (Alan Sheridan trans.). New York: Vintage Books.

———. 1980. *Power/Knowledge: Selected Interviews and Other Writings, 1972–1977* (Colin Gordon ed. and trans.). New York: Pantheon Books.

———. 1984. 'What is Enlightenment?' in Paul Rabinow (ed.), *The Foucault Reader*. New York: Pantheon Books.

———. 1986. 'Of Other Spaces' (unrevised text of a lecture given in 1967). *Diacritics* (Spring).

———. 1988. *Technologies of the Self: A Seminar with Michel Foucault* (Luther H. Martin, Huck Gutman, Patrick H. Hutton eds). Amherst: University of Massachusetts Press.

———. 1990 [1976]. *The History of Sexuality, Volume 1: An Introduction* (Robert Hurley trans.). London: Penguin, pp. 131–60.

———. 1991 [1978]. 'Governmentality', in Graham Burchell, Colin Gordon and Peter Miller (eds), *The Foucault Effect: Studies in Governmentality*. Hemel Hemstead: Harvester/Wheatsheaf, pp. 87–104.

FRANK, Andre Gunder. 1970. 'The Development of Underdevelopment', in Robert I. Rhodes (ed.), *Imperialism and Underdevelopment: A Reader*. New York: Monthly Review Press, pp. 4–17.

FRANKEL, Francine R. 1978. *India's Political Economy, 1947–1977: The Gradual Revolution*. Princeton: Princeton University Press.

FREIRE, Paulo. 1990 [1972]. *Pedagogy of the Oppressed* (Myra Bergman Ramos trans.). London: Penguin.

FREUD, Sigmund. 1956–74. *The Standard Edition of the Complete Psychological Works of Sigmund Freud* (translated from the German under the General Editorship of James Strachey, in collaboration with Anna Freud, assisted by Alix Strachey and Alan Tyson), 24 VOLS. London: Hogarth.

——. 1953a [1900]. 'The Interpretation of Dreams', in *The Standard Edition of the Complete Psychological Works of Sigmund Freud*, VOLS 4 and 5 (translated from the German under the General Editorship of James Strachey, in collaboration with Anna Freud, assisted by Alix Strachey and Alan Tyson). London: Hogarth Press, pp. 1–338, 339–627.

——. 1953b [1905]. 'Three Essays on the Theory of Sexuality', in *The Standard Edition of the Complete Psychological Works of Sigmund Freud*, VOL. 7 (translated from the German under the General Editorship of James Strachey, in collaboration with Anna Freud, assisted by Alix Strachey and Alan Tyson). London: Hogarth Press, pp. 123–45.

——. 1953c [1913]. 'Totem and Taboo: Some Points of Agreement Between the Mental Lives of Savages and Neurotics', in *The Standard Edition of the Complete Psychological Works of Sigmund Freud*, VOL. 13 (translated from the German under the General Editorship of James Strachey, in collaboration with Anna Freud, assisted by Alix Strachey and Alan Tyson). London: Hogarth Press, pp. 1–161.

——. 1953d [1917]. 'Mourning and Melancholia', in *The Standard Edition of the Complete Psychological Works of Sigmund Freud*, VOL. 14 (translated from the German under the General Editorship of James Strachey, in collaboration with Anna Freud, assisted by Alix Strachey and Alan Tyson). London: Hogarth Press, pp. 237–59.

——. 1955a [1919]. 'The Uncanny', in *The Standard Edition of the Complete Psychological Works of Sigmund Freud*, VOL. 17 (translated from the German under the General Editorship of James Strachey, in collaboration with Anna Freud, assisted by Alix Strachey and Alan Tyson). London: Hogarth Press, pp. 217–52.

——. 1955b [1921]. 'Group Psychology and the Analysis of the Ego', in *The Standard Edition of the Complete Psychological Works of Sigmund Freud*, VOL. 18 (translated from the German under the General Editorship of James Strachey, in collaboration with Anna Freud, assisted by Alix Strachey and Alan Tyson). London: Hogarth Press, pp. 65–143.

——. 1959. 'On Narcissism: An Introduction. Volume 1: Papers on Metapsychology', in *Sigmund Freud: Collected Papers*, VOLS 1–5 (General Editor Ernest

Jones; translation under the supervision of Joan Riviere). New York: Basic Books, pp. 30–59.

——. 1974 [1938]. 'Moses and Monotheism', in *The Standard Edition of the Complete Psychological Works of Sigmund Freud*, VOL. 23 (translated from the German under the General Editorship of James Strachey, in collaboration with Anna Freud, assisted by Alix Strachey and Alan Tyson). London: Hogarth Press, pp. 1–138.

——. 1982. *Sigmund Freud: Introductory Lectures on Psychoanalysis*, VOL. 1 (Angela Richards and James Strachey eds; James Strachey trans.). London: Penguin.

FUKUYAMA, Francis. 1992. *The End of History and the Last Man*. Harmondsworth and Middlesex: Penguin.

GANDHI, M. K. 1923 [1911]. *Hind Swaraj or Indian Home Rule*. Ahmedabad: Navjivan Press.

GANDHY Behroze and Rosie Thomas. 1991. 'Three Indian Film Stars', in Christine Gledhill (ed.), *Stardom: Industry of Desire*. New York and London: Routledge, pp. 107–131.

GANGHAR, Amrit. 1995. 'Films from the City of Dreams', in Sujata Patel and Alice Thorner (eds), *Bombay: Mosaic of Modern Culture*. New Delhi: Oxford University Press, pp. 233–45.

GHOSH, Sanjukta Tultul. 1992. 'Celluloid Nationalism: Cultural Politics in Popular Indian Cinema'. Ph.D. dissertation. Ohio State University, Columbus, Ohio.

GILCHRIST, John. 1798. *The Oriental Linguist: An Easy and Familiar Introduction to the Popular Language of Hindoostan*. London: Ferris and Greenaway.

GIROUX, Henry A. 1993. 'Reclaiming the Social: Resistance and Politics in Celluloid Culture', in Jim Collins, Hilary Radner, Ava Collins (eds), *Film Theory Goes to the Movies*. New York and London: Routledge, pp. 37–56.

GLEDHILL, Christine (ed.). 1985. *Home Is Where the Heart Is: Studies in Melodrama and the Woman's Film*. London: British Film Institute.

GOPAL, Madan. 1990. *Freedom Movement and the Role of the Press*. New Delhi: Criterion.

GOPALAN, Lalitha. 1993. 'Wogs, Natives, Heroes: Examining Cinema and National Identity'. Ph.D. dissertation. Univeristy of Rochester, Rochester, New York.

——. 2003. *Cinema of Interruptions: Action Genres of Conemporary Indian Cinema*. New Delhi: Oxford University Press.

GORDON, Colin. 1991. 'Governmental Rationality: An Introduction', in Graham Burchell, Colin Gordon and Peter Miller (eds), *The Foucault Effect: Studies in Governmentality*. Hemel Hemstead: Harvester/Wheatsheaf, pp. 1–52.

GRAMSCI, Antonio. 1971 [1929–35]. *Selections From Prison Notebooks* (Quintin Hoare and Geoffrey Nowell-Smith ed. and trans.). London: Lawrence and Wishart.

———. 1985 [1928–34]. *Selections From Cultural Writings* (Geoffrey Nowell Smith and David Forgacs eds; William Boelhower trans.). London: Lawrence and Wishart.

GRIMSTEAD, David. 1994. 'Vigilante Chronicles: The Politics of Melodrama Brought to Life', in Jacqueline Britton, Jim Cook and Christine Gledhill (eds), *Melodrama: Stage, Picture, Screen*. London: British Film Institute.

GUHA, Ranajit. 1983a. *Elementary Aspects of Peasant Insurgency in Colonial India*. New Delhi: Oxford University Press.

———. 1983b. 'On Some Aspects of the Historiography of Colonial India', in Ranajit Guha and Gayatri Chakravorty Spivak (eds), *Selected Subaltern Studies*. New York: Oxford University Press, pp. 37–44.

——— (ed.). 1983–94. *Subaltern Studies*, VOLS 1–8. New Delhi: Oxford University Press.

GUHA-THAKURTA, Tapati. 1992. *The Making of a New 'Indian' Art: Artists, Aesthetics and Nationalism in Bengal, c.1850–1920*. Cambridge: Cambridge University Press.

GUPTA, Nilanajana. 1998. *Switching Channels: Ideologies of Television in India*. New Delhi: Oxford University Press.

HALL, Stuart. 1981. 'Notes on Deconstructing the Popular', in Raphael Samuel (ed.), *People's History and Socialist Theory*. London: Routledge & Kegan Paul, pp. 227–39.

———. 1992. 'Cultural Studies and the Centre: Some Problems and Problematics', in Stuart Hall, Dorothy Hobson, Andrew Lowe and Paul Willis (eds), *Culture, Media, Language: Working Papers in Cultural Studies, 1972–1979*. New York and London: Routledge, in association with Centre for Contemporary Cultural Studies, UK, pp. 2–35.

HANDA, R. L. 1983. *Missing Links in Link Language*. New Delhi: Sterling.

HEUZE, Gerard. 1992. 'Shiv Sena and National Hinduism'. *Economic and Political Weekly* 27(40/41): 2189–94/2553–62.

HOBSBAWM, Eric and Terence Ranger (eds). 1983. *The Invention of Tradition*. London: Macmillan.

ILIAIAH, Kancha. 1996. *Why I am Not a Hindu: A Sudra Critique of Hindutva Brahminism*. Calcutta: Samya.

INDEN, Ronald. 1986. 'Orientalist Constructions of India'. *Modern Asian Studies* 29(3): 401–46.

IRSCHICK, Eugene F. 1969. *Politics and Social Conflict in South India: The Non-Brahmin Movement and Tamil Separatism 1916–1929*. Berkeley: University of California Press.

JACOBSEN, Mikkel Borch. 1991. 'The Freudian Subject, from Politics to Ethics', in Eduardo Cadava, Peter Connor and John-Luc Nancy (eds), *Who Comes After the Subject?* New York and London: Routledge, pp. 61–79

JAHAGIRDAR, Archana and Anupama Chandra. 1994. 'Shaping Up: The Modelling Business'. *India Today*, 31 October, pp. 187–94.

JAIN, Madhu. 1988. 'The Day of the Villain'. *India Today*, 30 November, pp. 148–61.

———. 1989. 'Return to Romance'. *India Today*, 15 May, pp. 132–9.

———. 1991. 'Cinema Turns Sexy'. *India Today*, 15 November, pp. 50–6.

———. 1994a. 'Joint Families: Change Amidst Continuities'. *India Today*, 30 September, pp. 80–92.

———. 1994b. 'Stress and Marriage'. *India Today*, 30 September, pp. 186–92.

———. 1994c. 'Today's Angry Young Indian'. *India Today*, 30 September, pp. 132–33.

JAMESON, Fredric. 1981. *The Political Unconscious: Narrative as Socially Symbolic Act*. London: Methuen.

———. 1989. 'Third World Literature in the Era of Multinational Capitalism'. *Social Text* 15: 65–88.

———. 1992. *Signature of the Visible*. New York and London: Routledge.

———. 1993. 'Postmodernism, or, the Cultural Logic of Late Capitalism', in Thomas Docherty (ed.), *Postmodernism: A Reader*. Cambridge: Cambridge University Press, pp. 62–93.

———. 1994. 'Postmodernism and the Market', in Slavoj Žižek (ed.), *Mapping Ideology*. London: Verso.

JAY, Martin and Jane Flax. 1993. 'On Fredric Jameson, Postmodernism, or, the Cultural Logic of Late Capitalism'. *History and Theory* 32(3): 296–311.

JEFFORDS, Susan. 1993. 'The Big Switch: Hollywood Masculinity in the Nineties', in Jim Collins, Hilary Radner and Ava Collins (eds), *Film Theory Goes to the Movies*. New York and London: Routledge, pp. 196–205.

JOSHI, P. C. 1985. *An Indian Personality for Television: Report on the Working Group of Software for Doordarshan*. New Delhi: Ministry of Information and Broadcasting, Government of India.

JOSHI, Svati (ed.). 1991. *Rethinking English: Essays in Language, Literature, History*. New Delhi: Trianka.

Journal of Arts and Ideas. 1987. 'Cultural Dimensions of Indian Nationalism'. Special Issue, 14–15.

Journal of Arts and Ideas. 1993. Special Issue on 'Careers of Modernity', 25–26.

Journal of Arts and Ideas. 1999. 'Gender, Media and the Rhetorics of Liberalization'. Special Issue, 32–33.

JUNG, Carl Gustav. 1967 [1912]. *Symbols of Transformation: An Analysis of the Prelude to a Case of Schizophrenia* (Richard Francis Carrington Hull trans.). Princeton: Princeton University Press.

KABIR, Nasreen Munni. 1999. *Talking Films: Conversations on Hindi Cinema with Javed Akhtar*. New Delhi: Oxford University Press.

KANT, Immanuel. 1963 [1784]. *On History* (Lewis White Beck ed.). Indianapolis: Bobbs-Merrill.

KAPUR, Geeta. 1987. 'Mythic Material in Indian Cinema'. *Journal of Arts and Ideas* 14–15: 79–108.

———. 1989. 'Ravi Varma: Representational Dilemmas of a Nineteenth-Century Indian Painter'. *Journal of Arts and Ideas* 17–18: 59–75.

———. 1991. 'The Place of the Modern in Indian Cultural Practice'. *Economic and Political Weekly* 26(49): 2803–06.

KARAT, Prakash. 1973. *Language and Nationality Politics in India*. Madras: Orient Longman.

KAVIRAJ, Sudipta. 1988. 'A Critique of the Passive Revolution'. *Economic and Political Weekly* 23(45–7): 2429–44.

———. 1990. 'Capitalism and the Cultural Process'. *Journal of Arts and Ideas* 19: 61–75.

———. 1991. 'On State, Society and Discourse in India', in James Manor (ed.), *Rethinking Third World Politics*. London and New York: Longman, pp. 72–99.

———. 1992. 'The Imaginary Institution of India', in Partha Chatterjee and Gyanendra Pandey (eds), *Subaltern Studies*, VOL. 7. New Delhi: Oxford University Press, pp. 1–39.

———. 1998. 'The Culture of Representative Democracy', in Partha Chatterjee (ed.), *Wages of Freedom: Fifty Years of the Indian Nation-State*. New Delhi: Oxford University Press, pp. 147–75.

KING, Christopher R. 1994. *One Language, Two Scripts: The Hindi Movement in Nineteenth Century Northern India*. New Delhi: Oxford University Press.

KING, Robert D. 1997. *Nehru and the Language Politics of India*. New Delhi: Oxford University Press.

KOMAL. 1989. 'Anil Kapoor'. *Film Information*, 7 January.

KOPPIKAR, Smruti. 1997. 'Murder in Mumbai'. *India Today*, 15 August, pp. 18–26.

KOSAMBI, Damodar Dharmananda. 1957. *Exasperating Essays: Exercise in the Dialectical Method*. Pune: People's Book House.

KRISHNAN, Srilata. 1996a. '"Feminists are Modern: Families are Indian": Women's Magazines and the Politics of Modernity'. Unpublished paper, part of doctoral thesis from the Department of English, University of Hyderabad.

———. 1996b. 'English or Hindi: The Brahmin's Mother-tongue'. Unpublished paper, part of doctoral thesis from the Department of English, University of Hyderabad.

KUMAR, Krishna. 1987a. 'Origins of India's Textbook Culture', in Nehru Memorial Museum and Library, New Delhi, and Centre for Contemporary Studies, New Delhi (eds), *Occasional Papers on History and Society*. New Delhi: Nehru Memorial Museum and Library.

———. 1987b. 'The Year of New Education'. *Economic and Political Weekly* 22(35) (29 August): 1481–2.

———. 1991. *The Political Agenda of Education: A Study of Colonialist and Nationalist Ideas*. New Delhi: Sage.

KUMAR, Avinash. 1999. 'History, Community, Consciousness: A Study of Hindi Journals, 1900–1930', in Tapati Guha-Thakurta (ed.), *Culture and the Disciplines: Papers from the Cultural Studies Workshops*. Calcutta: Centre for Studies in Social Sciences, Calcutta, pp. 55–69.

LACAN, Jacques. 1992 [1986]. *The Ethics of Psychoanalysis* (Jacques-Alain Miller ed. and trans.). New York: Norton.

LACLAU, Ernetso and Chantal Mouffe. 1985. *Hegemony and Socialist Strategy: Towards a Radical Democratic Politics*. London: Verso.

LOOMBA, Ania. 1989. *Gender, Race, Renaissance Drama*. Manchester: Manchester University Press.

———. 1992. 'Criticism and Pedagogy in the Indian Classroom', in Rajeswari Sunder Rajan (ed.), *The Lie of the Land: English Literary Study in India*. New Delhi: Oxford University Press, pp. 63–89.

———. 1993. 'Dead Women Tell No Tales: Issues of Female Subjectivity, Subaltern Agency and Tradition in Colonial and Post-colonial Writings on Widow Immolation in India'. *History Workshop* 36 (Autumn): 209–27.

MACAULAY, Thomas Babington. 1957 [1835]. 'Minute of 2 February 1835 on Indian Education', in G. M. Young (ed.), *Macaulay: Prose and Poetry*. Cambridge, Massachusetts: Harvard University Press, pp. 721–9.

MANI, Lata. 1987. 'Contentious Traditions: The Debate on *Sati* in Colonial India'. *Cultural Critique* (Fall): 119–56.

———. 1993. 'The Female Subject, The Colonial Gaze: Reading Eyewitness Accounts of Widow Burning', in Tejaswini Niranjana, P. Sudhir, Vivek Dhareshwar (eds), *Interrogating Modernity: Culture and Colonialism in India*, Calcutta: Seagull Books, pp. 273–90.

MANUEL, Peter. 1993. *Cassette Culture: Popular Music and Technology in North India*. Chicago: University of Chicago Press.

MARX, Karl. 1898. *The Eighteenth Brumaire of Louis Bonaparte* (Daniel de Leon trans.). London: International Publishing Company.

MAZUMDAR, Ranjani. 2007. *Bombay Cinema: An Archive of the City*. Minneapolis: University of Minnesota Press.

MERCHANT, Cyrus H. 1988a. 'Look Back in Anger'. *Stardust*, September, pp. 39–43.

———. 1988b. 'Love Triumphs'. *Stardust*, October.

MISRA, B. B. 1978. *The Indian Middle Classes: Their Growth in Modern Times*. New Delhi: Oxford University Press.

MISRA, Bal G. 1979. 'Language Movements in the Hindi Region', in E. Annamalai (ed.), *Language Movements in India*. Mysore: Central Institute of Indian Languages, pp. 70–9.

MODLESKI, Tania. 1987. 'Time and Desire in the Woman's Film', in Christine Gledhill (ed.), *Home Is Where the Heart Is: Studies in Melodrama and the Woman's Film*. London: British Film Institute, pp. 326–39.

MORSE, Margaret. 1986. 'The Television News Personality and Credibility: Reflections on the News in Transition', in Tania Modleski (ed.), *Critical Approaches to Mass Culture*. Bloomington and Indianapolis: Indiana University Press, pp. 55–70.

MULHERN, Francis. 1979. *The Moment of Scrutiny*. London: New Left Books.

MULVEY, Laura. 1975. 'Visual Pleasure and Narrative Cinema'. *Screen* 16(4) (Winter): 119–30.

———. 1989. *Visual and Other Pleasures*. London: Macmillan.

———. 1994. 'It Will Be a Magnificent Obsession: Melodrama's Role in the Development of Film Theory', in Jacqueline Britton, Jim Cook and Christine Gledhill (eds), *Melodrama: Stage, Picture, Screen*. London: British Film Institute, pp. 121–34.

———. 1996. *Fetishism and Curiosity*. London/Bloomington: British Film Institute/ Indiana University Press.

NAIR, Janaki. 1994. 'Of Dominated Cultures and State Protection'. *The Hindu*, 30 October, p. 7.

NEHRU, Jawaharlal. 1946. *Discovery of India*. New York: The John Day Company.

NIRANJANA, Tejaswini. 1990. 'Translation, Colonialism and Rise of English'. *Economic and Political Weekly* 25(15) (4 April): 773–9.

——. 1991. 'Cinema, Femininity and the Economy of Consumption'. *Economic and Political Weekly* 26(43) (26 October): 85–6.

——. 1992. *Siting Translation: History, Post-Structuralism and the Colonial Context.* Berkeley: University of California Press.

——. 1993. 'Whose Culture is It? Contesting the Modern'. *Journal of Arts and Ideas* 25–26: 139–51.

——. 1994. 'Integrating Whose Nation? Tourists and Terrorists in *Roja*'. *Economic and Political Weekly* 29(3) (15 January): 79–82.

NIVEDITA and Sandhya. 1988. 'Games Aamir Plays'. *Showtime*, November, pp. 45–7.

OBEYESEKERE, Gananath. 1999. 'Further Steps in Relativization: The Indian Oedipus Revisited', in T. G. Vaidyanathan and Jeffery John Kripal (eds), *Vishnu on Freud's Desk: A Reader in Psychoanalysis and Hinduism*. Delhi: Oxford University Press, pp. 147–63.

O'HANLON, Rosalind. 1988. 'Recovering the Subject: Subaltern Studies and Histories of Resistance in Colonial South Asia'. *Modern Asian Studies* 22(1): 189–224.

OMVEDT, Gail. 1996. *Dalit Vision*. Hyderabad: Orient Longman.

ORSINI, Fransesca. 1995. 'From Social Critique to Romance: The "Social" in Popular Hindi Fiction'. Paper presented at the seminar 'Consumption of Popular Culture in India'. School of Oriental and African Studies, London.

PADIKKAL, Shivarama. 1993. 'Inventing Modernity: The Emergence of the Novel in India', in Tejaswini Niranjana, P. Sudhir and Vivek Dhareshwar (eds), *Interrogating Modernity: Culture and Colonialism in India*. Calcutta: Seagull Books, pp. 220–41.

PANDEY, Gyanendra. 1990. *The Construction of Communalism in Colonial North India*. New Delhi: Oxford University Press.

PANDIAN, M. S. S. 1992. *The Image Trap: M G Ramachandran in Film and Politics*. New Delhi: Sage.

——. 1994. 'Deligitimising 1965'. *The Hindu*, 9 November, p. 7.

PATHAK, Rahul. 1994. 'The New Generation'. *India Today*, 31 January, pp. 72–87.

PATHAK, Zakia and Rajeswari Sunder Rajan. 1992. 'Shahbano', in Judith Butler and Joan W. Scott (eds), *Feminists Theorize the Political*. New York and London: Routledge, pp. 257–79.

PINES, Jim and Paul Willemen. 1989. *Questions of Third Cinema*. London: British Film Institute.

PINNEY, Christopher. 1995. 'Chromolithography, Locality and the Articulation of the "Popular": 1878–1995'. Paper presented at the seminar 'Consumption of Popular Culture in India'. School of Oriental and African Studies, London.

PRADHAN, R. C. 1987. 'Gandhi and the Language Problem in India', in Verinder Grover (ed.), *Gandhi and Politics in India*. New Delhi: Deep and Deep Publishers.

PRADHAN, Sudhi (ed.). 1985. *Marxist Cultural Movements in India: Chronicles and Documents*, VOL. 3. Calcutta: Rooplekha Press.

PRASAD, M. Madhava. 1993. 'Cinema and the Desire for Modernity', *Journal of Arts and Ideas* 25–26: 71–86.

———. 1994. 'The State and Culture: Hindi Cinema in the Passive Revolution'. Ph.D. dissertation. University of Pittsburgh, Pittsburgh, Pennsylvania.

———. 1995. 'Teaching Capitalism as Native Language'. Paper presented at 'The National Research Seminar on English Studies in the Nineties'. University of Hyderabad, Hyderabad.

———. 1996. 'Formal into Real Subsumption? Signs of Ideological Re-form in Two Recent Films'. *Journal of Arts and Ideas* 29: 27–43.

———. 1997. *Ideology of the Hindi Film: A Historical Reconstruction*. New Delhi: Oxford University Press.

———. 1998. 'The State in/of Cinema', in Partha Chatterjee (ed.), *Wages of Freedom: Fifty Years of the Indian Nation-State*. New Delhi: Oxford University Press, pp. 123–6.

———. 1999. 'Cine-Politics: An Approach to the Study of the Political Significance of Cinema in South India', in Pradip Bose and Bodil F. Frederiksen (eds), *Urban Culture and Democracy: Forms of Cultural Production*. Calcutta: Centre for Studies in Social Sciences, pp. 13–28.

———. 2007 [2004]. 'Realism and Fantasy in Representations of Metropolitan Life in Indian Cinema', in Preben Kaarsholm (ed.), *City Flicks: Indian Cinema and the Urban Experience*. London/New York/Calcutta: Seagull Books, pp. 82–98.

———. 2009. 'Fan Bhakti and Subaltern Sovereignty: Enthusiasm as Political Factor'. *Economic and Political Weekly* 44(29) (18 July): 68–76.

RADNER, Hilary. 1993. 'Pretty Is as Pretty Does: Free Enterprise and the Marriage Plot', in Jim Collins, Hilary Radner and Ava Collins (eds), *Film Theory Goes to the Movies*. New York and London: Routledge, pp. 56–76.

RAHMAN, M. and Anup Katiyar. 1993. 'Bombay Film Industry: Underworld Connections'. *India Today*, 15 May, pp. 114–23.

RAI, Alok. 1991. 'Out Here: A Teacher in the Provinces', in Svati Joshi (ed.), *Rethinking English: Essays in Language, Literature, History*. New Delhi: Trianka, pp. 298–321.

RAI, Amrit. 1984. *A House Divided: The Origin and Development of Hindi/Hindavi*. New Delhi: Oxford University Press.

RAJA, Sandhya. 1987. 'An Angry Anil Kapoor Threatens His Antagonists'. *Stardust*, August, pp. 49–51.

RAJADHYAKSHA, Ashish. 1980. 'Neo-traditionalism: Film as Popular Art in India'. *Framework* 32–33: 20–67.

——. 1987. 'The Phalke Era: Conflict of Traditional Form and Modern Technology'. *Journal of Arts and Ideas* 14–15: 44–77.

——. 1990. 'Beaming Messages to the Nation'. *Journal of Arts and Ideas* 19: 33–52.

——. 1993a. 'The Epic Melodrama: Themes of Nationality in Indian Cinema'. *Journal of Arts and Ideas* 25–26: 55–70.

——. 1993b. 'Satyajit Ray, Ray's Films and the Ray Movie'. *Journal of Arts and Ideas* 23–24: 7–16.

——. 1995. 'An Agenda for Indian Film Studies'. Unpublished paper presented at the study week on 'Making Meaning in Indian Cinema', Indian Institute of Advanced Study, Shimla.

——. 1997. 'The Four Looks and the Indian Cinema'. Unpublished paper.

——. 2006. 'The Curious Case of Bombay's Hindi Cinema: The Career of Indigenous "Exhibition" Capital'. *Journal of the Moving Image* 5 (December): 7–41.

——. 2007 [2004]. 'The "Bollywoodization" of the Indian Cinema: Cultural Nationalism in a Global Arena', in Preben Kaarsholm (ed.), *City Flicks: Indian Cinema and the Urban Experience*. London/New York/Calcutta: Seagull Books, pp. 111–37.

——. 2009. *Indian Cinema in the Time of Celluloid: From Bollywood to the Emergency*. New Delhi: Tulika.

—— and Paul Willemen (eds). 1994. *Encyclopedia of Indian Cinema*. London: British Film Institute.

RAJAGOPAL, Arvind. 2001. *Politics After Television: Hindu Nationalism and the Reshaping of the Public in India*. New Delhi: Cambridge University Press.

RAJAN, Rajeswari Sunder (ed.). 1992. *The Lie of the Land: English Literary Study in India*. New Delhi: Oxford University Press.

——. 1993. 'The Subject of Sati', in Tejaswini Niranjana, P. Sudhir and Vivek Dhareshwar (eds), *Interrogating Modernity: Culture and Colonialism in India*. Calcutta: Seagull Books, pp. 219–318.

RAMANUJAN, A. K. 1999. 'The Indian Oedipus', in T. G. Vaidyanathan and Jeffery John Kripal (eds), *Vishnu on Freud's Desk: A Reader in Psychoanalysis and Hinduism*. Delhi: Oxford University Press, pp. 109–36.

RISSEUW, Carla. 1992. 'Gender, Kinship and State Formation: The Case of Sri Lanka Under Colonial Rule'. *Economic and Political Weekly* 27(47): 46–53.

ROSE, Jacqueline. 2003. 'Freud in the Tropics', in *On Not Being Able to Sleep: Psychoanalysis in the Modern World*. London: Chatto and Windus, pp. 125–48.

——. 2004. *States of Fantasy*. Oxford: Oxford University Press.

——. 2005. *The Question of Zion*. New Jersey: Princeton University Press.

——. 2007. *The Last Resistance*. London: Verso.

RUSHDIE, Salman.1989. *The Satanic Verses*. London: Random House.

SADARANGANI, Deepak. 1988. 'Juhi Chawla: Who Says Guys Aren't Crazy About Me?' *Filmfare*, November, pp. 87–92.

SAFOUAN, Moustafa. 2000. *Jacques Lacan and the Question of Analytical Training*. (Jacqueline Rose trans.). London: Macmillan.

SAID, Edward W. 1978. *Orientalism*. New York: Pantheon.

——. 1979. *The Question of Palestine*. New York: Times Books.

——. 1993. *Culture and Imperialism*. London: Vintage.

——. 2003. *Freud and the Non-European*. London: Verso.

SANGARI, Kumkum. 1987. 'The Politics of the Possible'. *Cultural Critique* 30 (Fall): 157–87

——. 1990. 'Mirabai and the Spiritual Economy of Bhakti'. *Economic and Political Weekly* 25(27/28): 1464–75/1537–52.

——. 1991. 'Relating Histories: Definitions of Literacy, Literature, Gender, in Nineteenth Century Calcutta and England', in Svati Joshi (ed.), *Rethinking English: Essays in Literature, Language, History*. New Delhi: Trianka, pp. 32–123.

——. 1995. 'Politics of Diversity: Religious Communities and Multiple Patriarchies'. *Economic and Political Weekly* 30(51/52): 3287–3310/3381–9.

—— and Sudesh Vaid (eds). 1989. *Recasting Women: Essays in Colonial History*. New Delhi: Kali for Women.

SARKAR, Tanika. 1991. 'The Woman as Communal Subject: Rashtrasevika Samiti and Ramjanmabhoomi Movement'. *Economic and Political Weekly* 26(35): 2057–62.

——. 1993. 'A Book of Her Own. A Life of Her Own: Autobiography of a Nineteenth Century Woman'. *History Workshop* 36: 35–65.

SARKAR, Sumit. 1982. 'Popular Movements and National Leadership, 1945–47'. *Economic and Political Weekly* 27(14–16): 677–90.

——. 1985. *Modern India, 1885–1947*. Madras: Macmillan.

——. 1992. '"Kaliyuga", "Chakri" and "Bhakti": Ramakrishna and His Times'. *Economic and Political Weekly* 27(29): 1543–66.

SAVARKAR, V. D. 1917. *Who is a Hindu?* New Delhi: Bharatiya Sahitya Sadan.

SCHATZ, Thomas. 1993. 'The New Hollywood', in Jim Collins, Hilary Radner and Ava Collins (eds), *Film Theory Goes to the Movies*. New York and London: Routledge, pp. 8–36.

SEN, Ilina (ed.). 1990. *A Space Within the Struggle: Women's Participation in People's Movements*. New Delhi: Kali for Women.

SENGUPTA, Suddhabrata. 1991. 'Sexual Politics of Television Mythology'. *Economic and Political Weekly* 26(45): 2558–60.

SHANMUGAM, Kavita. 1988. 'One From the Heart'. *Filmfare*, March, pp. 54–6.

SIRCAR, Ajanta. 2009. *The Catgeory of Children's Cinema in India*. Unpublished draft manuscript submitted to the Indian Institute of Advanced Study, Shimla.

SPIVAK, Gayatri Chakravorty. 1985. 'The Rani of Sirmur', in Francis Barker (ed.), *Europe and Its Others*. Essex: University of Essex Press, pp. 128–51.

———. 1988. 'Can the Subaltern Speak?', in Cary Nelson and Lawrence Grossberg (eds), *Marxism and the Interpretation of Culture*. London: Macmillan, pp. 271–313.

———. 1992. 'Thinking Academic Freedom in Gendered Post-Coloniality'. The T. B. Davie Memorial Lectures, University of Cape Town, Cape Town, p. 3.

———. 1993a. *Outside in the Teaching Machine*. New York and London: Routledge.

———. 1993b. 'More on Power/Knowledge', in *Outside in the Teaching Machine*. New York and London: Routledge, pp. 25–52.

———. 1993c. 'Feminism and Deconstruction, Again: Negotiations', in *Outside in the Teaching Machine*. New York and London: Routledge, pp. 121–40.

———. 1993d. 'French Feminism Revisited', in *Outside in the Teaching Machine*. New York and London: Routledge, pp. 141–72.

———. 1999. *A Critique of Postcolonial Reason: Toward a History of the Vanishing Present*. Calcutta: Seagull Books.

———. 2003. *Death of a Discipline*. New York: Columbia University Press.

Stardust. 1988. 'Changing . . . Madhuri Dixit's Shocking New Lifestyle!' March, pp. 45–8.

STOKES, Eric. 1959. *The English Utilitarians and India*. Oxford: Clarendon Press.

STREE SHAKTI SANGATHANA. 1980. *We Were Making History*. London: Zed Books.

SUDHIR, P. 1993. 'Colonialism and Vocabularies of Dominance', in Tejaswini Niranjana, P. Sudhir and Vivek Dhareshwar (eds), *Interrogating Modernity: Culture and Colonialism in India*. Calcutta: Seagull Books, pp. 334–47.

SWAIN, Tony. 1993. *A Place for Strangers: Towards a History of Australian Aboriginal Being*. Cambridge: Cambridge University Press.

TAGORE, Rabindranath. 1912. *Gitanjali* (William Butler Yeats trans.). Boston: International Pocket Library.

TASKER, Yvonne. 1993. *Spectacular Bodies: Gender, Genre and the Action Cinema*. New York and London: Routledge.

TELLIS, Brian and Milton Frank. 1996. 'India Goes Pop'. *Femina*, December, pp. 10–38.

THAPAR, Romila. 1989. 'Imagined Religious Communities? Ancient History and the Modern Search for a Hindu Identity'. *Modern Asian Studies* 23: 209–31.

THARU, Susie. 1991. 'The Arrangement of an Alliance: English and the Making of Indian Literatures', in Svati Joshi (ed.), *Rethinking English: Essays in Literature, Language, History*. New Delhi: Trianka, pp. 160–80.

———. 1996. 'The Impossible Subject: Caste and the Gendered Body'. *Economic and Political Weekly* 31(22): 1311–15.

—— and K. Lalita (eds). 1991. *Women Writing in India: 600 B.C. to the Present*, VOL. 1. London: Pandora Press.

—— and K. Lalita. 1993. 'Empire, Nation and the Literary Text', in Tejaswini Niranjana, P. Sudhir and Vivek Dhareshwar (eds), *Interrogating Modernity: Culture and Colonialism in India*. Calcutta: Seagull Books, pp. 199–219.

—— and K. Lalita (eds). 1995. *Women Writing in India: 600 B.C. to the Present*, VOL. 2. New Delhi: Oxford University Press.

—— and Tejaswini Niranjana. 1996. 'Problems for a Contemporary Theory of Gender', in Shahid Amina and Dipesh Chakraborty (eds), *Subaltern Studies IX: Writings on South Asian History and Society*. New Delhi: Oxford University Press, pp. 232–60. [First presented as a paper at the 1993 Anveshi/Subaltern Studies conference, Hyderabad.]

THIONGO, Ngugi. 1986. *Decolonising the Mind: The Politics of Language in African Literature*. Portsmouth/London: Heineman/James Currey.

TRIPATHI, Salil. 1988. 'Hindi Film Industry: Good Times, Bad Times'. *India Today*, 31 May, pp. 80–92.

TRIVEDI, Harish. 1991. 'Reading English, Writing Hindi: English Literature and Indian Creative Writing', in Svati Joshi (ed.), *Rethinking English: Essays in Literature, Language, History*, New Delhi: Trianka, pp. 181–205.

TURIM, Maureem. 1993. *Flashback in Film: Memory and History*. New York and London: Routledge.

VANAIK, Achin. 1990. *The Painful Transition: Bourgeois Democracy in India*. London: Verso.

VASUDEVAN, Ravi. 1991a. 'Errant Males and Divided Females: Melodrama and Sexual Difference in the Hindi Film of the 1950s'. Ph.D. dissertation. University of East Anglia, Norwich.

———. 1991b. 'The Cultural Space of a Film Narrative: Interpreting *Kismet* (Bombay Talkies, 1943)'. *Indian Economic and Social History Review* 28(2): 171–85.

———. 1993. 'Shifting Codes and Dissolving Identities: The Hindi Social Film of the 1950s as Popular Culture'. *Journal of Arts and Ideas* 23–24: 51–84.

———. 2007 [2004]. 'The Exhilaration of Dread: Genre, Narrative Form and Film Style in Contemporary Urban Action Films', in Preben Kaarsholm (ed.), *City Flicks: Indian Cinema and the Urban Experience*. London/New York/Calcutta: Seagull Books, pp. 219–32.

VELICHETI, Rajiv. 1993. 'Women, Violence and Telangana: Changing Constructions in Telugu Popular Cinema'. Paper presented at the Anveshi/Subaltern Studies conference, Hyderabad.

VISWANATHAN, Gauri. 1990. *Masks of Conquest: Literary Study and British Rule in India*. London: Faber and Faber.

VITALI, Valentina. 2009. *Hindi Action Cinema: Industries, Narratives, Bodies*, New Delhi: Oxford University Press.

WILLIAMS, Raymond. 1973. *The Country and the City*. London: Chatto and Windus.

———. 1989. *The Politics of Modernism* (Tony Pinkney ed.). London: Verso.

———. 1990. *Television: Technology and Cultural Form*. New York and London: Routledge.

WOLLEN, Peter. 1981. 'John Ford', in John Caughie (ed.), *Theories of Authorship: A Reader*. New York and London: Routledge, pp. 102–08.

———. 1993. *Raiding the Icebox: Reflections on Twentieth Century Culture*. Bloomington/London: Indiana University Press/Verso.

ŽIŽEK, Slavoj. 1989. *The Sublime Object of Ideology*. London: Verso.

———. 1991. *For They Know Not What They Do: Enjoyment as a Political Factor*. London: Verso.

INDEX